Johnny Mize

Johnny Mize

A Biography
of Baseball's "Big Cat"

LEW FREEDMAN

McFarland & Company, Inc., Publishers
Jefferson, North Carolina

All photographs are from the National Baseball Hall of Fame,
Cooperstown, New York

ISBN (print) 978-1-4766-8593-9
ISBN (ebook) 978-1-4766-4539-1

Library of Congress and British Library
cataloguing data are available

Library of Congress Control Number 2022015370

Front cover: St. Louis Cardinals first baseman Johnny Mize at bat
(National Baseball Hall of Fame Library, Cooperstown, New York)

Printed in the United States of America

*McFarland & Company, Inc., Publishers
Box 611, Jefferson, North Carolina 28640
www.mcfarlandpub.com*

Table of Contents

Preface

In an era when baseball players were not as routinely large as they are in the 2020s, Johnny Mize was a first baseman who stood 6-foot-2 and weighed 215 pounds without weightlifting. For a big man, he was light on his feet, even graceful maneuvering around the bag and digging throws out of the dirt when fellow infielders were a trifle off in their aim.

Mize had the fielding skills to make the throwers look good and to help out his pitchers by protecting the first-base line as a gatekeeper to right field when an opposing hitter smacked one in his direction. It was this prowess with the mitt that gave Mize his nickname of "The Big Cat." The "Big" part was self-explanatory, a reflection of his size. The "Cat" part was a comparison, not to the ferocity of a tiger or lion, but to the dexterity and swiftness of a house cat making a sudden move.

Once, baseball nicknames were as commonplace as the names on the roster—just about everyone had one. Babe Ruth collected nicknames the way some kids collected baseball cards. Nickname labeling has somewhat died out, but at least in the case of Mize, he received one that made sense and was complimentary.

Mize once credited Joe Orengo, an infielder with the St. Louis Cardinals and New York Giants (two teams Mize also represented) between 1939 and 1945, for coining the nickname. "One day," Mize said, "the infielders were having a pretty bad time and were making some bad throws to me at first base. After digging a few out of the dirt, Joe Orengo called over to me, 'Atta boy, John, you look like a big cat.' Some of the writers overhead the remark and asked Joe about it later. The nickname has stuck with me ever since."[1]

It may be that Orengo realized he had uttered a popular phrase and stuck with it, since it was also reported that he said, "Ain't he a wonder? Why, he's a big cat."[2] Still other sources claim that one of Mize's early managers, Ray Blades, used the "big cat" description in assessing the first baseman.

Amusingly, Mize's teammate with the St. Louis Cardinals, Hall of

Famer Stan Musial, applied the Big Cat appendage to Mize with regard to his actions in the batter's box. "He'd just lean back and on his left foot, bend his body back and let the pitch go by. Then he'd lean back into the batter's box and resume his stance, as graceful as a big cat."[3]

Of course, that had nothing at all to do with fielding. Just maybe Mize moved like a "Big Cat," a lion, a tiger, a cougar, a jaguar, a leopard, or a panther, at all times, on the field, in the batter's box, and off, at least when he was young. By consensus, it seems, Johnny Mize was big and agile as a cat, none of which did him any harm on the baseball diamond.

In 1949, while Mize was still an active player, a movie was released titled *The Big Cat*. It was not a biopic about him. The cat in question was a cougar. The film featured just one actor whose name might resonate years later—Forrest Tucker. The Big Cat on the screen was not nearly the hit Johnny Mize was on the field.

Introduction

He carried a big stick. Johnny Mize wielded a bat like a club, a chunk of wood that when applied to a pitched ball sent it soaring to places difficult to track with the naked eye. Or so went the legend.

While Mize's athleticism on the field provided him with neat and necessary dance moves around the first-base bag and essentially was the root of his "Big Cat" nickname, the historians who read his statistics have been most wowed by his power.

Mize had the build of a strong man, a Ted Kluszewski–like muscle man before "Big Klu" broke into the game with his sleeveless baseball jerseys that would have been suitable for Mize, and as intimidating. A selection of Mize photographs highlights his muscles, and one can see how he possessed the firm strength to power the ball towards distant skies.

Young baseball fans do not know enough about Johnny Mize to appreciate his accomplishments. In an era when the home run has taken over the offensive game, someone who "only" smashed 359 of them doesn't stand out so much statistically. Mize is someone whose career (1936–1953), outstanding as it was, and as well-known as it was at the time, is rooted far enough in the past that only adults well into their Society Security years saw him play live.

Mize was a key figure for three cornerstone franchises of Major League Baseball, the St. Louis Cardinals, the New York Giants, and the New York Yankees. Yet as great as he was, his time was split and there was always another superstar on the roster, a fellow future Hall of Famer, whose fan links ran deeper.

In those communities, where baseball was king and the teams were beloved, Mize did not lack for day-to-day exposure when his exploits won a game or advanced the cause. But Mize did not possess the type of personality that endeared him to the sportswriters close to the teams. He was not a sit-around-the-locker-and-chat guy who made small talk or jokes in banter with the scribes. That did not come naturally to him.

Apparently, Mize reserved his friendliness for teammates, those

3

closest to him in the locker room, when the clubhouse doors were closed to outsiders. Those men seemed to be his best friends in the sport, not the sportswriters or the fans. He was somewhat private by nature, a trait that followed him to the end of his life.

The historical perspective of Mize's career was somewhat inhibited also by its timing. He was one of many stars whose career statistics were impacted by time spent in the service during World War II when he was at his peak. Players such as Ted Williams, Joe DiMaggio, and Bob Feller would easily have moved up lifetime numbers lists if they had not taken leave of the game for periods of three years or more when the United States needed them to don other uniforms. Mize was in the same category.

Young Johnny Mize with the St. Louis Cardinals. Mize broke in with St. Louis in 1936 after a long apprenticeship in the minors and became a star with the club.

Mize did not play Major League ball in 1943, 1944, or 1945. Not a single game. He took not a single at-bat. At the time, he was in his prime, 30, 31, and 32 years old. If they had not gone to war, it is routinely believed that Feller would have won 300 games, Williams would have collected 3,000 hits, and DiMaggio would have topped 400 home runs.

Late in life, Mize, who was born in the small town of Demorest, Georgia, reconnected with his roots and moved back to his hometown. There he became friends with Zell Miller, who was from the same part of the state, but who was serving as governor. Miller said that if Mize had not given three years of his career to the military, he would have hit 500 home runs. Maybe so. The total would have been within reach. "He was my hero," Miller said.[1]

As it was, Mize's lifetime statistics were eye-catching. Over 15 seasons in the majors, Mize batted .312. He won one batting title, led the National League in home runs three times, and led the NL in runs batted in three times. His single-season high for home runs was 51 in 1947 with the Giants during a period when topping 50 was a rarity.

Four times, Mize led the National League in slugging percentage, and he led once in runs scored and once in triples. He was a 10-time All-Star, on the last occasion chosen for the American League squad at age 40.

The description of behemoths stalking to the plate with their war clubs is a cliché, often accompanied by the words "feared slugger," as in making the hearts of weak-kneed pitchers go pitter-patter and inducing edgy managers to more vigorously chew their tobacco. Mize was one of those guys who fit the bill sufficiently for managers or pitching coaches to warn their throwers by saying, "Be careful with this guy."

One of the more amusing stories about Mize's power dates to his days in the military during World War II, not at a big-league ballpark. Mize was in the Navy with the rank of Specialist First Class when he was sent to Hawaii in 1944. He was serving with other baseball figures and during a game at the Naval Air Station Kaneohe, he hit a 425-foot home run against the 7th Army Air Force.

Major League pitcher Virgil Trucks was an eyewitness to Mize's performance there. "Mize hit several over the palm trees into the ocean," Trucks commented.[2]

The balls were last seen sinking to become possible toys for the sharks. Soon enough, Mize followed the homers to sea, visiting the familiar World War II locales of the Marshall Islands, Guam, Saipan, Palau, and Leyte.

You never could be too careful pitching to Johnny Mize. If he saw a bad pitch, he would make you pay. When Mize retired from playing, he was 40 years old and had just been a member of the New York Yankees for five straight world championships, enough to earn rings for every finger on one hand.

Whether the sportswriters were close to Mize or not, some among them had sufficient respect to send him off with predictions that he was headed to induction in the National Baseball Hall of Fame in Cooperstown, New York. They meant soon, as in soon after he became eligible after retirement. Only that didn't happen as predicted. Johnny Mize was welcomed into the Hall of Fame—eventually. Mize ended up being selected by the Veterans Committee in 1981.

When Mize stood up before the fans for his acceptance speech on August 2, 1981, one of the first things he did was make a joke about his long wait, setting the audience at ease, at least. "Oh, years ago the writers were telling me that I'd make the Hall of Fame," Mize said, "so I kind of prepared a speech. But somewhere along in the 28 years it took, it got lost."[3]

Mize, by then white-haired, had time for a rewrite and left his fans laughing.

1

Beginnings

Johnny Mize could always play. From the time he was a teenager, whatever level he signed up for, he was one of the best players on the diamond. He was one of those kids who stood out from the average wannabe players in the neighborhood. And he stood out later, when he signed a professional contract and became a star in the major leagues.

The Big Cat was always a stalwart hitter, to such a degree that his power and swinging for high average overshadowed his excellent fielding. A certain amount of his success was attributable to the natural gift of his athleticism, and a certain amount of his hitting came easily. But Mize always protested that hitters did not become great simply because the Lord reached out and touched them on a shoulder anointing them as The One. No, he insisted, it took hard work to excel in the big leagues.

The funny thing was that Mize the power hitter was a distant cousin of Ty Cobb and a distant relation of Babe Ruth, though that was by marriage. Mize was a cousin of Claire, one of Ruth's wives. The family tree seems oddly branched.

Mize was born in the small town of Demorest, Georgia, on January 7, 1913. Much later, after he was grown up and a baseball star of national renown, Mize co-authored a book about hitting. It was aimed at young people, to encourage them to commit to baseball, and it provided pointers on how to make a career out of the sport and succeed at it. The first chapter begins this way: "Hitters are made. They are not born."[1] He made his point right away, seeking to debunk any beliefs that all a big guy like him had to do was step up to the plate and smack the ball as far as he wished, without practicing.

He did swiftly make allowances, though, for the necessity of having some natural skill. "Of course," he wrote, "natural ability is paramount for doing anything well, but having an aptitude for hitting the ball is not enough."[2]

Mize's comments, as explained on the same page, were directed to fathers and sons about reality and added, "It is utter nonsense to claim a ballplayer's son can inherit the talents of his dad."[3]

The study of heredity by geneticists has come quite far since those words reached the public in 1953, but Mize was both right and wrong. There is much evidence to suggest that some abilities are in the genes, but there is no doubt that if the next generation does not cultivate them, it will go for naught.

Demorest is located in Northeast Georgia, in Habersham County, near the Blue Ridge Mountains. It was founded in 1889 and has never been confused with a metropolis. In 1900, the population was 560. When Mize was born and during his youth, there were about 700 residents. The population didn't top 1,000 until after World War II. Even during the second decade of the 2000s, Demorest's population was only 1,823, though the most recent estimate does number over 2,000.

The community was originally a farm, run by one family, dating back to 1829. When Demorest became a town, it was named after a man who strongly backed Prohibition. In the early years of the 20th century, Demorest was best known as the site of Piedmont College, still a staple of the town today.

Mize's youth was not an especially smooth one. His parents, Edward and Emma, separated and his mother moved to Atlanta. Mize stayed with a grandmother in Demorest, and she raised him. When Mize first became interested in sports, it was tennis, not baseball, that first attracted him. Tennis was his initial high school sport at Piedmont Academy, and he won a county championship swinging a racquet instead of a bat. This despite those distant relations tearing up the sport and being viewed as baseball luminaries 1 and 1A, Cobb and Ruth, Ruth and Cobb, possibly the greatest two players of all time.

While a little bit later Mize would have the word "Big" incorporated into his nickname, until he experienced a growth spurt, he was not that big. Once he gained heft between the ages of 13 and 15, he began packing on the muscle. The physical stature helped Mize adjust to baseball, and when he began swinging that other implement, it's possible that he benefited from the hand-eye coordination of wielding a tennis racquet.

The teenager became better known in his hometown (although in a town that size, everyone certainly knew everybody anyway) as he filled out and took up baseball. It seemed Mize did his best baseball work for Piedmont College while attending Piedmont Academy, the high school he was enrolled in.

Legend has it that although he was only about 15 years old, Mize actually suited up for the college and was a slugging star for two seasons. Occasionally, Mize was contradictory in his comments about playing for the college instead of the high school, perhaps because with the passage of years, something that once was routinely acceptable might have had its legality questioned. But there seems little doubt that he was a high school–aged student on a college team. Mize noted that he could get away with doing that because Piedmont College was not a member of any national governing body for collegiate play such as the NCAA or NAIA, which came along later. In his own book about hitting, Mize said, "The fact is, when I was 15 and a sophomore at high school, I played on the varsity baseball team for the college. I could do this because Piedmont College didn't belong to any athletic conference and therefore there were no rules governing eligible players."[4]

Much the way elementary school–aged boys look up to high school players, the local high school players admired the Piedmont players. They represented the best game in town. Mize, his brother, and playmates from the neighborhood, who all enjoyed baseball, would watch the Piedmont team practice. Mize wrote of their helping the team by stationing themselves beyond the outfield fences to retrieve baseballs the older guys swatted.

This was in the mid- to late-1920s, at the same time Babe Ruth was turning the home run into a popular weapon to be emulated in the majors. Not so many years before that, when Ty Cobb was in his heyday, the home run was a much rarer commodity. Teams were playing what Cobb referred to as "scientific" baseball, advancing the runner towards home one base at a time with singles, walks, bunts, and stolen bases.

Baseball was the National Pastime. No American boy grew up with the aspiration to play professional hockey or basketball (they probably only vaguely knew the rules of those sports), or rarely even football. Baseball was the thing, the only game that really mattered.

Mize the tennis player (unusual enough), gave baseball a try as a fifth-grader at age 11. His first position was catcher, and he was foolish enough (his own description) and daring enough to set up behind the plate without wearing a mask. That did not last long. After accumulating the usual collection of cuts and bruises for lack of protection, Mize realized this was neither the proper approach required nor the proper position for him.

By the time Mize and his group were aiding Piedmont, though, home runs were the hot item in the sport, and especially in practice the team slugged its share of balls out of the park. At other times, Mize and his gang were allowed in the outfield itself to chase down fly balls the college players stroked during batting practice. Coach Harry Forrester didn't mind having the crew around and felt there was no harm in encouraging them in baseball as long as they didn't get in the way of what he was trying to accomplish with his team.

"We couldn't hurt doing this and it was wonderful practice," Mize said.[5] Of course, for teenagers, the association with the older players was a source of pride as well. They were made to feel part of things, a bit closer to the action than the other town fans.

When the team packed up its gear for the day, often broken bats were left behind. Mize and the other boys gathered them up and put them back into use. As was common in neighborhoods across the United States over the decades, those boys who couldn't afford new equipment from sporting goods stores improvised. The Mize family did not have the wherewithal to indulge the boys with such purchases, and if they wanted to play ball, they had to supply themselves.

Before Mize was old enough to hang out with the crowd at Piedmont, he and his brother created their own baseball entertainment. Their bat was a sawed-off broomstick, and instead of a baseball they used a tennis ball. Mize apparently had plenty of those around. They stayed out playing until the sun set and they could no longer see well enough to hit a pitched ball.

Mize's high school was so small that it didn't regularly field a baseball team. There just weren't enough boys who had the will and the skill to play. From time to time, a high school-aged boy stood out enough to be recruited to the Piedmont College team, Mize said, though he was hesitant to push himself into that mix. Once he experienced his growth spurt, however, he was physically as large as many of the college players.

It seems that the reality of the situation was that Forrester took note of this and essentially coerced Mize into trying out for the college team even though he was just a sophomore in high school. Forrester was a former minor league baseball player who was Mr. Everything at the school, coaching all sports. He probably possessed a pretty good eye for talent that would translate up to a higher level of play, though it is unlikely he looked over Mize and proclaimed, "There goes a Hall of Famer."

Mize surprised himself, if not Forrester, by quickly making a mark on the team. "I had pretty good luck pinch-hitting and pretty soon I was playing regularly," Mize said. "Harry stationed me in the outfield, where I liked to play at that time."[6] Of course, he had been chasing those batting practice fly balls, and that provided experience out there in the wide, green pasture. First base came later.

Hitting came right away. Mize became a two-year player for Piedmont College, even while he was working his way academically through high school, and he batted over .400 both seasons. This hitting success by Mize at such a young age impressed Forrester.

During that era, there was no sophisticated scouting, of course no video, and no highlight tapes. Major League teams dispatched roving scouts to the hinterlands to discover talent. The big clubs, all 16 of them at the time, eight in the National League and eight in the American League, also were the beneficiaries of tips from men like Forrester, former pros now coaching in remote areas, keen eyes focused on diamonds in the rough, or polishing them on teams they led.

It may be that the early deprivation, being forced to swing at a ball with a broom, led to Mize's firm belief that hitters should carefully select their bats. In his instructional missive to youngsters, he addressed that point. "The first thing is to get a bat that feels good to you," Mize said. "The weight and the length of the bat and the type of handle and model must be just right. The bat is the tool of the hitter. Take great care in selecting your bat."[7]

Many years later, when he was in the majors, Mize was such an acknowledged aficionado of bats, it seemed he might have been in demand by the Louisville Slugger factory to design them. Teammates teased him for bringing so many bats with him on road trips that it created imbalance in the club's luggage count. One joke ran that while all of the other players' bats fit into one trunk to be loaded onto the train, Mize's bats occupied another trunk on their own.

In 1940, when Mize reported to spring training with the St. Louis Cardinals in St. Petersburg, Florida, and walked into the clubhouse, he saw 43 bats lined up for him and noted that the clubhouse manager who had to deal with the batches of bats was, in Mize's words, "vigorously complaining that they occupied an entire bat trunk. I asked him how [I was] expected to work without my tools, for which he had no answer." Teammate Don Gutteridge took in the scene and commented, "When you hit .350, they buy you all the bats you want."[8]

When he could afford to, when broomsticks were no longer a necessity, Mize cared deeply about his bats. He had a virtual Crayola box full of choices to rely on in different circumstances. Not every player was as studious, adaptable, or picky about choosing a bat each time around in the order. Many players experimented, found their stick of choice, and stuck with it. Mize thought in broader terms. To him, it was just a matter of responding to a different pitcher's strengths with the appropriate weapon.

Gutteridge, who played with Mize in St. Louis, was an infielder better known for his glove work during a 12-year big-league career than his hitting, though his lifetime average was a respectable .256. Gutteridge was less a student of hitting than a wry observer of Mize's hitting and fixation on bats.

"He had bats of different sizes and weights, 34 ounces, 37, 40," Gutteridge said. "The harder the thrower, the lighter the bat. Gutteridge said. Mize sometimes switched lumber mid-game, even when facing the same pitcher in later innings."

Gutteridge quoted Mize about a particular left-hander the Cardinals were facing in Sportsman's Park who seemed to have Mize's number. "Next time I get up there, I'm gonna get one of those light bats and I'll get around on that high fastball. You watch," Mize told Gutteridge. "So," Gutteridge recalled, "the next time up he hits the first pitch out onto Grand Avenue outside of old Sportsman's Park. He comes back to me and says, 'See, I told you.'"[9]

That was an example of experience and acquired wisdom coming together, an educational process that made Mize smarter at the plate than he had been as a youth at Piedmont.

2

The Minors

Those who watch a local phenomenon play in any sport, especially if he later becomes famous, may or may not have selective memories. But they do savor memories of when the kid was young, and they claim they knew he was going to be special all along.

In Johnny Mize's case, the local sports fan understood he was precocious, or else he would not be representing the college team on the diamond. But localized greatness does not always translate to immortal greatness.

The favorite stories his neighbors recalled about Mize were about how darned far he could hit a baseball. You remember the time when Johnny smashed that ball over the college administration building? You remember the time old Johnny lay into one pitch and airmailed it out to Route 441? Maybe they did remember such happenings, and maybe they exaggerated them. According to one account, when Mize was living back in Demorest as a senior citizen, he pretty much pooh-poohed the tales as being a bit polished up for popular consumption. That did not disguise the reality that young John Mize, also called "Big Jawn" by some when he was just becoming known in the game, could belt a ball.

The first building blocks of a reputation for Mize stemmed from his .400-hitting success for Piedmont College. Then he played summer ball and others got a look at his skills. Piedmont coach Harry Forrester was savvy enough to recognize that Mize was the real deal and that he could have a career in professional baseball.

In the late 1920s, and for years before and after, the St. Louis Cardinals were the team of the South. St. Louis was the western-most city in the United States to harbor a big-league team, and the club's reputation was burnished by powerful radio signals that broadcast the team's achievements to a wide geographic area.

When it came to providing a personnel tip to a Major League team, naturally enough Forrester thought of the Cardinals before any of the others. He wrote a letter to Branch Rickey, ultimately a Hall of Fame executive who gained considerable fame in the game due to a mix of exploits, but who at the time was general manager of the Cardinals.

Certainly, Rickey had numerous such pen pals willing to drop him notes about this can't-miss-kid and that can't-miss-kid. In an era even before baseball was watched on television, never mind the electronic and technological advances that enable young players to lobby for themselves by recording video highlights and the like, there were no shortcuts to seeing a player play. The only thing to do was go see him play in person. Rickey sent his brother, Frank Rickey, on the road to seek out Mize and grade his stuff.

After school was out for the summer when Mize was 17, he hooked up with a semi-pro team identified with Toccoa, Georgia. This was always a hit-or-miss proposition for the traveling scout. Much depended on whether the player was in top form on a given day. The player might be supremely talented, but on the night of his viewing could wake up with a stomachache, be out of sorts, and strike out three times. Nah, the kid can't hit, the scout may determine, and label the player as not worth signing.

Or the kid might catch lightning in a bottle the day the scout slipped into the crowd with his binoculars and notepad, just in time to see the burly prospect smash three home runs and a double.

The pressure was on the scout to get it right—which was the true player?—especially if his time was limited and he could hang around this particular ballpark only briefly. Frank Rickey was apparently a sharp scout who could discern subtleties and weigh strengths and weaknesses dispassionately. He saw Mize play just one time and reached plus-and-minus conclusions. In the field, he thought Mize was on the slow side for an outfielder, but in game situations showed off mature smarts. He liked that Mize did not seem to make mistakes while running or when throwing the ball back to the infield, but also at the plate. In the batter's box, Mize was selective, not swinging at bad pitches.

Frank Rickey determined that Mize was worth taking a chance on. He was only 17 and had plenty of time to smooth any rough edges and improve. It also wasn't that Mize's acquisition would force someone else off a roster altogether. At the time, Branch Rickey was building the Cardinals' farm system, introducing the new concept of rounding up every minor league prospect available, almost cornering the market, and building a championship team from within. Eventually, Commissioner Kenesaw Mountain Landis decided that what Branch Rickey and the Cardinals were doing to capture all of the young talent went too far. Landis ordered the Cardinals to free many young players from their contracts.

During the summer of 1930, Branch Rickey was collecting autographs (on contracts) as zealously as today's sports memorabilia collector. One signature he obtained was Mize's, who was signed and sent to St. Louis' Class C team in Greensboro, North Carolina.

One coincidence of Mize joining the Cardinals' outfit was that, as a young hitter, this soon-to-be connoisseur of batting implements regularly employed a Rogers Hornsby model. At that time, Hornsby, owner of the second-highest lifetime batting average in big-league history behind Ty Cobb, was indisputably the greatest Cardinals player of all-time.

The Greensboro Patriots were in the Piedmont League, and when Mize shipped in, he did a lot of sitting. Still just 17, his first professional season consisted of appearances in only 12 games, getting just 31 at-bats. He did not hit a home run, and his batting average during this abbreviated assignment was a minuscule .194.

Mize really did nothing to distinguish himself or to prove that the Cardinals made a sharp move by adding him to the organization. It was obvious that if he had a future in the game, he would need some seasoning, so it was no surprise that Mize was sent right back to Greensboro in 1931 to get some more playing time.

Big difference. Appearing in 94 games, Mize batted .337 this time around with nine home runs. He was still one of the youngest guys around, only 18 years old, young enough that he could still have been in high school. The team liked what it saw from that lively bat. At the time, however, Mize was still an outfielder. He wasn't getting any faster, though, or expanding his range much.

Long before there was any such thing as a designated hitter, a role Mize would certainly have fit at the tail end of his career, a ballplayer had to demonstrate all-around skills to make the cut in the majors. That meant he had to pull his weight in the field as well as at the plate.

Pleased by the progress shown by that .337 average but concerned over Mize's lack of mobility in the outfield, the Cardinals promoted him to Class B Elmira in the New York-Penn League for the 1932 season when he was 19. But they also gave up on the notion of Mize as a Major League outfielder, transferring him to first base to learn a new position. It was definitely the right move. Mize may not have possessed open-field speed to dash across the outfield, but he had the innate quickness to make slick moves around the bag.

That year he played in 106 games, and the fielding switch did not distract him at the plate. Mize batted .326. He still had the big stick. There was no rushing through the minors, skipping many, or any steps, for a young player, in the early 1930s, especially if he belonged to a franchise overstocked with talent operated by an administrator like Branch Rickey who wanted to disperse his men across the country.

There were few roster spots opening up as St. Louis competed in three World Series between 1930 and 1934, winning two, while being the most colorful team in the majors. The "Gashouse Gang" won big and was bigger than life for fans who loved the prominent players such as Dizzy Dean, Joe "Ducky" Medwick, and "The Fordham Flash," Frankie Frisch.

During his earliest days in professional baseball, Mize was serving an apprenticeship. The slugger with the high average, who would end up writing a book on how to hit, was still enrolled in his own studies of how to hit. Playing in the minors is like going to school, attending college, learning new things to apply to innate knowledge.

Major League clubs are more impatient in the 2020s than they were in the 1930s, when there were many more minor league teams than there are now. If the Cardinals were accused of holding back players who could have filled spots on other teams' rosters, then so be it, until Landis intervened. But Mize was stuck on a slow path to the big-time.

Mize turned 20 in 1933 and split the baseball season between two teams. The Cardinals moved him up to the Rochester Red Wings of Class AA, though Rochester later became a fixture in AAA. In 42 games at that location, Mize did his usual reliable job with the bat, hitting .352. Yet he was shipped out, back to Greensboro again, by then affiliated with Class B, for the rest of the campaign. Mize showed up in 98 games for the North Carolina team and hit .360. For the first time, he truly began to show off his power in professional ball, smacking 22 homers for Greensboro.

By then, it was obvious that Mize could hit. Except for that initial, short trial in Greensboro at .194 (when he was incidentally paid less than a dollar per point on his batting average, at a rate of $150 a month), he hit at least .300 for 14 straight seasons after that.

The Cardinals remained in no hurry to promote Mize, waiting for him to develop into a ballerina covering first base, which he ultimately sort of did, and for a roster spot to clear, which it also ultimately did. Also, by starting out so young, Mize had some growing up, as in maturing, to do, when youngsters were not often given seats in the dugout before they were in their 20s, though it happened.

Coming out of the spring in 1934, it was back to Rochester for Mize, back to AA. Another stretch with the Red Wings produced .339 hitting for the now 21-year-old. More eyes were on the big club than the minor-league team that year, however. It was another banner St. Louis championship season with the Cardinals capturing the World Series. The first baseman for the champs was Ripper Collins, then 30, and there was little to complain about his work. Nothing to gripe about at all. If Collins was even aware of Mize, he certainly was unlikely to spend energy worrying about him swooping in and stealing his job. Collins played in all 154 games for the winners, batted .333, tied with Mel Ott for the National League title with 35 home runs, and knocked in 128 runs. Collins was a switch-hitter whose .615 slugging percentage also led the league. He had a fabulous season in 1934. Johnny Who?

Collins was not a youngster, but he wasn't fading, either. In 1935, he batted .313, crashed 23 homers, and drove in 122 runs. The All-Star Game was a new showcase on the sports landscape around that time, and Collins was chosen to represent the NL in 1935, again in 1936, and still again in 1937, albeit for the Chicago Cubs that year.

The point was that the Cardinals had Mize spend a lot of time and energy becoming a first baseman, but there was no room when the funnel narrowed. When it came to protecting the bag at Sportsman's Park, Collins' foot was firmly planted on the base.

Ripper Collins did not make his big-league debut until he was 27, so he was in no hurry to vacate. The odd thing about his place in history was that there was a Rip Collins playing in the American League, who also played first base. Rip Collins was eight years older, but their careers did overlap in the majors in 1931.

The St. Louis Collins, fittingly since this was the Gashouse Gang, was known for his lighthearted, playful ways, an expert practical joker who could entertain the clubhouse. To be singled out as one of the creators of offbeat mayhem in the Cardinals' operation was saying something. "[Branch] Rickey always accused me of being the ringleader," Collins said. "I never could understand why he picked on me. Unless it could have been because there was considerable truth in his allegations."[1]

Ripper's name was first applied when he was a young man better known as Jimmy. He was playing the outfield one day when a batter smashed a ball off a fence, hitting a nail, and ripped open the cover. When Collins made a comment about that, he acquired the "Ripper" moniker.

As much of a fun guy as he was, including being one of the Cardinals' regulars who sang on the radio, Collins was battling time and the ever-looming figure of Mize. At least most would believe so.

Sometimes Rickey groomed a player for years. Other times he was happy to turn around a young player for cash, buy someone else, and start over. During the 1934 season, Mize was relegated to just those 90 appearances in Rochester because of an injury. He tore a muscle connected to his pelvic bone and was sidelined. Still, Mize's slugging body of work enticed the Cincinnati Reds to make a $55,000 offer for him.

Rickey agreed to the terms, but Cincinnati wanted insurance. If Mize was not healthy enough to go, the deal was off. Slow to heal, Mize had not yet regained 100 percent form, and the swap was cancelled. The Cardinals' team doctor insisted that Mize was well enough to play, though the player knew better. In 1935, he had difficulty swinging the bat and bending low for ground balls, and once again he could not complete the season because of the same groin injury. Somehow, Mize still batted .317 despite this aggravation, but he was in trouble.

After all of the promise shown, and all of the minor-league toil, now that he was on the cusp of making the majors, Mize worried he might never cross over the last hurdle. He was still only 22 years old. In his mind, he believed he might have to retire. Discouraged, he returned to Demorest for the off-season, doubtful that just rest would allow his leg to heal.

The Cardinals and the team surgeon, Dr. Robert Hyland, came up with a plan for an operation. Mize was willing to try anything, even if the surgery did not promise a sure-fire solution. Yet Hyland's work did

Johnny Mize (left) posed with St. Louis teammates (left to right) Enos Slaughter, Jimmy Brown, Walker Cooper and Terry Moore before a game.

rescue Mize's career. The player improved sufficiently to show up for spring training in 1936. Due to the iffiness of his health, the Cardinals decided it was pointless for Mize to sit on the bench in Rochester recuperating when he might gain more from sitting on the bench watching in St. Louis. That low-key approach made him a major leaguer at last. This was Rickey's call, and Mize long after recalled the thinking that he would "maybe get to pinch-hit there [in St. Louis]. I tell people I'm the only guy who played in the major leagues because I couldn't play in the minors."[2]

The 1936 season was the turning point for Mize, making it to the top, at last, the hard way. That rookie year, Mize stuck with the Cardinals. He and Ripper Collins were together, sharing roster spots and one first baseman's job. After that season, St. Louis traded Collins to the Cubs to give the position to Mize full-time in 1937.

3

The Majors—Rookie Year

Johnny Mize's long minor-league apprenticeship ended in 1936. Except for fond memories of his regularly knocking the stuffing out of the ball, there is not much record of him pining for the sights in Rochester, New York, and Greensboro, North Carolina, in his future years.

He invested as much time in Rochester and Greensboro as it would have taken him to earn an undergraduate and Master's degree at a university somewhere, but when he did earn his sheepskin he was qualified to move up in his profession.

Most of the time Mize spent in the minors overlapped with the Great Depression, a depressing time indeed across the United States. In that sense, he was fortunate to have a job when upwards of 25 percent of Americans were unemployed, losing homes, and going hungry.

Branch Rickey may have sought superstar talent, but he was not eager to pay superstar wages, even in the best of times. During the Depression, it was not in his heart or nature to spend big. He had supreme faith in his ability to identify first-class players and build and rebuild ballclubs by making essential moves when it became necessary.

The Cardinals were in a boon stretch of success, the franchise making itself into a power in the 1920s and seeing the victories carry over into the 1930s. Mize was in the organization already, but in the minors when St. Louis won the World Series in 1931 and 1934. The most recent National League pennant, which led to a triumph over the Detroit Tigers in seven games, was two years in the rearview mirror when Mize joined the team.

St. Louis was definitely expected to contend in 1936. The Cardinals did not have the same strengths in the lineup as they did in 1934, but they were still well-stocked with weapons. Mize was on the roster, but without a set starting position, although everyone knew most of his playing time would come at first base. It was also suggested that his useful stick could be deployed as a pinch-hitter whenever manager Frankie Frisch needed a left-handed swinger.

In this manner, subbing for Ripper Collins, thrown up to the plate for a single at-bat cold off the bench 21 times, Mize spent most of his rookie year, although as always, when given the chance to hit, he hit. Mize batted .329 that season in 126 games, spending most of his time at first base, in addition to those pinch-hit calls.

The Cardinals opened the 1936 season against the Chicago Cubs on April 14. Mize sat. Big Jawn made his Major League debut on April 16 in the same series against the Cubs. He was a pinch-hitter for pitcher Paul "Daffy" Dean in the 5–3 loss, striking out in the bottom of the ninth inning to end the game. It was definitely one of those unheralded starts.

"Do I remember my first big-league at-bat?" Mize was asked years later. "Sure. I struck out on three pitches from the Cubs' Larry French. I took the first two and I swung at the third. That was no time to go up and pinch-hit when there's two out in the ninth, nobody on and you're a few runs behind."[1]

At that time, Mize couldn't have helped reflecting on how his longtime passion for the game had finally placed him in the majors. After the years of learning the sport as a youth and toiling in the minors, at last he was wearing the uniform of a big-league team.

"I played baseball every chance I got," he said of his early days in Georgia. "In the mornings, before grammar school, during recess, after school and during the summer."[2]

Mize's next St. Louis chance occurred on April 20 when the Cardinals beat the Cincinnati Reds, 8–7. Again used as a pinch-hitter, this time Mize walked and scored a run. Mize had another 0-for-1 box score line as a pinch-hitter against the Reds on April 23.

On April 25, St. Louis' opposition switched. Against the Pittsburgh Pirates, albeit in a 12–5 loss, Mize recorded his first major league hit. Still being used exclusively as a pinch-hitter by manager Frank Frisch, Mize came to the plate in place of pitcher Jim Winford. He belted a two-run double to left field, stroking the offering from Pirates pitcher Jim Weaver. There were just 4,500 witnesses at Sportsman's Park on a Saturday, presumably because the Cardinals were just 3–5 at the time, not quite looking like pennant contenders.

Mize, who would bang 359 of them during the course of his career, hit his first big-league homer on April 30 against the New York Giants. It was a home game at Sportsman's Park, but again attendance was very light, rounded off at 3,000 fans. St. Louis won, 3–2, despite being out-hit, 11–5. The game zipped along, lasting just 1 hour and 37 minutes.

Mize got a start at first base and went two-for-three in the game, slugging a home run and a double in support of Paul Dean. Dean went the distance, allowing those 11 hits but being stingy about letting the

Giants runners cross the plate. The homer represented the winning run in the seventh inning.

New York tied the game, 2–2, in the top of the seventh, then brought in Harry Gumpert to pitch in relief of Al Smith. Gumpert was a right-hander who had a long career, pitching for 15 years in the bigs and winning 143 games. Gumpert, whose nickname was "Gunboat," was beginning an 11–3 campaign in 1936, one of 10 times he won in double figures in a season.

Once Mize got going, taking Gumpert deep, he began showing his ability as a power hitter, ending up with 19 homers his rookie season. He also knocked in 93 runs. By the end of that season, it was clear that Mize was a major leaguer for good, and his minor-league stays were in his rearview mirror.

Despite his strength, Mize had not been a really noticeable power hitter in the minors. He clubbed his share, but was not Ruthian, at least not yet. "But Mr. [Branch] Rickey told me I should have hit more home runs," Mize said. "I told him I don't go for home runs, but if he wanted me to, I would."[3]

With a reputation already established as a fun-loving, entertaining team, the Cardinals were two years removed from their 1934 World Series crown, but seemed perfectly capable of winning another National League pennant.

Mize was young but eager, joining a team heavy on star power and veteran talent. Joe Medwick held down an outfield spot and was a potent offensive weapon with 18 homers, 138 runs batted in and a .351 average in 1936, the type of numbers that carried him into the Hall of Fame. Frankie Frisch was manager, though at 38 was not the full-time second baseman. He could wield the stick when he had to, however. Terry Moore was one of the greatest fielding center fielders of all time. Leo Durocher was the shortstop. Better known for his managing later, he had already played on championship clubs with the New York Yankees, and his .286 average in 1936 helped gain him selection to the first of three All-Star teams. Pepper Martin hit .309, stole 23 bases, and was a marvelous offensive instigator, jump-starting rallies.

Mize said the Gashouse Gang he joined was well-named, though he thought much of the name stemmed from Martin's behavior. Being a teammate with Martin brought considerable excitement.

"That came from Pepper Martin sliding head first, and the dirty uniforms, and the general style of play," Mize said of the famous nickname applied to that bunch. "It was a good name to give them. Martin was the main one, I guess, when you come right down to it. He was the chief wild man and joker."[4]

As a rookie, Mize was quiet around his teammates. He was just happy to be in the majors after his long apprenticeship in the minors. He let his bat doing his talking, and his bat spoke loudly. Medwick was used to being the big cheese run-producer, and even though he should have welcomed assistance, some thought he began to show signs of jealousy towards Mize as a new big swinger in the clubhouse.

"John wanted to drive in runs, and so did Medwick," said infielder Don Gutteridge, "and there was some times when John was on base and Medwick got a hit and he thought John should have scored. Then, Medwick would get on him. But Joe was kind of arrogant. We called him the 'Mad Hungarian' because he was mad all the time."[5]

The Cardinals had a strong team in 1936. In 1935, the year after capturing the Series, they finished second in the NL with a 96–58 record, one more victory than in 1934, but they couldn't repeat. The feeling going into 1936 was that it should be St. Louis' turn again.

No one entertained baseball fans, or sportswriters, more than Dizzy Dean as the face of the Gashouse Gang. He led the league in wins with 30 in 1934, but also malapropisms. His nickname was at the core of the Cardinals' image. Dean was almost as good in 1935 as the year before, winning 28 games with 29 complete games while throwing 325 1/3 innings.

Dean was only 26 in 1936, in his prime, and looking as if he could keep up his remarkable work for some time. He did not disappoint in 1936, going 24–13. He threw another 315 innings and, as an illustration of how he was relied on, Dean was called upon in relief often enough to accumulate the equivalent of 10 saves today.

Dean was one of those singular personalities of baseball history, almost too good to be true as a chatterbox and hurler both. His brilliance on the mound didn't last, though he is forever remembered for his 30-win season, due to injury. As a television commentator, his gift of gab lasted much longer in public forums, on the air and as a speaker at banquets.

The problem for the 1936 Cardinals was that Dizzy Dean didn't have much help in the rotation. Pursuing a pennant was futile without more backup. Roy Parmalee and Jim Winford each won 11 games, and they were the only others with double-figure victories. Paul Dean, also known as Daffy, and Dizzy's younger brother, wasn't healthy enough to finish better than 5–5.

"Daffy" was a nickname of convenience, to complement older brother Dizzy's moniker, not because Paul really earned it. He was more steadfast than goofy. Dizzy was the jokester. Paul went along for the ride. When sportswriters tried to pump him for information, Paul said,

"Diz does enough talking for both of us. Whatever he says is OK with me."[6]

Dizzy Dean talked early and often. He made bold predictions, and the duo lived up to them. In 1934, he announced in spring training that they would win the pennant for the Cardinals. Dizzy won his 30 games that year, the last man to do so in the National League. Daffy won 19 that season, so the prognosis was pretty much accurate.

They once pitched a four-hit shutout (Dizzy) and a no-hitter (Paul) back-to-back in a double-header. Dizzy said, "I wish Paul would have told me he was going to do that. I'd a done the same thing in the first game." Paul got the last laugh that time, saying with a chuckle, "Once in a while I got to do something to top him."[7]

"We always seemed to be one good starting pitcher short of a pennant," Mize said of his days with the Cardinals, just a little bit too late to share in the prime glory. "If Diz hadn't gotten hurt when [Earl] Averill's liner hit him on the foot in the 1937 All-Star game … well, who knows?"[8]

The Cardinals were good in 1936, but not as good as they were the preceding years and not as good as they needed to be to claim the pennant. St. Louis led the National League in runs batted in, slugging percentage, and stolen bases. That showed there wasn't much wrong with the offense. It was the pitching, behind Dean, that didn't provide much assistance. The Cardinals finished with an 87–67 record, tied with the Chicago Cubs for second place behind the pennant-winning New York Giants, who finished 92–62.

Overall, 1936 was a good break-in season for Mize. He was ensconced in the majors and he wasn't budging. The Cardinals realized he was a gem and a keeper, and they traded away Ripper Collins while giving the first baseman's glove to Mize full-time starting in 1937.

4

Cardinals Stardom

In the 1930s, baseball was king. Baseball was the sport that everyone cared about, with boxing, horse racing, and football ranking somewhere back on the fandom scale. That meant if you became a top-shelf baseball player in the majors, fans everywhere knew your name and learned about you. For Mize, he began to gain a following as a rookie in 1936, but he became a star in 1937. There was really no long lag time.

Every city supported its big-league club, but some hotbeds were more passionate than others. During that era, New York had three major league clubs in the New York Yankees, New York Giants, and Brooklyn Dodgers, with split allegiances amongst the populace. New York was also the media capital of the world, so every time a player laid down a bunt, he received disproportionate attention.

Philadelphia had two teams, one in the National League and one in the American League, as did Chicago and Boston. Those big cities featured numerous daily newspapers, each devoting ample space and manpower to the coverage of the ball clubs.

St. Louis fit the bill as well. The Browns were in town representing the AL, and the newspapers were as aggressive as they were most places. By becoming a full-time starter at first base for the Cardinals, Johnny Mize became a public property of sorts. He was replacing Ripper Collins, a solid contributor, so there were some expectations attached to his performance level.

Stepping into the lineup on a regular basis, Mize became an elite figure on a team that had a strong and vociferous fan base. The spectators demanded a lot, and he was the right guy to fulfill their expectations and the expectations of management. He had seemed to be a man in waiting for an eternity anxious for this chance, and he jumped on it, taking over at first base and emerging as the team's next big-time hitter.

The timing, if a little slow in Mize's mind, was just about perfect for the Cardinals. Mize was a coming-into-his-prime 24 years old that season, and in a 154-game season, he played in 145. He totaled more than

600 plate appearances, and his power numbers were attention-getters. Mize clubbed 25 home runs and drove in 113 runs while batting .364 on 204 hits. Collins was not missed in St. Louis.

From the days of Babe Ruth on, when the "Sultan of Swat" was revolutionizing the game with his bombardment of home runs, the homer has been associated with free swingers, sluggers who strike out more than the average contact hitter as a trade-off for their ability to hit the ball a long distance. Mize came ready-made, though, with a sharp eye, a player who could bash the ball, but who was as discerning as one of those banjo-hitting middle infielders. It was not all that common a combination.

Mize espoused a somewhat conservative approach to hitting when he penned an instructional book on hitting for youngsters. "The most important point to remember when learning how to hit is just meet the ball," he said. "Don't swing for the fences. I have always believed you can teach someone to be a good hitter if he is meeting the ball. But you can't teach the boy who continues to swing hard and miss all the time."[1]

While Mize had confidence in his ability, he was not a player who showed off, who drew a lot of attention with verbal outpourings, and on a team like the Gashouse Gang, he did not stand out for any antics. Except for the occasional clubhouse friction with Joe Medwick, Mize mostly minded his own business and was more an observer of the situations behind the scenes than at the center of them.

On a team like this, loaded with strong personalities and veterans who had won championships, it was most likely the best way to behave as he broke in and becoming accepted as one of the Cardinals. His image among most teammates was of a laid-back guy who brought help to the lineup with his bat.

"Johnny was always smiling," said Hal Epps, an outfielder who spent parts of a few seasons with the Cardinals when Mize was a member of the team and hailed from the same region of Georgia, "and if he had a bad moment, I didn't know about it. He had a good attitude. Easygoing. Nothing seemed to bother him much."[2]

One way to fit in with the Gashouse Gang was to laugh at the jokes told and the actions promulgated by the stars. The Cardinals definitely liked to win, but they also wanted to have a good time while they did so. If they felt circumstances warranted, they were not shy about stretching the boundaries of mature behavior, either.

Having time on their hands while on a road trip could be a dangerous equation for the Cardinals. Mize recalled one occasion when St. Louis was in Philadelphia to play the Phillies, but the game was called on account of rain and the team was stuck in its hotel with nothing to do. When these opportunities for mischief sprang up, third baseman Pepper Martin was often an instigator.

Martin preferred action over inaction, doing something physical rather than lying around in his room reading Shakespeare. "When Pepper was idle, you just knew that a situation was going to load up," Mize said.[3]

As the rain poured down in Philadelphia, Martin enlisted the partnership of Dizzy Dean (who was always game for a good practical joke) and at least one other teammate. They scrounged up workman's caps, overalls, and tools, said Mize,

> and went downstairs to remodel the hotel. They went into the barbershop and told the barber they had to take his sink out. He chased them out and they went into the dining room. They started crawling under the tables where people were eating and began hammering and moving things around. This went on until the complaints reached the front desk.
>
> This went on until the hotel manager came around to see what was going on, but by that time the boys were gone. They would do things like that. Anytime, anyplace.[4]

In Mize's telling, it sounded very much like a Marx Brothers routine. Such foolishness seems quite different from the modern way ballplayers supposedly waste time by playing video games, or otherwise employ telephone technology while they are sitting around their hotel rooms.

Mize was the low-key newcomer on this team of outgoing personalities, who had a history together, who had a history with the Cardinals, a good history producing solid winning seasons and championship results, and who were well-known to the fans.

Sometimes it seemed as if Mize was just sitting back and watching the circus pass by as he established himself as an integral member of the team and a budding star. But most of the sub-plots off the field for the 1937 Cardinals did revolve around others.

Foremost was the drama surrounding the Dean brothers. When Dizzy was at the heart of a matter, one could be sure something unusual, or at least something eye-catching, was in the works. And he pretty much did speak for younger brother Paul when issuing his proclamations to the press.

This was the spring of the Great Holdout, the Deans versus management, seeking new contracts with big bucks penciled in. Still just 27 entering that 1937 season, Dizzy was coming off a 24-victory 1936 campaign. Daffy had gone 5–5, and it wasn't even clear if he was healthy. This limited Dizzy's bargaining power when he made outrageous statements to sportswriters as part of his pre-season strategy.

Dean informed president and owner Sam Breadon that he would not play for the St. Louis Cardinals in 1937 for less than $50,000. With America trying to drag itself out of the Great Depression and with baseball attendance down across the country because the patrons did not have much disposable income, Breadon was not inclined to shell out.

Dean declared that if he did not receive the $50,000, he would walk away from the sport that had made him famous, coming out of small-town Arkansas as either Jerome Hanna Dean or Jay Hanna Dean before everyone began calling him Dizzy. This was both a bold and empty boast. He had accomplished much in a few years, and the musical accompaniment to his achievements were the words that flowed from his mouth. One common phrase Dean uttered in his drawl was that if he did it, it wasn't bragging.

As mid–March came and went, and with salary negotiations stalled, Dean told the inquiring minds of the press box, "I will never pitch another Major League baseball game."[5] This brought raised eyebrows from the writers, but no tears from Breadon, who didn't believe him.

A vocal public participant in the back-and-forth was Pat Dean, Dizzy's wife, who spoke up when questioned, even if it was somewhat of a rarity for a spouse to take part in such negotiations in newspaper sports pages.

A couple of months ahead of spring training, she actually foreshadowed the testy talks in an interview. She explained how the couple had $100,000 in the bank and a new home and didn't need baseball's money for survival. Pat Dean also made it sound as if previous years of dealings with Branch Rickey had left her cold. Rickey was often the front man in protecting Breadon's money, and this ultimately would come into play when other players, including Johnny Mize, were seeking raises.

"Branch Rickey signed us last year only because we didn't have enough money to tell him to quit bothering us and go on back to St. Louis and do his fancy talking and shouting where we couldn't hear him," Pat Dean said. "This year things are different. We've got enough in the bank to live on the rest of our lives and we don't sign for one penny less than $50,000. It's 50 grand or we don't pitch."[6]

This was drawing battle lines early, considering the Mrs. spoke in January. Blunt towards the Cardinals, she was conciliatory towards the fans. "I would like the American baseball fans to know just how we stand," she said. "They pay us our living and they have a right to know. You tell 'em that the only trouble between us and the Cardinal bosses is that they don't want to pay us what we deserve. We draw thousands of dollars through the gates, and believe me we are worth a lot more than they want to pay us."[7]

Calling Dean's bluff once Dean hit training camp in Florida, and taking his ego down a peg or two, when the pitcher wrote a letter of what was called resignation, but was technically of retirement, to St. Louis to be forwarded to the National League offices, the Cardinals graciously said okay.

That left the return volley in Dean's court, and he said, "That's very nice of them to give me my release. They've been very fair about it all. It was just what I expected them to do. That means I am definitely through with baseball."[8]

None of Dean's ploys paid off, and he was smacked in the face by reality. He wasn't going to win this battle, and since baseball had made him famous, gave him a forum, and made him comparatively well off compared to the average American worker, he was better off pitching than trying something else. So he signed a contract with St. Louis for $25,000.

When the terms were revealed, Dean was not in the house. Breadon made the announcement, saying Dean had called him after midnight to suggest they work things out and they did so. Dean was still on the roster for 1937. Alas, it was a troubled year and he finished 13–10. The season was even worse for Paul Dean.

Daffy appeared in one game and did not get anybody out in his sole appearance, ending with an earned run average of infinity based on the three runs he surrendered. He recorded a 0–0 record for the season. Daffy was injured all year and was never as effective as he had been earlier in the 1930s.

The decline of the Dean brothers was a huge blow to the Cardinals' pennant chances that season. Dizzy was a sure bet for 20-plus wins but didn't get there. Daffy, if healthy, was a likely bet for 15-plus wins. The holes in the pitching staff could not be patched.

Of course, no one could foresee what befell Dizzy Dean during that 1937 season. He was cruising along with a 12–7 record and was chosen for the National League All-Star team. Dean was on the mound when the Cleveland Indians' Earl Averill stepped into the batter's box for the American League. Averill tattooed one of Dean's pitches right back at him. The line drive hit Dean in the left foot, smashing into a big toe.

This was a painful moment for Dean, more painful than he might have imagined because it triggered a landslide of events. In the type of half-sensible, half-offbeat comment regularly uttered by Dean, his reaction to the doctor's analysis of his injury was "Fractured? Hell, the damn thing's broken."[9]

This was an injury that should not have led to the consequences it produced. Dean had his heal-up layoff, but he returned to the mound too quickly. To ease pain still emanating from the toe, he altered his pitching motion. That was his fatal mistake. In doing so, he put extra strain on his right shoulder and caused an injury that forever reduced his effectiveness as a thrower. In a matter of months, Dean went from a $50,000 pitcher to essentially a $5,000 pitcher, though it took a little bit longer to figure that all out.

Although he did not see nearly as much of Dean at his finest, Mize did garner enormous respect for his talents. He was hesitant to rate

Johnny Mize (right) with his good friend Stan Musial, a fellow Hall of Famer and the most revered St. Louis Cardinal of them all. Musial always said the team made a mistake trading away Mize and that error contributed to the loss of one or two pennants.

Dean as the best he saw, but he did have him in his top three. "Dean enjoyed the clowning and cutting up as much as anybody," Mize said. "But when he wanted to pitch, he could pitch. If he said he was going to shut them out today, why, he'd come pretty close to doing it. He was one guy who could pop off and back it up. Was he the best pitcher I ever saw? Well, when you've faced guys like [Carl] Hubbell and [Bob] Feller, too, it's hard to tell which one is the best."[10]

Those were all good candidates to be considered the best pitcher in the Johnny Mize era in baseball. All three are Hall of Famers, with Dean and his cut-short career having a record of 150–83, Hubbell, who just missed being a teammate with the New York Giants, going 253–154, and Feller going 266–162.

Hubbell was a spectacular pitcher, angular in build, and unlike power pitchers, he did not have a sturdy lower body. There was a running joke that Hubbell was so skinny he lacked a caboose of any note, and he agreed. "You gotta have a better anchor than I did," Hubbell said. "I didn't have any behind."[11]

As tough as Mize viewed Hubbell as a mound foe, he was fortunate Hubbell had recorded his most famous mound exploit long before Mize represented the American League in the All-Star Game. In the 1934 contest, Hubbell, twirling his trademark screwball, struck out five Hall of Famers in a row: Babe Ruth, Lou Gehrig, Jimmie Foxx, Al Simmons, and Joe Cronin.

For all of his respect for King Carl Hubbell, Mize did produce one very memorable game against him. On July 13, 1940, Hubbell was not as crisp as usual against the Cardinals, allowing six earned runs on 12 hits in 6⅓ innings. Mize belted Hubbell for a single, double, and home run. Then, in the bottom of the ninth inning, Mize tripled off reliever Red Lynn, which gave St. Louis a 7–6 win and enabled him to hit for the cycle.

The 1937 Cardinals had no such superstar pitcher in the lineup for that season, only a diminished Dean, and that cost the club. Mize was on the rise, the most notable new addition to the Gashouse Gang. But the team was beginning to falter.

Rather than contend for an NL pennant the way the previous Cardinals clubs of the 1930s had, this bunch finished 81–73 and in fourth place.

5

Low-Key Johnny Amid the Wild Men

What a collection of characters the comparatively unassuming, often stand-back-and-watch Johnny Mize joined in St. Louis, if only the tail end of the group that nine decades later still is referred to by a nickname and is regarded as one of the most colorful bands of ball players ever assembled—and one that was not merely humor-provoking, but successful.

Mize was late to the Gashouse Gang party, but he wasn't too late. He shared the lineup with many of the star individuals who brought such joy and entertainment, such high-caliber baseball and hijinks to St. Louis.

A boy who overcame some hardships growing up and who in his late teens into his early 20s was someone who seemed to receive only belated appreciation from his team, Mize was not the kind of guy who was going to be out front waving a flag as the grand marshal of a parade. There were others on the roster better suited to that.

What he did bring to St. Louis was a big bat, and he was someone who was such a fine player that he represented the beginning of an era of change, the new guy who could help ease the transition from the champs of the recent past to the next generation of players who could bring more glory to the St. Louis Cardinals. Mize was glad to be there, and he spent little time proving he belonged in the line-up full-time in 1937, at the job he was gifted at first base.

The Cardinals could be rambunctious even on their own, without an opponent. One sportswriter of the era wrote, "They fight among themselves and use quaint and picturesque oaths. They are not afraid of anybody. They don't make much money and they work hard for it. They will risk arms, legs and necks, their own, or the other fellow's, to get it. But they also have a lot of fun playing baseball."[1]

This was true on the main counts. Dizzy Dean needled his fielders, blaming them for errors that cost him games, and the irascible Joe Medwick and Dean were ready more than once to throw punches at one another. In between, they all had fun. But they were also very good at what they did.

Mize joined good company, with the savvy Frank Frisch as manager, even as his days as a player-manager were waning at 39 after a 1936 season when he batted .274. He used himself in the lineup sparingly in 1937, only playing in 17 games. That year, too, it was Pepper Martin's turn to give up full-time work in the field, though he did bat .304 in 98 games.

However, Mize's observation that the Cardinals always seemed to be just one pitcher away from a pennant was accurate. The most-used starters of 1937 were trying to make up for Dean's woes. Some did their share, but the team had no true stopper as a regular. Dean's 13–10 mark was still better than most, and his low earned run average, just under 2.70, was better than all. Bob Weiland went 15–14 with a 3.53 ERA. Lon Warneke's 18–11 record was first-rate, but his ERA of 4.53 was not. Si Johnson was 12–12 and 3.32. Mike Ryba made for a fifth starter, kept because Dean was idle so much. Ryba was 9–6 with a 4.13 earned run average. They were serviceable as a group, but not outstanding.

Dean seemed more than brittle physically that year. He seemed in danger of going off the deep end. He verbally lashed out at National League President Ford Frick, got suspended, seemed on the verge of signing an apology letter, and then backed off. Once again, some folks wondered if Dean's injury was not in his toe or shoulder, but in his head. It was not exactly a prudent move to label the chieftain of the league as one of the two biggest crooks Dean knew of, along with a certain umpire.[2]

One minute Dean was holding out for more money and saying he planned to retire if the Cardinals didn't pay him what he felt he was worth, and the next he announced that he was going to sue Frick and the league for $250,000 "if I'm deprived of making a living, which is pitching for the Cardinals."[3]

Dean supposedly said he was misquoted by a sportswriter, but he would not apologize in writing, announcing, "I ain't signin' nothin'."[4]

This all took place not very long after Dean got into a fight with a different sportswriter and punched him in the face. One sports columnist remarked that the writer was fortunate Dean's wife, aka "Mrs. Dizzy," hadn't done the swatting. Apparently, it was believed that she was tougher than Mr. Dean. It was definitely hard to keep up with the Deans.

Those iffy earned run averages sometimes meant there was a need to get pitchers out of the game before they allowed a couple of touchdowns. When the other hurlers were being roughed up, Mize said, Mrs. Dizzy, Pat Dean, would yell from the stands for Frisch to put in her hubby to drench the flames.

"I can remember games where our starting pitcher got knocked out and we'd send in a reliever or two and every one of 'em would get hit pretty hard," Mize said. "Diz's wife Pat would be sittin' in the stands at Sportsman's and we'd hear her yell, 'Put Jay in there! Put Jay in there! He'll get 'em out!' She always called him Jay, not Dizzy."[5]

There was still some latent and periodically sometimes true craziness left in the old gang, but slowly and steadily, the old Cardinals were passing from the scene. Martin, still present and accounted for, even changed. He had been known as "The Wild Horse of the Osage." By 1937, he was leading a musical group made up of Cardinals as the house band. They called themselves "Pepper Martin's Marvelous Musical Mississippi Mudcats." Which, keeping it close to home, sounded Daffy enough. A *New York Times* sports columnist suggested that Martin's new nickname should be "The Wild Bull of the Orchestra Pit."[6]

Martin started on harmonica, switched to the guitar, and directed traffic. Lon Warneke played the guitar. Bob Weiland played a jug. Frenchy Bordagaray, a utility player on the field, also seemed to be a utility musician, dabbling with several instruments.

"Why, we play everything—we play anything—whether we know it or not," Martin said of the group's repertoire. At times the same may have appeared true of how they were performing on the diamond. A sportswriter commented that he saw manager Frisch with his fingers in his ears when the Cardinals were playing—music, that is—but it would not have been surprising if he transferred his fingers to his nose as they played out the 81–73 season that some believed ahead of time was a potential pennant year.

It might be noted that some of the antics of these Cardinals were not far different from the Gashouse Gang's habits off the field, with the difference being that the earlier crew had its playfulness immortalized because it was winning, and the latter group was criticized because it was not winning enough.

Don Gutteridge, who had a lengthy career in baseball, coaching as well as playing, was not a youngster by the time he reached the majors for a short while in 1936, but was supposed to be fully formed by 1937. However, he started off hitting slowly, and Frisch was close to exiling him to the minors when Gutteridge had a heart-to-heart with the boss and pleaded for a little more patience. "I know what's wrong with me," Gutteridge told Frisch on a train ride between series. "You see, ever since I could read a box score, I was a Cardinal. Then, when I got a chance actually to play third base for my favorite club, it sort of struck me all in a heap. I was so anxious to make good that I've been trying too hard. But now that I've got it all figured out, if you just give me a little longer, I know I'll go up there to hit loose as a goose."[7]

Frisch said he would give Gutteridge one more chance, but if he did not come through, he would be demoted to Columbus, Ohio. Gutteridge ended up batting .271 that season, so he might have been right about what had been holding him back.

One thing about Mike Ryba was that he proved over and over again how much he loved the game and how willing he was to be employed in any manner by a creative manager. In the minors, he made appearances at all nine positions. There was no designated hitter, or he likely would have tried that, too.

Ryba was a 32-year-old rookie in 1935, and his 9–6 season was the second-best of a career that lasted through 1946 with the Boston Red Sox before he stayed in baseball as a coach, manager and scout. He returned to the Cardinals as a coach for several years in the 1950s.

There were a couple of other oddities on Ryba's resume as well. He got a late start in pro ball because he worked in coal mines first. When he was toiling in the minors for years (shades of Mize), Ryba won Most Valuable Player awards in the Middle Atlantic League, the Western Association, and the American Association. A few years later, after the Cardinals lost interest in him and Ryba was trying to work his way back to a major league job, he won the MVP award in the International Association. That was some record. Also, Ryba both pitched and caught in both the American League and the National League, not something a club would dream of trying today. His lifetime pitching mark was 52–34 and his lifetime average was .235, though he never did hit a big-league home run.

Ryba admitted he needed to put to use different muscles when assigned the two tasks, though he seemed not terribly exorcised by the challenge. "But once I was warmed up I never found any trouble throwing from the rubber or behind the batter."[8]

Ryba, born in De Lancey, Pennsylvania, favorably compared the lifestyle of being a coal miner and a ballplayer, noted that he met his wife when sent to the minors one time, and although when he managed in the minors he also had to drive the team bus, he didn't mind doing that. "But baseball to me was a vacation after my days in the coal mines and I never minded the hard work," he said.[9]

Still, the Cardinals needed pitchers who could pitch more than pitchers who could catch. While the team was gradually being

re-shaped, Mize was emerging as a pivotal hitter. Mize did not pontif-
icate verbally around the batting cage about hitting rights and wrongs
and hitting style, but he absorbed ideas, assimilated them into his own
approach, and later became confident enough to write a book on hitting,
dispensing advice.

The book was aimed at youngsters and their fathers, urging them
to develop their swing in the proper way, though no one prohibited a
struggling big leaguer from buying a copy and studying the pages rather
than taking college-level courses in how to hit. Although Mize was
just beginning to establish his reputation in 1937, by the time the book
came out, his body of work spoke for itself. His credentials were in the
numbers.

When Mize first broke into the majors, he swung a 40-ounce bat.
To the denizens of the game in the 2020s, that would be equivalent to a
Fred Flintstone club, a caveman club. By the end of his career, when he
was 40 years old, Mize had downshifted to a 36-ounce bat and choked
up on it about an inch. Not being as strong or as quick led to Mize's
adjustment.

Over the years, hitters worked closely with bat companies, most
notably Louisville Slugger, to tailor their bats to their preference. Mize
discussed one point rarely heard, at least not in public, especially among
those conscious of endorsements. "A great many professional ballplayers prefer the handle of one model and the barrel of another," Mize said.
"Therefore, the bat companies will, for the most part, make up bats to
the individual player's specifications."[10]

Mize was not a one-bat guy in his prime. He was not superstitious
enough to stay with one bat at all times but liked to adjust to circumstances and the type of stuff he was likely to see from a given pitcher.
When younger, pre-majors, and even being a big guy, the Big Cat sometimes even wielded a 34-ounce bat. He explained:

> Most ballplayers use two different weight bats during the season for the fol-
> lowing reasons. No. 1, it is wiser to use a lighter bat against a fastball pitcher
> and a heavier club when you have a pitcher who doesn't throw as hard. No. 2,
> The weather and your physical condition greatly affect the choice of which
> weight bat should be employed. On those hot, humid days that sap your
> strength [and St. Louis had plenty of those], particularly in the later innings,
> it is wise to use a lighter bat. While on a cool day, when you have a lot of
> energy, it is better to use the slightly heavier one. This major-league system
> applies to younger and older boys alike.[11]

What impressed experts through the years of Mize's career was
his bat control, how this home run bopper so rarely struck out. One
year when Mize smacked 43 home runs, he struck out just 49 times.

When he slammed 51 homers, he struck out just 42 times. When he hit 40 home runs, that season he struck out 37 times. The man with the terrific vision never came within hailing distance of striking out 100 times in a year, never doing so more than 57 times. Babe Ruth struck out between 80 and 93 times in a season eight times. Even the discerning Hank Aaron was in the 90s three times, and Willie Mays fanned at least 80 times in a year seven times.

As the 1937 season began, the thinking in the St. Louis Cardinals' front office was that they still had a pennant contender. Ripper Collins might be missed, but Johnny Mize loomed as a trusted, long-term replacement.

Opening day, April 20, was at Cincinnati. Mize was in the starting lineup and went two-for-four as St. Louis won, 2–0. Mize drove in one run and scored the other. It was a nice season's debut, a little reminder proving that indeed he belonged. Somehow, Dizzy Dean pitched a shutout despite allowing 13 hits. Just keeping everyone dizzy.

It was more of the same, only better, in the second game, a 14–11 St. Louis victory. Mize went two-for-four again, but with three runs scored and two runs batted in. He hit his first home run of the season in the second inning. Two games into the season, Mize was batting .500. Obviously, the average would not stay at such a lofty level, but it was a good look-at-me beginning.

For that matter, April was a look-at-us month for the Cardinals. They went 7–1, and Dean already had three wins. Mize closed the month the way he opened it, with two runs scored and two RBI, although his average was down to a much more believable .333.

Only one day into May, after a loss to the Chicago Cubs, Mize raised his average by 20 points. The only problem was that the defeat heralded a much more leveled-off performance for the Cardinals. They came out of May with an 18–18 record, in fourth place in the National League, a much more realistic status report of the team's capabilities that season. Mize was still hitting .345. It wasn't his fault St. Louis wasn't winning more often.

Post-Memorial Day, however, the Cardinals seemed to jell. They began rolling, living up to the hopes of the front office and the fans. After beating the New York Giants, 9–4, on June 25, The Cardinals were 35–22, in second place and just a game out of first. Mize was batting .353. Then, just as abruptly, things went haywire. Between that win and July 3, St. Louis lost six games in a row. When the All-Star Game came around on July 7, it was a good time for a break.

The All-Star Game was conceived as a one-time special event by *Chicago Tribune* sports editor Arch Ward in 1933 as publicity to tie in with Chicago's Century of Progress World Exposition world's fair. The game proved so popular it became an annual institution.

The 1937 game was played at Griffith Stadium in Washington, D.C., an American League home game. President Franklin D. Roosevelt was in attendance and threw out the first pitch. The National League team was managed by the Giants' Bill Terry, and the AL team was managed by the New York Yankees' Joe McCarthy.

Among the luminaries on the AL squad were Lou Gehrig, Joe DiMaggio, Lefty Grove, Jimmie Foxx, Hank Greenberg, and Charlie Gehringer. Featured players on the National League team included Mel Ott, Paul Waner, Carl Hubbell, Gabby Hartnett, and Ripper Collins, by then with the Cubs. He was still hitting well.

Despite their up-and-down season, the Cardinals were well represented. Joe Medwick, Pepper Martin, Dizzy Dean, and for the first time, Johnny Mize, were St. Louis selections. Everything was just ducky for Medwick, who was hitting .404 at the time and slugging .738 with 17 home runs.

This was one All-Star contest the Cardinals wished Dean skipped. It was the game when Cleveland's Earl Averill's liner struck Dean in the foot, breaking a toe, and launching the series of developments that ultimately wrecked his career.

Demonstrating how reliable Mize had been at the plate, he was chosen as the NL starter at first base. Through regular-season games of July 5, Mize was batting .358, and his on-base percentage was .420.

The game itself was won by the American League, 8–3. Unlike more recently played All-Star Games where managers generally only play the selected starters for three innings and keep substituting liberally throughout the game, in the early days of the All-Star Game, starters went all the way. Managers used a sprinkle of pinch-hitters and did change pitchers when it was warranted.

So in his first All-Star appearance, Mize started for the National League at first base, came to the plate four times and went 0-for-four, although he did garner an RBI. Medwick went four-for-five with a run scored and an RBI. As a footnote, Ripper Collins came to the plate once and got a hit.

As the season (and Mize's subsequent years with the Cardinals) went on, there was no lamenting the loss of Collins in favor of Mize. This season showed why Mize was given the job, even if Branch Rickey and the Cards made him wait a long time to get a shot at it.

The Cardinals hinted of making a move in the pennant race in late June and around the All-Star break, but then became stagnant. They seesawed back and forth during July, sometimes getting up to seven games above .500, sometimes dropping to as little as two games over .500. They played just well enough to stay above water, but they made no surge toward the front of the pack.

July ended with St. Louis at 47–42. August was a little bit better. The optimists in the stands at Sportsman's Park (although the clientele was somewhat limited that season with just 430,811 paying customers, coming out of the Depression), felt okay as September arrived. The Cardinals were 65–54 in third place and just 7½ games out of first. That was not a hopeless situation at all.

On September 23, after beating the Brooklyn Dodgers 8–4, St. Louis was 13 games above .500 at 79–66. But for those, such as poet T. S. Eliot, who coined the phrase, and others who believe April is the cruelest month, they were not hanging around the 1937 Cardinals in September. Rather than rallying when they needed to, St. Louis began to come unglued. The Cardinals lost four in a row to start the month.

Then, pretty much consigned to third or fourth place, the Cardinals began losing ground with erratic play. As autumn beckoned and the leaves fell, so did the Cardinals. They lost four in a row to end the month as well, and five out of six. Early in October, St. Louis lost their final two games of the season and finished 15 games out of first place.

What became clear that season was that much of the future depended on the continued slugging of 24-year-old, second-year man Johnny Mize, whose average rose after the All-Star break. The Big Cat blasted 25 home runs, drove in 113 runs, collected 204 hits, and batted .364. He was the new stick in town.

6

Hitting Your Best

There are some famous batting stances remembered over time, from ones belonging to Johnny Mize's old teammate, Stan Musial, to the Boston Red Sox's Carl Yastrzemski. Some young player might look at their style in the batter's box and figure if it worked for them, it might work for him. Chances are the answer is no. The distinctive stances helped make them Hall of Famers, but they were one of a kind. More often, the beginning hitter studied Musial and Yaz and their quirky positioning and concluded, "How the heck do they do that?"

It wasn't for everybody. Nobody talks about Mize's stance so many years after his playing days concluded, but his fundamental approach was as sound as it got, and he was a hitter extraordinaire, as he proved right away in his major league career.

"Be natural," Mize wrote.

Be comfortable. These are the most important rules to remember. Assume a stance whereby you can shift your weight from one foot to the other in a manner that is both natural and comfortable. After you have learned to shift your weight properly and feel natural and relaxed, then you can apply a crouch and open or close your stance. Be cautious when you are doing this, in order that you do not sacrifice your free and natural movement. Remember that scouts, managers and coaches, judge you on your ability to hit and not your ability to look fancy at the plate. Trying to copy the stance of your favorite ballplayer is not good practice.[1]

Musial and Yaz would be Exhibit A and Exhibit B for such cases. Indeed, likely the first scouts, managers, and coaches who saw them almost surely believed they had their hitting success despite the stances they used and couldn't wait to dig their mitts into hands-on renovation. It is a testimony to the success of those players, and probably the stubbornness to their commitment to what they knew worked for them, that they endured as big-league stars with their own mannerisms.

By 1938, it was apparent that Mize was the hitter of the future for

St. Louis. The old guard was fading out. Mize was still on the way up. He had made his point emphatically in 1937.

The other big bat still in the lineup belonged to Joe Medwick. Medwick, born in Carteret, New Jersey, in 1911, was just 26 and was still a core producer as one of the remnants of the Gashouse Gang. At 5-foot-10 and 187 pounds, Medwick was no Big Cat in physique, but he was strong, and over the prime of his 17-year career, he was one of the best players in the game.

Medwick generated some terrific numbers for the Cardinals, then the Brooklyn Dodgers, and ultimately elsewhere, in some late-career stops. His lifetime average was .324 and Medwick batted over .300 every year between 1932 and 1942. He was a seven-time All-Star for the Cardinals and won the 1937 National League Most Valuable Player award as well as taking the Triple Crown, the last National League player to do so.

That season Medwick won the batting title with a .374 mark. He hit as many as 64 doubles in a season, collected at least 200 hits four times, and recorded a 154-RBI season. Mize and Medwick were not best friends, but they were teammates into the 1940 season, when the Cardinals traded Ducky Medwick to the Dodgers.

Medwick had earned the favor of Cardinals fans many times over with his productive bat, and he earned it as a stalwart standing up to the enemy by proxy in the 1934 World Series when the Detroit Tigers, and their fans, took him personally. St. Louis pummeled the hosts in the seventh game of the Series, relying heavily on some of Medwick's 11 Series hits, and Tigers backers became so resentful that he was showered with abuse from the Navin Field fans in the left field grandstand.

Medwick was pounding the daylights out of the Tigers, almost single-handedly ruining the hopes and dreams of a city. The repeated smashes that sent him around the bases were all fair reactions to the tosses of regretful Tigers pitchers. In Game 7, Dizzy Dean was pitching a shutout and by the seventh inning the Cardinals were leading the downtrodden Tigers, 10–0, in the deciding game.

In the course of bashing a triple, scoring Pepper Martin, Medwick sought purchase for his foot on the third-base sack as he slid. Detroit third baseman Marv Owen barely missed stepping on Medwick's appendage, though he went through imitation tag motions without the ball. The Cardinal let Owen know he didn't like the fielder's action, and there was some back-and-forth with minimal harm done and nothing to warrant umpire interference. Medwick promptly scored on another St. Louis hit.

However, Tigers fans were worked up, grumpy because of the score, and irritated by the perceived contretemps between Medwick and Owen. When Medwick took his position in the field in left, many in the crowd of 40,000 seemed to be annoyed by his continuing presence.

Armed with a wide assortment of projectiles, fans, who seemed ridiculously well-stocked, unleashed in Medwick's direction grapefruits, oranges, lemons, apples, bananas, eggs, and other assorted eats that would have made for a healthy meal. They also threw newspapers that had been crushed down in size and even bottles. It was a private hailstorm on Medwick.

Medwick tried to preserve his stoicism and was described as keeping his head up and his jaw set and bravely weathering these autumn storm clouds without an inflammatory response. "They wouldn't do that if Joe had a bat in his hand," said his manager, Frank Frisch. "He'd kill somebody."[2]

It was good for humanity and the baseball establishment that Medwick did not have a bat with him. He hurt no heckler, and he was not hurt by the items thrown at him. This harassment went on for some time, and each time cleanup crews rid the field of the garbage, more materialized in the palms of the throwing fans who sought to bury Medwick all over again. This led to a lengthy delay in play, some said a half-hour.

A particularly interested and peeved witness to the circumstances was Commissioner Kenesaw Mountain Landis, sitting in a box seat, not left field. He summoned Medwick over and they had a chat. Then he ruled that Medwick had to leave the game so it could finally be finished. Imagine the controversy if the commissioner had removed the Cardinals' hottest hitter and the Tigers had rallied against very long odds with an 11–0 deficit to come back and win the whole thing. But that did not happen. Everyone but the Tigers survived.

This story followed Medwick around the rest of his career and the rest of his life, really. Decades later, when a mellower Medwick was approached by sportswriters to chat, he was once introduced to a reporter from Detroit. Someone nearby said, "Duck." As in look out for those flying vegetables. Medwick deftly retorted, "That's why they call me Ducky,"[3] which wasn't true at all, but it was an example of his sharp wit in the moment.

This was evidence of the fiery nature of Medwick, one of the traits that made him such a fine ballplayer. But the scenario remains one of the more infamous in World Series history. More recently, a commissioner would probably have threatened to stop the game and forfeit it to St. Louis to admonish the home fans.

Decades later, in 1975, when Medwick passed away during spring training, the headline on the *St. Louis Post-Dispatch* sports editor's column read, "Fiery Medwick Took No Gaff from Friend or Foe."[4]

The tribute obituary relayed a story about Medwick's incendiary nature, revolving around some tense times the slugger experienced with his pitcher, Dizzy Dean. Dean was not above criticizing teammates' fielding when an error proved costly. Teammates didn't appreciate that outlook.

During one game in the 1930s in Pittsburgh against the Pirates, Medwick, due to misjudging the ball, came up short on catching a fly ball that bounded around after landing somewhere besides his glove. It resulted in three Pirates scoring. Dizzy Dean was furious, and bringing brother Paul along as reinforcement, menaced Medwick. In shades of what Frisch was suggesting could have happened in Detroit, Medwick picked up a bat in self-defense and exclaimed to the Deans, "All right, step right up, boys, and I'll separate you." There was no bloodshed and an inning later, during his turn at bat, Medwick smacked a grand slam. After returning to the dugout, he said to Dizzy, "OK, you big-footed, pig-eared, so-and-so, there's your three runs back and one more. Now let's see you hold the lead."[5]

Dean grumped that Medwick, who had gotten into fistfights with other Cardinals, always wanted to settle matters with violence when all Dean did was stir things with words. You couldn't have a decent argument with the guy, Dean felt, because he was cocking his fist at the first insult. As someone with the somewhat benign nickname of "Ducky," these were rather extreme habits.

Ducky. There were two ideas on how Medwick's moniker originated. One was that when he was playing in the minors in Houston, a girl in the stands called him "Ducky Wucky" because she thought he walked like a duck, which may have been true. The longer version was the reason behind why he walked like a duck. Medwick walked in such a fashion supposedly as the result of a limp from an old injury that affected his gait (some might have thought it was a swagger).

Briefly, Joe Medwick was also Mickey King, a fake name he employed when he was finishing high school and still thought he might want to play college football at Notre Dame and preserve his eligibility after taking money for playing baseball. Given the amateur rules in place at the time, he would not have been able to steamroll players on the gridiron as a student if he had been found out. But he gave up the football idea and went with professional baseball.

Although Mize was unlikely to give Medwick unvarnished praise despite his hitting prowess, he brought his own peculiar stance with him to the plate as one not to be emulated.

Medwick batted right-handed, and when he prepared to swing against a pitcher's best offering, he raised his left foot and angled it in the direction of third base. Some called that "hitting with his foot in the bucket," a no-no for sure in the Mize advice column. Somehow, it never hindered Medwick. It was just not for others.

Like Mize, Medwick succeeded a very able player with the Cardinals at his position in Chick Hafey, who batted .317 lifetime and won a batting title for St. Louis. Medwick's rise to prominence was concurrent with the Great Depression, when teams were extra conscious of saving money and keeping salaries low. Owners always had the upper hand in those days, anyway, but this was an extra excuse to avoid paying raises. Medwick took the brunt of this, but his outspoken nature took over after his spectacular 1937 season, when he led the league in batting with that .374 mark, ripped 31 home runs with his career-high 154 runs batted in, won the MVP Award, and led the league in 12 categories, including 156 games played in a season originally scheduled for only 154.

You could almost hear his thoughts out loud decades later, on the order of: "Now let's see what they come up with to keep from giving me a raise." Medwick showed up for contract dickering with Branch Rickey armed with all the statistics any player could want. When Rickey said perhaps Medwick should meet with owner Sam Breadon, Medwick said no way. "Oh, no, you don't, Mr. Rickey," Medwick said. "I want to negotiate with you. For years, you've been telling me what I've done wrong. Now, I'd like to hear what you think I did wrong this year."[6]

Medwick made no more than $20,000 a season during baseball's lean years. He once said Rickey shaved with a sharp razor without cream as he negotiated with the player, gushing blood all over. Whether it was supposed to demonstrate that the tough times indicated that Rickey couldn't afford to lather up, or he just wanted to show he was tough, it had the effect of hurrying Medwick along in the proceedings.

The disagreement between player and franchise came down to a difference of $2,000—and Medwick was meeting with Breadon by then. Breadon told Medwick the money was a matter of principle, and he would rather throw it out the window than give him the raise he sought. Medwick retorted, "Mr. Breadon, if you ever threw $2,000 out the window you'd still be holding onto it."[7]

Medwick credited his phenomenal 1937 season to getting married in 1936 to wife Isabelle and her quelling his bad habits. He didn't go out and carouse. "This past season I had peace and contentment and plenty of rest. I had the right kind of food. I had somebody and something to fight for."[8] Medwick always seemed to have a reason to fight, but that did not appear to be what he meant.

The Cardinals' penurious outlook bugged Medwick. His own philosophy, espoused when he made the majors, was "Base hits and buckerinos," as in if you collected enough of the former, you would be paid off with a fair share of the latter. It was annoying to learn this was not true.[9]

Neither side of the conversation was likely to produce close personal friendships, but there was a message in there from management to all players in drawing a hard line. After all, nobody else on the team could match what Medwick had done, and if the Cardinals weren't going to reward him, other players had no chance to obtain the big payday. This debate had to be one watched keenly by Mize. He was coming up on the outside as the Cardinals' most important hitter, and he could see there might well be a ceiling on his earnings.

Happily married or not, Medwick never had another season to match 1937. Winning the Triple Crown by leading the National League in homers, runs batted in and average, as well as just about every other number they kept track of at the time was a one-time thing. But Medwick was still a star in 1938, even if he shone a few watts less brightly. His follow-up year consisted of 21 home runs, 122 RBI, 47 doubles, and a .322 average. He "only" led the NL in two categories that season, doubles and runs batted in, and he was chosen for the All-Star team again.

Medwick left no room for anyone to lead the league in anything in 1937, but Mize was right behind him, Lou Gehrig to Medwick's Babe Ruth. That year, Mize swatted 25 home runs with 113 runs batted in and a .364 average, which would be the highest of his career, along with 40 doubles. They were very much 1 and 1A sluggers that year.

In 1938, Mize, like a racehorse coming up on the outside on the stretch, out-hit Medwick in some areas. Mize led the NL in three categories, including triples with 16 (rather remarkable for a big man who really had to hustle around the bases) and slugging percentage at .614, while also compiling a .337 average. Ernie Lombardi, the future Hall of Fame Cincinnati Reds catcher, won the batting crown with a .342 average, and Mize was second. Medwick's .322 was fourth that year. Mize was third in home runs and fifth in RBI with 102.

These were the days when Mize was earning his stripes and reputation as a terrific hitter, as a player others looked to for instruction and advice because of the easy way he seemed to knock the stuffing out of the ball.

7

Home Runs in Bunches

As time went along, Johnny Mize became a bigger slugger than he had been. He did not think of himself as a home-run specialist, but when the season closed, he always had his share of moon shots. His rookie year, playing in two-thirds of the St. Louis Cardinals' games, he stroked 19 homers. In 1937, as a full-timer, Mize slammed 25 homers. The next year, he bashed 27.

One notable aspect of Mize's power outbursts, however, was his ability to harness them in clusters. The longstanding (and often-tied) record for most home runs in a big-league game is four. Mize is not one of those who share the mark. However, he has his own distinction in the big swingers' club—he mashed three home runs in a game six different times.

Sometimes it seemed that the Big Cat would climb out of bed, stretch his muscles, show up at the ballpark with mischief on his mind and his batting eye at 20–10 and decide, Hey, how about a show? Six times. When Mize retired—and for years afterwards—this was a record he held on his own. He still holds a share, but during his slugging career, mainly with the Chicago Cubs, Sammy Sosa also smacked three homers in a game six times. Joe Carter, Mark McGwire, Dave Kingman, and Carlos Delgado had three homers in a single game five different times. Only once in baseball history have two players pulled off the accomplishment. In 2001, Milwaukee Brewers teammates Richie Sexson and Jeremy Burnitz each ripped three home runs in the same game.

On September 25, Milwaukee did not even run up the score that much, defeating Arizona, 9–4. Sexson hit 45 homers that season and Burnitz 34. Mize is also one of only three players to slam three home runs in one game for three teams, joined by Kingman and Alex Rodriguez.

Mize recorded his first three-homer game on July 13, 1938, in a game between the Cardinals and Boston, which was called the Bees at the time instead of Braves. Both teams brought losing records into the game at Sportsman's Park, and not a huge number of fans were interested enough to turn out. Attendance was 7,846 for the afternoon game. Starting on the mound for Boston was Jim Turner, later a venerable pitching coach with the New York Yankees. Mize went three-for-four at the plate with five runs batted in. He touched Turner for homers in the fourth, sixth, and eighth innings. One would think Turner might have been lifted from the game after being on the receiving end of such a personal onslaught. But unfortunately for the Cardinals, their pitching was worse, and Turner got everyone else out. Boston won the game, 10–5, meaning Mize's big blows produced less pleasure than they might have.

He remembered them pretty well, however. Many years later, Mize recounted the feat and how pleased he was with it, but also lumped it together with his other five three-homer days. "I remember something about each and every game," Mize told the Baseball Hall of Fame in a first-person story for its newsletter under a feature headlined, "My Greatest Day in Baseball."[1]

Mize did not go into tremendous detail about the event, which had occurred 43 years earlier, but at 69 years of age he had the pertinent details correct in his mind.

I suppose one's first three-homer game provides a special thrill. I had never hit three in the minors, but mid-way through the 1938 season the Cardinals were hosting Boston. The Bees had piled up an early lead and they coasted to an easy win, but I tagged Jim Turner for three consecutive drives batting fifth in the order behind [Joe] Medwick.[2]

The odd thing was that after going a lifetime without exhibiting such a concentrated explosion of power, Mize soon did it again.

He did not provide many specifics about that day for some reason, merely summing up the achievement this way: "A week later I hit three more in the second game of a double-header against the Giants, and I remember us sweeping the twin-bill."[3] Mize could have been more colorful in his description for the historical minded.

It wasn't as if the original three-homer game touched off a spree by Mize. After that accomplishment, he had eight home runs on the season. Exactly a week later (Mize was right), on July 20, the Cardinals hosted the New York Giants in a doubleheader and swept it. St. Louis won the first game, 7–2. Mize was 0-for-four at the plate, though he drove in two runs.

The Cardinals' record was still under .500, and the Giants brought a 50–32 mark into the second game. St. Louis disposed of them again, 7–1. This time Mize crushed New York pitching, going three-for-four with five runs batted in. He homered twice off starter Slick Castleman and once off Bill Lohrman.

Even with Mize's periodic swinging of a really big stick, the Cardinals were sinking. He arrived in the majors with St. Louis at just the wrong time. In 1936, the Cardinals went 87–67 and definitely thought of themselves as pennant contenders, as a team ready to grab another flag. In 1937, they finished 81–73, slipping backwards in the standings.

In 1938, it became clear to all that the Cardinals were no longer among the elite in the National League. St. Louis finished 71–80 and sixth in the league. This was the end of Frankie Frisch's managerial tenure. The team was 63–72 when coach Mike Gonzalez replaced him, going 8–8 to wrap things up.

Although not as well-remembered by the average baseball fan as he should be, Gonzalez, whose first name was Miguel, was a pioneering Latin American player, coach, and fill-in manager at a time when the Latin influence in the major leagues was almost non-existent. Gonzalez was born in Havana, Cuba, in 1890 and reached the big leagues with the Boston Braves in 1912 as a catcher, playing in just one game that season. He walked once that day, with no hits.

Gonzalez was not a star behind the plate, but found steady work, mostly as a backup. He caught more than 1,000 games in the majors spread over 17 years and batted .253, with time on the rosters of the Cardinals, Cincinnati Reds, Chicago Cubs, and New York Giants. When he took his final major league swings, Gonzalez was 41 years old. A regular in Cuban winter ball, during a period of strong prejudice against dark-skinned individuals in big-league baseball, Gonzalez was light-skinned enough to be allowed into the big-league club.

Although it was on a temporary basis, Gonzalez was the first Latino major league manager. He was called on to fill in for the Cardinals in a similar manner again in 1940. Respected as a smart baseball man and teacher, Gonzalez was a bigger cheese in Cuba, where he won championships as a manager and eventually even owned his own team.

Although his biggest stage as a manager in the United States came when he was employed by St. Louis, years before, future Hall of Fame skipper Joe McCarthy recognized Gonzalez's savvy. Although Gabby Hartnett was the Cubs' catcher of the year and a future Hall of Famer himself, McCarthy frequently subbed Gonzalez in for the prodigy. At the time he said, "There aren't many players who can't out-hit Gonzalez, and maybe he doesn't spiel our language so well [Gonzalez's first language was Spanish], but somehow he makes those pitchers understand him and they'll learn about pitching to a hitter from him."[4]

Gonzalez was 39, toiling in the high minors and very much nearing the end of his playing days when the Cardinals' Branch Rickey brought him to St. Louis. Although placed on the active roster, Gonzalez did not play much for the high-octane Cardinals in the early 1930s, but he acted as a bullpen coach when staffs were smaller. Anyone who got to know Gonzalez recognized his baseball smarts.

While Gonzalez understood and spoke English, he also spoke it with an accent and had his own idioms. He is credited with one of baseball's most famous scouting phrases ever expressed as an offshoot of his periodic linguistic challenges. Scouting for the New York Giants and reporting to manager John McGraw about a prospect, Gonzalez said succinctly, "Good field, no hit."[5] There were times Americans did not understand his accent, but everyone knew exactly what he meant in this case.

Gonzalez considered Frank Frisch a good friend and mentor and was disappointed when the Cardinals fired the "Fordham Flash," truly signifying the end of the Gashouse Gang era. But it would be neither the first time, nor the last that the Cardinals relied on Gonzalez to remedy a problem. Managers were replaced, but Gonzalez stuck through more than one dugout administration. Nearly a decade after Frisch departed, Gonzalez played a major role in perhaps the most famous single play in franchise history.

The Cardinals' ups and downs meant that Mize ended up with a new crew of teammates and a new generation of players who had not been part of the hot spell with Frisch, Pepper Martin (in his heyday), Ripper Collins, and Dizzy Dean. The front office had to face it that some fresh construction work was required to restore St. Louis' foundation as a true pennant contender. The fans, by their absence, were certainly letting their opinions be known by keeping their money in their pockets. Home attendance in 1938 was an abysmal 291,418.

The St. Louis Cardinals organization had become used to winning. Although it had not been one of the early success stories in the first part of the 20th century, by the late 1920s that had changed. The ownership and leadership decided they liked the feel of winning and wanted to keep it up. With the exception of the New York Yankees, since the Roaring Twenties, the Cardinals have been baseball's top championship franchise.

It took from 1892 to 1926 for the Cardinals to capture their first pennant. But the Cardinals won the National League crown in 1926, 1928, 1930, 1931 and 1934, and three of those pennants resulted in World Series championships. St. Louis leadership believed that if the Cardinals were not finishing first, they should be challenging for first.

Branch Rickey's philosophy of building from within, of virtually cornering the market on young prospects and developing fresh replacement talent over the years through the minors, was so aggressive that Commissioner Kenesaw Mountain Landis eventually stepped in, and in 1938 forced the Cardinals to release players to give them the opportunity to play elsewhere in the majors. If not for that drastic step, one might wonder what type of a dynasty St. Louis could have built.

Nonetheless, as the Gashouse Gang guys aged out, the Cardinals needed high-quality new guys. Johnny Mize certainly filled that description, but some of his new teammates became significant contributors, too.

Although he was never much of a power hitter, Terry Moore, who came to the big club in 1935 and staked a flag of ownership in center field, has long been regarded as one of the greatest outfield fielders of all. He ranged wide, covered territory that overlapped both left and right field, and caught everything that was hit in his vicinity. Moore spent 11 seasons in the majors, alas also with three seasons missed due to military service during World War II. He was a four-time All-Star with a lifetime batting average of .280. Moore won more games for St. Louis with his glove than his bat, and he was a rare player appreciated more for his fielding skill in the outfield than for his hitting.

Many years later, future Hall of Famer and Cardinals manager Red Schoendienst, who was a teammate in St. Louis in 1946, praised Moore as a clubhouse leader likely to lead the league in intangibles. "When he was on your club, all the manager had to do was put up the best lineup he knew how," Schoendienst said.

> Terry Moore took care of the rest. If he didn't think somebody was hustling enough, he'd come up to you, grab you [by the shoulder], pinch you and he'd just look at you. He'd say, "I didn't think you hustled enough." Terry was so damn strong. He'd keep pressing harder and harder and all of a sudden you'd see the guy would go down on his knees. He'd never forget it. Terry was no rah-rah guy. He just knew how you should play the game.[6]

Moore must have been stronger than many knew because his listed measurements were 5-foot-11 and 195 pounds. Solid, but not scary imposing.

It was probably no accident that Moore was team captain. He was never a slugger, and perhaps that is why those who are not aficionados overlook him when listing great center fielders. Players like Tris Speaker, Willie Mays, and Mickey Mantle overshadow him. They were better hitters. Moore cast a giant shadow on the grass he covered.

"I always thought more about fielding than hitting," Moore said years after his playing days. "I didn't take as much pride in hitting as I should have. It seemed I could win more ball games with good fielding. Show me a club with a bad outfield and I'll show you a second-division club."[7]

A little bit later in his career, in the 1940s, Moore shared a Cardinals outfield with Stan Musial and Enos Slaughter, two future Hall of Famers. The Cardinals won big with the three of them in the lineup. But that was after St. Louis rebuilt.

If every game was filmed in the 1930s, Moore would have made more than his share of highlight reels for his fielding. He claimed that his most memorable catch came in 1936, his second year in the NL, against the New York Giants. He was chasing a line drive swatted by Mel Ott. New York had the bases loaded and Moore sprinted for the ball and stuck out his right hand in an attempt to knock it down and prevent it from rolling all of the way to the wall.

"I got a real good jump on the ball," Moore said. "Running full speed, I tried to slap the ball down, but the ball stuck in my bare hand. After that catch, I threw the ball to third base to get a double play because the runners were tagging up. Later, I caught a lot of others in my bare hand. I have very big hands and I would just reach out when I couldn't get to the ball with my glove. In fact, I used to practice catching bare-handed."[8]

In 1939, Moore was selected for his first All-Star team. He made only two errors all season and had the distinction of hitting two inside-the-park homers in one year. Before entering the military, Moore was present for the resurrection of the Cardinals in the early 1940s under manager Billy Southworth. The Cardinals won pennants in 1942, 1943, 1944 and 1946. If not for the wartime disruption, Moore believes St. Louis would have done even better. "If the war hadn't come along," Moore said, "I think we would have won six or seven pennants in a row. We were that good."[9]

Jimmy Brown was another of the kind of player handy to have on a roster at all times because he could do many things well, though perhaps not great. Hailing from North Carolina, Brown was an infielder who played for North Carolina State and did not break in as a Cardinals rookie until 1937, when he was turning 27.

Through 1937, the inimitable Leo Durocher was the Cardinals' shortstop, after he had passed through the New York Yankees dynasty spearheaded by Babe Ruth and Lou Gehrig, and well before he became a famous manager of the Brooklyn Dodgers and New York Giants. He had stopped in St. Louis long enough to shout and holler and instigate enough practical jokes to become an accepted member of the Gashouse Gang.

Durocher made an All-Star team for St. Louis before a trade to

Brooklyn, leaving a vacancy sign on the shortstop position for the 1938 season. Brown did not own the slot that season, but he badly wanted it full-time. A sore arm that he believed was healed had interrupted his progress.

In spring training in March of 1939, Brown made it clear that he wanted to take charge at short. Johnny Mize happened to walk into an interview Brown was giving to a sportswriter just as the player was asked, "What are you going to play this year?" Brown replied, "Short-stop. What did you think I'd play?" Mize, who stood 6-foot-2, teased Brown, who was 5–8. He was seeing Brown for the first time after the winter break and ribbed him with, "Hello, you runt, glad to see you." Brown brought Mize into the conversation, asking, "Who's going to play short for the Cardinals?" Mize shot back, "Why, you are, of course. With your arm OK, nobody can beat you out."[10]

Brown stroked nine triples in 1937, hit .301 in 1938, and made one All-Star team for the Cardinals before entering the service. He only played one season post–World War II, at 36, before embarking on a long minor-league managing career.

A rookie addition in 1938 was a major difference-maker for the Cardinals, a fresh face who took over for departing Gashouse Gang figures. Enos Slaughter, 22, broke in and batted .276 with 10 triples to begin a long run, first with the Cardinals, and in the majors overall. His career culminated with election to the Hall of Fame.

Slaughter was born in North Carolina in 1916, and his nickname was "Country" because not even 19 seasons in major cities of the United States in the majors took the country out of him. That didn't even count three years in the middle in military service, another player who lost part of his baseball prime to the war.

Slaughter hit 169 home runs in his career and scored 1,247 runs. That was an indicator that his strength was in his feet. The 10-time All-Star never stopped hustling as he concluded his career with a .300 average on the dot. That was typical of his personality. Long into senior citizen status, Slaughter still raised tobacco. At 75, it was suggested that he might consider slowing down and not making so many public appearances, or working full-time, but he said pshaw to that. "Then what in the hell would I do?" he said. "I'd go crazy."[11]

Of course, Slaughter's name is most famously associated with a running play that won the Cardinals a World Series championship in October of 1946 over the Boston Red Sox. It was a play that even earned a name: "Slaughter's Mad Dash for Home." Slaughter was on first base in the seventh game of the Series when Harry Walker hit a sinking shot to left-center field that became a double.

Boston's star center fielder, Dom DiMaggio, had been lifted from the game with a pulled hamstring muscle, replaced by the lesser-known Leon Culbertson. There were two outs when Harry "The Hat" Walker hit the ball to the outfield between Culbertson and Ted Williams in left. Culbertson fielded the ball as Slaughter ran all-out, never slowing around third base. Culbertson's throw in hit shortstop Johnny Pesky, the cut-off man, and to this day there are arguments about whether Culbertson's throw took too long to reach Pesky, or Pesky held the ball too long. Pesky's relay throw to catcher Roy Partee pulled him up the third-base line. In any case, Slaughter became the hero of the moment, never slowing down until after he crossed the plate. Third-base coach Mike Gonzalez—the old coach who was interim manager after Frankie Frisch—actually attempted to hold Slaughter because he believed he would be out at the plate, but the player ignored him and steamed right past the bag.

"He must have sprung wings," Pesky said. "I would have had to have a cannon for an arm."[12]

Somewhat unusually given the renown attached to that play, Slaughter did not claim it as his biggest thrill in baseball, or even in a World Series game. He selected a nice throw from right field. St. Louis was facing the New York Yankees in the second game of the 1942 World Series.

"We had lost the opener and needed this game," Slaughter said. "We led by a run in the eighth inning when Tuck Stainback ran for Bill Dickey with one out and tried to go to third on a single to right. I threw to third and Stainback was out. The next batter hit a long fly and that runner on third would have tied the game. We won it and won the next three to take the Series."[13]

So the Cardinals were trying to follow their formula of bringing homegrown talent to the majors to fill the gaps as the older guys aged out. Catcher Mickey Owen, 22, took over behind the plate. With Mize, Medwick, Moore, Slaughter, and more, in 1938, no member of the St. Louis starting lineup was older than 26.

There was one problem: None of the younger, successful newcomers was a starting pitcher, and four of the five most frequently used pitchers in the rotation were between 28 and 34. None had the makings of another Dizzy Dean (who was gone, trying to stage a comeback with the Cubs), and Daffy Dean was only 3–1 that year and just about flamed out.

One season later, with most of the same faces in place, however, behind a new manager, and following the lead of their best hitter—Johnny Mize—the Cardinals experienced a notable resurgence.

8

1939

By 1939, the St. Louis Cardinals' Gashouse Gang of lore was basically in the rearview mirror. Most of the notable names were gone. Johnny Mize represented the succeeding generation of team stars. He was in his fourth season with the club and his third season as the fixture at first base. He had been chosen for one All-Star team, in 1937, and even though he was not selected in 1938, no one thought he regressed. After all, he led the National League in slugging percentage at .614, batted .337, and was tops in triples with 16.

In 1939, however, Mize graduated to another level of hitter, one not merely admired by St. Louis fans, but noticed by all fans—and opponents. Like any rookie or newcomer, Mize had been an unknown quantity to most hurlers as a fresh face. But after he had been around a little while, they formed opinions.

One pitcher who developed a certain attitude of fear that trotted itself out each time Mize came to the plate was Cincinnati star Paul Derringer. "The toughest hitter in the National League is Johnny Mize," Derringer said that season. "At least I think so. The guy murders me. He's the best hitter of a good ball I've ever seen. He'll take a pitch that's no more than an inch inside or outside and never even quiver his bat. He'll make you come in with that pitch. And then, when you do...."[1]

Mize had grown into such a headache for Derringer that each time it was Mize's turn in the order, the pitcher felt the urge to down a couple of aspirin.

> I was pitching to him in our last night game at home, and thought I was doing pretty well. I kept firing high fastballs to him. He fouls off about six of them in succession. He had me at the three-and-two count then, so I came in with a curve. I've thrown curves that didn't break and I've thrown some damn good ones, if I do say so myself. Well, this one I threw to Mize was as good a curve as I ever threw. And what do you think that big so-and-so did? He stood up there and followed the ball all the way past the break and hit it when it was sweeping down on him. Where did he hit it?

Man, he hit it way past the exit gate in Cincinnati and that's a good 400 feet from the plate.[2]

Although Mize had already batted higher once, in 1939 his .349 average led the league. He became a batting champion. He also led the National League in home runs for the first time, with 28, knocked in 102 runs, and again led the NL in slugging percentage at .626. Now, if anyone discussed the best hitters in baseball, Mize's name was mentioned near the top of the list.

Though he did not write a book about it until later, it was then that Mize really began earning the right to dispense hitting advice to young hitters. He did not keep jotting down notes for later, but his notebook was in his head. He worked out what he had to do, remembered what he had to do, and recalled what he had to do when he stepped into the batter's box.

"There are two phases of a proper baseball swing," Mize said. "The beginning, as you move forward to meet the ball, and the point of contact as bat meets ball. Most important when beginning your swing into the ball is the position of your arms and elbows. As a left-handed hitter, I have always kept my left elbow as close to my body as I could, and pointed straight down when awaiting the pitch. This allows me to swing into the ball with my bat perfectly parallel to the ground."[3]

Mize set his tone for the year in the Cardinals' first game of the season. St. Louis won, 3–2, over the Pittsburgh Pirates, and Mize went two-for-three. So he was batting .667 after one day, the April 18 opener. Mize hit his first home run of the season on April 23 off Clay Bryant of the Chicago Cubs in a 6–5 loss. Mize ended April with a .310 average. The Cardinals concluded the month 5–4. Fans responded to a chilly April with their own big chill. At one Sportsman's Park game, paid attendance was just 1,994. After the disappointing losing season of 1938, the fans did not yet trust the new Cardinals.

The Cardinals did have a new manager, though, given authority by the team powers to turn things around. Ray Blades did not have the name recognition of Frankie Frisch, though he might have been as known in St. Louis as interim manager Mike Gonzalez. Blades was very much a known quantity to the Cardinals' decision makers.

Blades, born in 1896, was first spotted as a talented player by Branch Rickey in 1913. However, at the time Rickey was managing the same-town St. Louis Browns of the American League. Blades eventually signed with the Cardinals and, while not breaking in as a rookie, mostly as an outfielder, until 1922 when he was 25, spent 10 years with the team.

Known as a fiery competitor, Blades recorded a .301 lifetime major league average with a .395 on-base percentage in 767 games. He stayed in the chain as a minor-league manager—with high-level teams—between 1933 and 1938, where his temperament made him enemies. Soon enough he angered big leaguers by banning drinking. He was very much a disciplinarian, essentially the contrarian to the atmosphere established by the Gashouse Gang.

But Blades hurriedly shaped a winner, leading the Cardinals to a 92–61 record and into contention for a pennant. The 21-game improvement in the standings was not necessarily expected. As April showed, the turnaround was not instant, but it was gradual, and by the end of May, St. Louis was 22–14. Mize was a .300 hitter and so was Joe Medwick, the mainstays in the center of the order. But they were aided by Jimmy Brown, and perhaps most surprising of all at that point of his career, by a seemingly rejuvenated Pepper Martin, who was filling in a little bit everywhere, including center field. As of Memorial Day, he was batting .352.

The Cardinals stuck around second or third place through June, finishing the month when summer began with a 33–27 mark. Blades was pushing the right buttons or pulling the right tricks out of his baseball cap. Mize was hitting .325, and his on-base percentage was .430. Pitchers were wary of giving him good looks at their throws.

By then, Enos Slaughter was pretty much a star, too, having moved alongside Mize and Medwick as a hitter you could count on. He was hitting .309 going into July. It was clear he belonged, and even if he wasn't going to slug that many home runs, he was always getting on base, always slashing those singles and doubles. Slaughter was just 23 and would bash 52 doubles that year, boosting his average to .320. He also drove in 86 runs and eked out 12 homers. Basically, he was always doing some kind of damage to the opposition.

Slaughter could have ended up elsewhere. In his last minor-league season, he and another outfielder were tearing up their leagues. Rickey realized they both had value, both had big-league futures, but there was really room for just one of them. He traded the other guy, who never challenged Slaughter for supremacy again. Slaughter played with the Cardinals through 1953—and he played longer than that. When he reached his 40s, players teased Slaughter that he was going to stay in the majors so long he would receive his pension before he retired.

Where once Slaughter's nickname was "Country," after 20-plus years in the majors some began calling him "Old Folks." Slaughter was okay with the jokes, but he didn't let them pass without a response, either. Star Braves pitcher Lew Burdette once made a crack at Slaughter's expense when he heard the outfielder being asked to remember back to the beginning of his career and recount the thing he learned that most led to his success. "Remembering from the start of Slaughter's career?" Burdette said in 1959. "No one can remember that far back. Slaughter was growing old the same year Al Smith was running against [Herbert] Hoover [for president in 1928]."[4]

Slaughter took the ribbing but answered seriously. "Well, maybe I have been around a long time," he said, "but I'll tell you one thing. I had to work like the devil to get up here, and now I'm working like the devil to keep someone else from coming up and grabbing my job."[5]

Although he did not stick with the Cardinals, nor in the majors, nearly as long, completing his playing career in 12 seasons, infielder Don Gutteridge, a great fan of Mize's, outlived them all, living to be 96 years old and not passing away until 2008. He stayed in baseball for years off the field as a coach and scout and never even singled out a specific number one thrill, because every minute he spent in the game was a thrill. "Every game was special when you go to put on that uniform," Gutteridge once said.[6]

Gutteridge hit .269 in 1939, but in those days as a shortstop and third baseman, he committed too many errors. A little later, when he switched to second base, his glove improved.

By the All-Star break, the Cardinals were just hanging in the race with a 35–33 record in third place, eight games behind the league-leading Cincinnati Reds. Mize, who went four-for-nine in a double-header with two home runs and five RBI, leaving him at .339, was still sizzling on the last day before the All-Star contest.

The pitching was better, and that made a difference. A tip of the Cardinals cap went to right-hander Curt Davis, who was a 30-year-old rookie in 1934 and all of a sudden became a 22-game-winner at 35 in 1939. Davis broke in with the Philadelphia Phillies and won 19 games as a rookie, but this trip through the summer with the Cardinals was the only time in his 13-season career that he won more. Coincidentally, in his first season with the Cards in 1938, Davis had the same earned run average he did in 1939, but his record was just 12–8. Also in 1939, Davis saved four games.

For a guy who had such a late start in the majors, Davis accomplished many things, including winning 158 games overall and making two All-Star teams. Davis might well have a become a big leaguer earlier, but he was held hostage by the San Francisco Seals in the Pacific Coast League because he was so valuable. The club just would not sell his contract to a major league outfit. When the Seals first offered him around, they demanded $45,000, but nobody would meet the price.

Davis excelled in San Francisco, but he was not happy being held back. "I feel those San Francisco owners deprived me of thousands of dollars in salary," he said.[7]

During the 1938 season, Davis pitched a beauty of a game against the Brooklyn Dodgers, one he said was really a no-hitter with only an official scorer's singular call ruining that. In the second inning, Ernie Koy laid down a bunt and sprinted for first. Johnny Mize darted in to pick it up, grabbed the ball, and tossed it to Davis, who dropped it. Davis the pitcher blamed Davis the fielder, saying an error should have been called on him. Instead, the official scorer ruled that Koy would have beat out the play anyway. It turned out to be the Dodgers' only hit.

Davis regularly won 10 or more games, though he rarely was the top ace on a staff. He was less an overpowering pitcher than one who specialized in good control with an array of pitches. Catcher Mickey Owen, then behind the plate for St. Louis, said of Davis, "Every ball he throws sinks, sails or spins. And they do it at the last second."[8]

Davis was on the edge of exasperation when the Seals held onto him so long, and he resented it mightily. "Any young ballplayer with sense wants to make the major leagues," Davis said. "This is necessary if he is to reach the peak of his profession. Besides, the majors offer about all there is in the way of reputation and financial rewards. When I worked my way to the top of the Coast League pitchers, I felt that I had earned my right to advance. Frankly, I was about ready to quit baseball for good when my opportunity came to join Philadelphia."[9]

Mize was correct that for many years the Cardinals had Dizzy Dean and no one else. This season they had Curt Davis and no heavy-duty second banana. But they did have some depth on the mound. Righty Bob Bowman, who had a short career and never had another top-notch year, finished 13–5 with a 2.60 earned run average. Bill McGee went 12–5 in one of his two noteworthy pitching seasons. Bob Weiland was only 10–12, but his ERA was 3.57.

Lon Warneke went 13–7. He had done well with the Cubs and continued to do well with the Cardinals, coming close, if not quite matching his peak years.

Mort Cooper was 12–6 with a 3.25 earned run average. That year the Cardinals could call on a mix of arms to make things happen. Accuracy came naturally to Cooper, who was also a very sharp trap-shooter. In a 1935 contest, he broke 196 out of 200 targets. Cooper started shooting when he was six and said that if he practiced as much with a gun as he did with a baseball, he would be able to contend with the best shooters in the country at any time.

Cooper was 26 and still ripening as a hurler. A few years later, he would be one of the best pitchers in the National League, in 1942, 1943, and 1944 winning more than 20 games each season and twice leading the NL in victories. In 1942, in one of the two seasons when Cooper won 22 games, his 1.78 earned run average was the best in the league. Given that he also threw 10 shutouts that season, the combination made him the league's Most Valuable Player.

A family member of the farming Coopers of Atherton, Missouri, some 250 miles from St. Louis, Mort was brilliant for a while but was hindered by frequent arm woes. When healthy he did big things for the Cardinals, and also recommended his brother, Walker Cooper, the catcher, to the team.

It only cost the club $75 for Mort's signature, and when his younger brother was turning into quite a player, too, he informed the team, "You guys were pretty square to give me that $75, so I'll tell Walker to sign for nothing."[10]

Taken together, this group gave manager Ray Blades a collection of arms to work with so St. Louis fans could once again think the team had the goods to come through with a pennant.

The Cardinals still suffered from the Dizzy Dean hangover. Dean's greatness was supposed to carry St. Louis for longer than it did. It also cast a gigantic shadow, even after he was injured and could not pitch at a high level anymore. Even after he was shipped to the Chicago Cubs in 1938, where he went 7–1, and followed with a 6–4 record in 1939, Dean still had star power and magnetism. In the late 1930s, he was one of the rare sports figures who could command payments as a product endorser. Although his right arm was not what it once was, Dean's chatty demeanor and charisma hung in there with the baseball fan.

Collier's magazine gathered material to show its readers how much money Dean received for putting his stamp of approval on an item for sale. These were not huge sums of money for endorsements by modern-day standards, but they were good paydays in the late 1930s. His affiliations listed were: Tobacco: $250; harmonica, $50; cereal, $300; Dizzy Dean pants, $438; Dizzy Dean watches, $100; "Me and Paul" sweatshirts featuring Dizzy and brother Daffy; and for appearing in a cartoon cigarette advertisement, $500.[11] Oh, for the days of Dizzy, they pined in St. Louis.

Mize was now a veteran, confident he could hit daily in the big leagues and proud he was in the forefront of the team's offense. He felt his average really demonstrated that he was an all-around hitter (and had been) and not merely a home-run threat. At the end of July in 1939, Mize was hitting .333 and the Cardinals were improved over the Cardinals of recent vintage, when they were losing.

St. Louis was 48–42 at the end of that month, but August was kind. The Cardinals started the month with eight straight wins, added to two in a row ending July. Although there was a short losing streak that month, too, the Cardinals were making noise. By the end of August, they were 68–51, in second place, and just 5½ games out of first. St. Louis was in a pennant race.

Mize did his part during St. Louis' good stretches of the month. He finished the month batting .360. He was hitting so well, teams started pitching around him. During an August 26 doubleheader sweep of the Phillies, Mize walked twice and got two hits in the first game, and he walked four times and stroked one hit in the other game. His on-base percentage was up to .454.

The Big Cat was gaining admiration and earning his status of being able to inform others how to hit. Mize said he often heard talk of people comparing swinging a bat in baseball with swinging a club in golf, though perhaps the main thing they had in common was the word "swinging."

> However, one capital rule regarding a golf swing that differs greatly from baseball is the follow through. The only time you see a batter follow through is when he has missed the ball. In golf, you hit a lighter ball that is stationary. There is no problem in swinging the club all the way through. In baseball, you are hitting a much heavier ball, moving rapidly, and you can't swing the bat through like a golf club.
>
> Most of your power hitters are pull hitters. This is only normal because when you pull a ball, you are throwing the weight of your entire body into it with the greatest possible force, by swinging your bat in a direction that pulls your body.[12]

The 1939 season marked Joe Orengo's first appearances in a St. Louis Cardinals game. Orengo was a 24-year-old middle infielder from San Francisco who played in seven games before becoming a full-time player in 1940. He was the one who bestowed Mize's nickname upon him, a spontaneous reaction to Mize's fancy footwork around the first-base bag. There were a couple of origin stories about how Mize came to be called the Big Cat, but he said Orengo came up with the phrase.

"The man responsible was Joe Orengo, who played second base," Mize wrote in his book on hitting. "One day infielders were having a pretty bad time and were making some bad throws to me at first base. After digging a few out of the dirt, Orengo called over to me, 'Atta boy, John, you look like a big cat.' Some of the writers overheard the remarks and asked Joe about it later. The nickname has stuck with me ever since."[13]

Orengo was also a certified butcher, and he did not exempt himself from butchering the throws to first base that day.

On July 29, the Cardinals were in fourth place in the National League. When they defeated the Dodgers twice by 5–2 scores in a double-header on July 30, they leap-frogged into second place. They were still 12 games out of first. But once St. Louis gained that high spot in the standings, it was never shoved aside. The Cardinals spent all of August in second place, but they kept whittling the lead all of September, too. The chase of the Cincinnati Reds was made in earnest, and St. Louis closed to within 2½ games of first place as late as September 27, but could never quite pull even with the Reds.

Manager Ray Blades pushed buttons and wrung high-quality play out of most of the roster, but when St. Louis ran out of time, the Cardinals had a record of 92–61, sitting 4½ games behind Cincinnati. It was a good enough showing that the upper echelon of management and fans could recommit their faith to the belief the Cards were on the cusp of another championship run.

On the flip side, none of the top-hitting contenders could catch Mize. When they ran out of games and time, Mize was batting .349. Sitting in a second-place tie for the batting title were Mize's teammate, Joe Medwick, and Cincinnati's Frank McCormick, with .332 averages. Mize won the home run title with 28, and McCormick won the RBI crown with 128.

Mize long remembered a humorous incident at the plate that season when the Cardinals were facing the Cubs in Wrigley Field in Chicago. There was much debate at the time that the outfield backdrop for hitters was not quite fair because it distracted them from seeing the pitch coming out of the thrower's hand.

When Frank Frisch was managing the Cardinals, Mize said, he did not want to hear any of his batters using the backdrop as an excuse for not getting good wood on the ball. Indeed, he said he would fine them if he heard them complaining. Mize wrote:

Bill Lee was on the mound when I came up to bat the first time. Their catcher [future Hall of Famer] Gabby Hartnett said to me, "John, how on earth can you hit with that bad background?" I said, "Well, I'll have to see how it goes today." And I promptly doubled to the opposite field. When I came up again in the fourth, Hartnett said, "How did you do it?" And I replied, "Gabby, I just so happened to get the bat on the ball." Then I belted one of Lee's curves over the right-field wall. In the seventh, I stepped in again, and Gabby grumbled, "Don't tell me you can't see in this ballpark." And I tripled off the vines in right field. Well, when I came up in the ninth, Hartnett shook his head. "John," he said, "you're really giving it to us today." I smiled and hit Lee's first pitch for another home run. A double, a triple and two home runs in four at-bats. One doesn't forget that kind of an afternoon.[14]

It was a season for Mize to savor. He led the NL in two key hitting categories, and his team was on the rise. He felt secure in his place with the Cardinals and felt sure that even the penny-pinching financial negotiator, Branch Rickey, would recognize his accomplishments.

"In 1939, I led league in batting with .349," Mize said. "Naturally, after a year like that you look forward to talking contract. But when I sat down with Rickey, he said, 'Well, your home run production stayed pretty much the same.' No mention of my batting average."[15]

Much like Medwick, who felt scorned in the financial realm after his own brilliance on the field was taken for granted, Mize walked away disgruntled. There were no alternative options for a player in those days. He could bargain with only one team, so it was essentially a take-it-or-leave-it situation on contracts.

Reviewing Mize's career, one could pretty much point to this moment when his relations with the Cardinals began to run cold and sent out the first hint that he might not be a St. Louis Cardinal forever.

9

St. Louis Shakes Things Up

On paper and in the numbers, things were on the upswing for the Cardinals—even if Johnny Mize would have told everyone to swing levelly. The team's second-place finish in 1939, with 92 victories, stamped the club as a pennant threat once again. Mize was one of the best hitters in the National League. So was Joe Medwick.

Ray Blades was hardly a warm personality, but his no-alcohol rule, temper flare-ups, and do-it-my-way style was something St. Louis seemed to respond to during that season. The question now was whether he could take them all the way. It quickly became apparent that he could not, and that the smoothness of performance by so many Cardinals the year before could not be sustained.

Most of the pitchers could not match their previous showing, and Curt Davis devolved from an All-Star to a faint presence. At 36, he went 0–4 after winning 22 games a season earlier. Mort Cooper had a losing record at 11–12. The sterling right arm let Davis down. When arm problems sidelined him, the Cardinals ditched him. They did this at the same time they rid themselves of Medwick, a mainstay hitter who appeared in 37 games with a .304 average before they bundled him off to the Brooklyn Dodgers, not so much for useful players who could help immediately, but because of St. Louis owner Sam Breadon's receipt for an estimated $125,000 in cash, though some said the amount of money moving to the Cardinals was in the neighborhood of $200,000.

Medwick had been carrying a grudge against Branch Rickey for a while, almost three years since his fruitless negotiating session for a good raise after his tremendous 1937 season. There never was a thaw between the two men during the rest of Medwick's St. Louis stay.

The player had a built-in attitude problem in the minds of the front office anyway, and he was easy enough to rile. Medwick was not warmly observed by the sportswriters for this reason, either. Medwick was set in his ways and felt he knew Joe Medwick's strengths and weaknesses better than anyone else. "I've always hustled for the good of the team,"

Medwick said. "But I always felt that the best way I could do it was by having the best batting average I could get. There's no sentiment in this game and by helping myself I'm best helping the team."[1]

During his days in St. Louis, Medwick was definitely superstitious. For someone expressing so much confidence in his hitting, it seemed he was inwardly insecure, or at least brought an oddball habit to his philosophy. Medwick believed that every hairpin he discovered in team hotels represented a hit at the plate. No one could explain the connection between the two things, but his faith was unshaken; once, in a Pittsburgh hotel lobby, Medwick found a bounty of lost hairpins and achieved a hit representing each one discovered.

Medwick did not keep his proclivity a secret, and one day a St. Louis sportswriter thought he would test the theory outside of the Medwick orbit. The sportswriter noted that Cardinals star Pepper Martin was in a slump and, as a ruse to help him escape it, he spread hairpins around a hotel lobby. But before the writer could bring Martin in on the search, Medwick took control, finding the hairpins one by one and stashing them away. The sportswriter tried to halt Medwick, but he would have none of that. "Oh, no," Medwick said, "Let him find his own hairpins."[2] After all, they were worth their weight in base hits, and no hitter could spare any.

Medwick was a Cardinal from 1932 through about one-quarter of the 1940 season, or June 12. He batted over .300 for St. Louis nine times, including that partial season, with a high of .374 in 1937, when he led the league. He may not have been beloved by sportswriters, or all of his teammates and all of the fans, but Medwick put in yeoman service, and his absence created a big hole in the lineup. Only one of the acquisitions from the Dodgers moved into the starting lineup. Ernie Koy took over an outfield position, joining Enos Slaughter and Terry Moore in the pasture, and batted .310.

As a team, the Cardinals still hit .275, but without relying on Davis and Cooper, the pitching stagnated despite some good years out of Lon Warneke and Bill McGee, who both went 16–10, and Clyde Shoun, who went 13–11.

Still, the Cardinals were somewhat in disarray after a sloppy start that saw them go 4–6 in April, sink to 10–18 in late May, and somewhat shockingly fire Blades in June with a 14–24 record. It was a swift fall for Blades. His immediate replacement was Mr. Reliable, Mike Gonzalez, fill-in manager again, though he only went 1–5 before the new fella came in.

St. Louis's hire on a permanent basis was Billy Southworth, who ushered in a new era of success in what became his Hall of Fame career as a skipper. After the 15–29 start to the 1940 season, Southworth led the Cardinals to a 69–40 mark the rest of the way. After being around 15 games below .500, St. Louis finished 15 games above .500 at 84–69. Big change.

Southworth had been around the game a long time. He was born in 1893 in Harvard, Nebraska, and made his major league debut as a player in 1913 for the Cleveland Indians. He completed his playing career with the Cardinals in 1929 and had a lifetime .297 batting average. He played little with St. Louis that season, but he became interim manager for 90 games for the first time after leading Rochester to a minor league championship in 1928. He had gone in that leadership direction after a rib injury in 1927 was apparently going to end his playing days.

More than a decade later, and always prized for his skills by the Cardinals, Southworth had had a discouraging parting from the organization in the early 1930s after returning to Rochester and serving in Columbus, Ohio. During that period, Southworth was a heavy drinker, though not an acknowledged alcoholic, who faced and had to cope with several personal family problems and tragedies, including the death of his wife. There was no announcement of why the Cardinals were separating from him, but there was speculation that it related to his alcohol consumption. A short stint as coach with the New York Giants under manager Bill Terry ended badly when the twosome engaged in a fistfight. Southworth worked outside of baseball for a couple of years and then returned to the minors to manage.

Southworth began leading youthful players to minor-league crowns and drinking nothing stronger than Coca-Cola. Cardinals leadership looked at Southworth as a favorite son gone straight and rehabilitated. They brought him back to the organization in 1939 and back to Rochester, where he made the Red Wings winners again.

Now, here was Southworth again, finishing off what Blades started and beginning a more established stint for the club in the dugout. At his hiring press conference, Southworth said, "All I want is a fighting chance to make good. I'm going up with an open mind. I plan no drastic changes. There is nothing wrong with that team that spirit and hustle can't fix. I'm ambitious and I like to be on a winner."[3]

St. Louis finished nearly 30 games over .500 in Southworth's 109 games at the helm in 1940. One guy Southworth could count on was Johnny Mize. While Mize did not defend his National League batting title, he did hit .314, and he was more of a monster of a power hitter. His 43 home runs were a career high to that point, and he led the NL in that category. He also led the NL in runs batted in with 137 and in slugging percentage with .636. He was chosen for his third All-Star team.

This was Mize's greatest home run year to date, and twice in 1940, once early in the season, once late, he smashed three homers in a single game. The first time occurred on May 13, at Crosley Field in Cincinnati, part of a four-game series ending on a Monday. Mize referred to this game as "a mix-up in scheduling. The strange thing about it was no umpires showed up for the game. It was a make-up affair."[4]

One game was tacked onto the originally scheduled series because on April 23, a St. Louis-Cincinnati game could not be played because the field was flooded. That whole series was thrust into the make-up mode of rescheduling because of that incident. Someone forgot to work out the details with the league to send an umpiring crew to Crosley for the 3:30 p.m. game. Some 6,606 fans got the word and bought tickets, however.

Larry Goetz, who umpired in the majors for more than 3,200 games between 1936 and 1957, lived in Cincinnati, was available, and was pressed into service. Each team volunteered someone affiliated with its organization. Jimmy Wilson, the former catcher who was a Reds coach, umped that day, as did St. Louis pitcher Lon Warneke. Warneke had been the losing pitcher in the second game of a doubleheader the day before, so was resting his arm and would not be called on to pitch.

It became a peculiar game, too. The Cardinals and Reds battled for 14 innings, and the contest concluded in an 8–8 tie, no decision. Mize started at first base and nearly single-handedly finished the game in overtime innings. He smacked three hits in five at-bats, all of them home runs, scored four runs, and drove in four runs.

Southpaw Johnny Vander Meer was on the mound for the Reds in the second inning when Mize pounded the ball the first time, a solo shot to center field. In the top of the fourth inning, Mize nailed Vander Meer again with a blast to deep right field that also brought home Medwick, who had singled.

That gave the Cardinals a 3–0 lead. Mize was safely walked in the fifth inning, and by then it was 4–4. The Reds had built an unsteady 7–5 lead when Mize came up again in the sixth. This time he was intentionally walked by Elmer Riddle. The Cardinals came out of that turn at bat tied at 7–7 again, and the game headed to extra innings.

In the top of the 13th, facing reliever Milt Shoffner, Mize smacked his third home run of the day, this time to left field. That made three homers knocked out of the park in three different directions. The Cardinals led, 8–7, and were in position to win. But the Cardinals couldn't hold back Cincinnati and it was tied again, 8–8, after 13 innings. The teams played one more inning, and the game was halted because of darkness. Mize hit three home runs in one game and his team couldn't even win. Seems like one of those baseball anomalies that come around in a long season.

For his next trick, Mize ripped three home runs in a game once again that season, though much later. On September 8, the Cardinals faced the Pittsburgh Pirates in a home doubleheader when it was once more the Johnny Mize show at the plate. Or should have been. The teams had the same record of 66–61, and they struggled in the same manner inning by inning this day.

Just as a glimpse of what kind of game this was, the Pirates started the game with three runs in the top of the first inning, and the Cardinals fought back with five runs in the bottom of the first. That lead held for about 10 minutes as the Pirates added five more runs in their half of the second inning. Pittsburgh had two more three-run innings, and the Cardinals had a four-run inning. No pitchers' duel in this one.

Mize's first home run of the afternoon came in the third inning. Leading off against Dick Lanahan, Mize swatted the ball out of play to deep right. Lanahan was still on the mound in the fourth inning when Mize came up again and blasted another homer. Enos Slaughter was on base, so it was a two-run shot. The ball followed a similar trajectory, again leaving the park via right field.

There was a new fellow on the mound in the sixth inning when Mize strode into the batter's box again, bat twitching, eyes focused on the throws of Johnny Lanning. Goodbye, Mr. Spalding, as one fictional announcer commented in a movie. Mize's third homer, with Terry Moore aboard, kept up the same old traffic pattern, following the right-field route. Complementing the three-homer showing, Mize scored four runs and drove in six. And not even such a muscle-flexing day at bat like that for Mize ensured a Cardinals victory. "But we lost a slug-fest, something like 16–14," Mize noted years later.[5]

St. Louis lost by precisely that score. Pittsburgh amassed 21 hits in that game. Cardinals pitching was not terribly sharp for those nine innings. Those were all momentous slugging days that stuck in Mize's memory. Years later, after a stint in the American League, and in retirement, Mize said one home run–related thrill was his slamming a four-bagger in every big-league park in both leagues; that is, all of the ones available to him during his playing days. Most of those stadiums disappeared over time, replaced by new, more sophisticated parks. And, of course, both leagues expanded so there are nearly twice as many teams now.

The arrival of Marty Marion at shortstop at 23 in 1940 was another major personnel addition from a farm system that kept on producing. Marion first swung a bat for the Cardinals' organization at age 19 and was seasoned until ready at AAA Rochester. For sure, Marion was not rushed. He wasn't a high-average hitter even in the minors, but wielded a good enough bat when he did reach the Show. As a rookie, the player called "Slats" hit .278, so he was not a liability at the plate.

The "Slats" description stemmed from Marion being viewed as a skinny guy, variously referred to as being 6-foot-2 or even 6-foot-4 and weighing as little as 155 pounds and as much as 170.

This was the beginning of a 13-season big-league career that featured seven All-Star selections. Marion also won the National League's Most Valuable Player Award in 1944. He helped spark the stars who surrounded him on the roster, but Marion has never been elected to the Hall of Fame despite many backers who believe he belongs. Much appreciation of Marion's skill centers on his continuous brilliance in the field. He earned several nicknames that sprung from his prowess with the glove, including "The Octopus," "Mr. Shortstop," "The Vacuum Cleaner," and the witty, but slightly more subtle "The Groundskeeper."

This pretty much amounted to Marion being as graceful and acrobatic as a ballerina in the field, one who could reach any ball hit in the vicinity and do something slick or wise with it. "He could go in the hole better than anyone I saw," said Hall of Fame teammate Stan Musial. "He had the most accurate arm you ever saw."[6]

Marion, who was born in South Carolina and attended high school in Atlanta, where he was a member of three state championship teams, had a grandfather preacher who wanted Marion to follow in his footsteps. Instead, Marion found a different calling, a baseball player not necessarily receiving quite the same reverence as a profession. "He never did like that too well," Marion said.[7]

Later in life, perhaps miffed at the short shrift the Hall of Fame seemed to give to glove men, Marion was peppered with provocative questions in an interview, and he did not shy away from boosting himself against the best of his era and those who came after, from Pee Wee Reese and Phil Rizzuto to Luis Aparicio and Ozzie Smith. "You want me to brag?" Marion said to his inquisitor. "I don't think I ever saw anybody that could do it better than me. There ain't nobody."[8]

Marion was added to an already strong lineup that at the beginning of the season included Mize and Joe Medwick, Moore, Slaughter, and Mickey Owen. Then Medwick was sent out of town. Mize was durable, playing in 155 games and with power numbers such as 43 home runs and 137 runs batted in, plus a .314 average. He was in his prime at 27.

The outfit was soon to be joined by lefty-slugging Stan Musial, one of the greatest players of all time who could truly do it all with a bat. Only the first time Musial ran across Mize, the newcomer was still thought of as a pitcher.

Musial, who grew up in Western Pennsylvania coal country, was signed by the Cardinals as a 17-year-old and spent a couple of seasons focused on winning games with his arm in Class D. In a 22-year big-league career, Musial actually appeared in one game as a pitcher. He had long before given up on the notion that he was going to strike people out for a living. One of the people who convinced him of that was Mize, though not with verbal direction.

In the spring of 1940, Musial was just one of many prospects in Columbus, Georgia, waiting to be assigned to a Cardinals minor league team for the summer. One day, he was summoned and told he was probably going to pitch against the Cardinals, the major leaguers, in an exhibition. Musial was already beginning his transition to becoming an outfielder on the suggestion of Burt Shotton, who later managed the Brooklyn Dodgers to pennants, and he wanted no part of throwing to the best players around.

"I didn't start against the Cardinals," Musial said, "but it wasn't long before I was needed." The Cardinals tapped other minor leaguers for six runs, and Musial was rushed into the game. "I retired the side without further scoring and felt pretty good about it. Maybe Burt Shotton was wrong. Maybe I could still pitch."[9]

The thought did not last long.

"In the second inning, I changed my mind," Musial said. "Or rather [Terry] Moore and [Johnny] Mize changed it for me. Moore hit a long home run with a man on base and Mize hit a homer that went farther. I got through three more innings, all scoreless, but I had few illusions left."[10]

Mize had that effect on a lot of pitchers, and they were making a living at the major league level, not just trying to catch on in the minors. It wasn't long before Musial became a Cardinal, not as a pitcher, breaking in at 20 for a dozen games. He came on strong immediately, hitting .426 in 49 plate appearances and making some dazzling catches in the outfield.

His emergence was a shock to Moore and Mize, who did not even recognize him from the mound showing of months earlier. Musial was conversing with Moore about five months later and mentioned how things had changed so quickly for him when Moore burst out laughing and exclaimed, "You're not that kid left-hander." Moore called to Mize, standing nearby watching a clubhouse card game, and brought him into the chat, saying, "Hey John! You won't believe this! Musial is the lefthander who threw us those home-run balls in Columbus this spring." As for Musial, he said, "Neither Moore, nor Mize, I might add, ever let me forget it."[11]

Teased or not, Musial learned something about hitting by watching Mize and later in life praised him for his style with the bat, pretty much confirming the Mize knowledge dispensed to others. If "Stan the Man" Musial spreads your gospel, it must be admitted you pretty much know what you're talking about. "Johnny Mize had a classic swing," Musial said. "It was smooth, seemed effortless, yet Big John had a good follow-through and was one of the best home-run hitters baseball has known."[12]

Musial didn't get to play with Mize for very long, but Mize remained in the National League for some years after his departure from St. Louis, and Musial admired him from across the diamond. It also sounded as if Musial didn't think much of the Cardinals trading Mize away. "Johnny Mize had the best eye of any hitter I've seen in the National League," Musial said. "He was a slugger who could be as finicky as a leadoff man. John had a big, lazy swing and just got the bat on the ball, but used a big, heavy bat and had a nice follow-through that furnished great distance. The trades by which the Cardinals lost him and Walker Cooper cost us pennants."[13]

Musial later picked Mize as his choice as his personal All-Star at first base for the National League.

Mize did not hit nearly as many home runs in 1941 as he had in 1940, but he was still an All-Star for the NL, and he put up all-star hitting statistics. He batted .317 with 100 runs batted in and led the National League in doubles with 39. His homers dipped to 16, but that was the only major difference in his work.

This was Billy Southworth's first full season in charge of the Cardinals, and the club went 97–56 to finish second in the pennant race. This was more than a tentative run at first place. The Cardinals spent the first few days of the season in first place in April, moved back into first for most of the first week in May, and took over first again on May 21. St. Louis stayed there straight through June 4. The Cards spent a couple of days a half-game out of first and moved back into first for the rest of the month. From July 22 through August 13, they were also in first.

Back and forth things went in the standings, with the Cardinals slipping into first place for a few days near the end of August and in early September, but pretty much chasing the Brooklyn Dodgers to the finish line throughout September. The Dodgers took the pennant by 2½ games. The excitement was back in St. Louis, even if the Cardinals could not capture the flag.

It was a terrific season. Six pitchers won at least 10 games. Howie

Slugging Johnny Mize as he looked with his second team, the New York Giants. Mize, who led the National League in home runs four times, bashed his career high of 51 for the Giants.

Krist, whose career was over by the time he was 30, went 10–0. Lon Warneke and Ernie White won 17 games each. There were no Dizzy Deans, but it was good work by committee. Musial's explosive late-season play generated thrills. Southworth being in command produced major dividends. The set-up for 1942 was supremely buzz-worthy.

The future of the St. Louis Cardinals was not yet written, but it seemed to be as enticing as the recent past glories recorded by the Gashouse Gang.

Too bad Johnny Mize would not be part of it.

10

Giants and War

For a few years, Johnny Mize had believed he should receive a larger salary from the St. Louis Cardinals as a reward for his performance on the field. Each year, he sat down to negotiate terms of a new contract with general manager Branch Rickey, and each year he walked out of the front office disappointed by the outcome. Management had full control of players in Mize's era, and it did not matter much at all what a player thought about fairness. The offer was what the offer was, and if a player was not ready to accept the price being offered, the team seemed ready in almost all instances to let him walk away and go into retirement.

Salaries were not widely publicized at that time, either. Teams did not want players comparing what they made from the team, and often enough players were probably embarrassed to admit what they accepted to keep playing. It was not 100 percent clear what Mize made from the Cardinals for the 1940 season, it being reported by *The Sporting News* as one of two figures, either $15,000 or $17,500.

One dollar in 1940 was the equivalent of $18.61 in 2021, and even if Mize was making $17,500 at the time, his current-day salary would be nearly $326,000. That is hardly peanuts, but by the standards of the modern ballplayer, he would be grossly underpaid. The Cardinals were on the rise again, rebuilding into a fresh power and a team that come 1942 would be favored to win the National League pennant. Looking at things from the cheap side, St. Louis either decided it could win a championship without Mize, despite all of his contributions through the 1930s, or they just did not want to put up with the aggravation of him voicing disappointment over his salary.

On December 11, 1941, just four days after the Japanese bombed Pearl Harbor, plunging the United States into World War II, the Cardinals traded Mize to the New York Giants. They obtained right-handed pitcher Bill Lohrman, who went 1–1 for the Cardinals before being shuffled back to the Giants. They obtained first baseman Johnny McCarthy, who never played a game for the Cardinals. And they obtained catcher Ken O'Dea, who did stick around the Cardinals for four part-time seasons. Owner Sam Breadon probably got more pleasure out of the $50,000 New York added in. The trade was flashy for St. Louis in terms of bodies coming over, but not even taken together the trio of players, plus the bucks, added up to one Mize.

"I'll tell you what the talk used to be about [Branch] Rickey," Mize said. "Stay in the pennant race until the last week of the season and then get beat. I heard some talk to the effect that that was what he preferred. That way he drew the crowds all year and then later on the players could not come in for the big raise for winning the pennant and maybe the World Series. I don't know if it's true or not, but that was the talk."[1]

The player from small-town Georgia had never been part of any other professional organization and had developed an affinity for St. Louis. He met his wife, Jene, there. In fact, her father was a friend of Breadon's. Mize said the Cardinals owner gave the couple a $500 wedding present—and then Rickey held it against him in the next year's negotiations. "He said, 'Well, you made $7,500 last year,'" Mize claimed Rickey said. "'No, I only made $7,000.' Rickey said, 'Oh? Where's that $500 that Breadon gave you?' That was Rickey."[2]

Mize was surprised to be traded, although if anywhere, he was sure he was headed to the Brooklyn Dodgers. Manager Leo Durocher, who was an ex–Cardinal, called him up and asked how he felt about playing for that team. He touched base with Mize on December 7, Pearl Harbor Day, four days before Mize was shipped to the Giants.

It was somewhat miraculous that Durocher even contacted Mize in that period before cell phones. Mize was out of town, far out of town, on a bird-hunting trip to the Ozarks and was staying at a lodge. A guy at the place sought him out, and Mize's father-in-law got on the phone to pass on a message to call Durocher.

When the man summoning Mize to the phone handed him the receiver, he said, "By the way, the Japanese have bombed Pearl Harbor."[3] Mize said he didn't believe him. "I thought he was nuts. Didn't pay him any attention."[4]

Mize and Durocher spoke, and Durocher informed the slugger that he was trying to swing a deal for him and wanted to know if he would be happy to play in Brooklyn. "I told him it didn't mean a damn to me where I played," Mize said.[5] Whether Durocher took that as an endorsement of life under him or not, no trade was consummated.

Almost immediately, Mize's mind was on other things. He stepped into his car, turned on the radio, and discovered the telephone messenger was right about the news on war breaking out. "That was a hell of a piece of news and I didn't know what to think about it," Mize said.

"When something like that happens, you don't know what's coming next until it comes."[6]

That summed up the United States' situation for the next four years, when the country was on full-time war footing with the true fate of the free world up in the air for some time, not just as a figure of speech, or part of a serious political speech.

"Four days later, I was traded to the Giants," Mize said.[7] Maybe he did care where he played, or at least what ballpark was his home field. "I wasn't too crazy about playing in the Polo Grounds because I wasn't that much of a pull hitter. Maybe if I'd got there earlier in my career I might have become a pull hitter to take advantage of that short right-field, but after hitting straightaway for so many years, I didn't want to start changing around."[8]

Mize was going to undergo big changes anyway, his affiliation shifting from St. Louis to New York, but still with the National League. He may not have listed the Polo Grounds as his favorite stadium to play in, but he was still in his prime, still an All-Star, and not a player being dumped because he could no longer perform. At no time was that hint given by the Cardinals or even by Mize's least preferred baseball administrator, Branch Rickey. They were merely moving into separate orbits, though with the same goal of winning NL pennants and representing the NL in the World Series in 1942.

Mize was 29 during the 1942 season, his first with the Giants. He was slotted into the first-base position and appeared in 142 games. His average dropped slightly that season to .305, but his home runs jumped again, this time to 26, and his 110 runs batted in was tops in the league. Once again, Mize was an All-Star, chosen for the fifth time.

The 1942 Giants were a solid team. New York was managed by Mel Ott, in his first season in charge. However, Ott also remained an All-Star outfielder in the lengthy playing career that began in 1926, when he was 17. Ott played 22 years and was elected to the Hall of Fame based on his performance.

Bill Terry, another future Hall of Famer, concluded his managing career with the Giants in 1941 after succeeding the legendary John J. McGraw in the dugout. New York finished 74–79, in fifth place. Ott himself, with 27 homers, was the club's leading power hitter. The only other regular who produced big whacks at the plate was first baseman Babe Young, who stroked 25 homers and drove in 104 runs. This raised the issue of why New York pursued another first baseman instead of filling other needs.

Yet the 1942 Giants were comparatively transformed. Mize was the only .300 hitter, though Ott was not far behind. Ott, who blasted 511 home runs in his career, the first National League hitter to reach the 500 mark, swatted 30 homers that season, drove in 93 runs, and batted .295.

Ott and Mize complemented one another nicely in the batting order. Ott was definitely one of the greatest players in Giants franchise history. Despite breaking into the majors several years before the All-Star game was created, he was selected for the National League roster 11 times. He also collected 1,860 career runs batted in with a lifetime .304 average. He was a six-time home run champ and six times led the league in walks. His lifetime on-base percentage given his 1,708 career bases on balls, was not surprisingly a gaudy .414.

The fiery McGraw loved Ott like a son, and Ott was definitely young enough to be his son when he made his major league debut, or even his grandson. Ott was not brash like his mentor; he was sometimes called "Mild Mel," and maybe it was because he was a shy youth around older men. Ott was born in Gretna, Louisiana, and his ball-playing talents were identified quite early.

Ott was playing high school ball when he got word that the president of the New Orleans Pelicans minor league team of the Southern League wanted to offer him a tryout. The club did not realize that the youthful then-catcher was just 15 years old. When he showed up in New Orleans, his face gave him away. So did his wardrobe. He still wore short pants, not long pants.

He stuck around for a few days and showed off keen knowledge of the game, even if he was ridiculously young. The president of the team evaluated him, saying, "You are too light, too short, too small, and too young to play with my Pelicans."[9]

Ott was fixed up with a semi-pro team affiliated with a lumber company, and the boss there shipped him McGraw's way for a look-see soon enough. Mostly, Ott sat on the bench in 1926 and watched baseball, briefly appearing in 35 games with 60 at-bats. He had never seen a big-league game until he dressed for one. Ott struck out his first two times up but got a hit in his third at-bat. As sparingly as he was used, Ott would be inserted into a game for a few swings and ended up batting .383 in that short, educational season.

McGraw saw the potential in Ott and nurtured it. As an 18-year-old, Ott was eased into more games, 82 of them. By 1928, Ott was pretty much a full-timer on the field and hit .322. He had briefly dabbled as an infielder when he was smaller, but McGraw made him an outfielder. In his earliest Giants days, before getting the chance to start, McGraw made the kid sit next to him perpetually, for all games. He was the teacher's pet, but it was very much a time for learning.

Ott did develop one of the oddest of batting stances. He would have completely ignored Mize's precepts on hitting. Ott was a lefty swinger who, when he saw an approaching pitch, lifted his right, front foot to hit. Not recommended by most strategists, but Ott made it work. McGraw was viewed as single-minded in pursuit of talent and victory and never hid his feelings. Ott was not a yeller, even when he inherited the Giants manager position once removed from McGraw.

He was a man of many interests beyond the ballfield, including playing golf and following racehorses, didn't mind taking a drink, loved attending the movies, spent free moments doing crossword puzzles, and liked playing gin rummy. The rest of the time he devoted to the Giants organization.

As many home runs as Ott hit, he did not seem built for it, much the opposite in size from Mize. Ott stood 5-foot-9 and weighed in at around 170 pounds. He hit three in one game only one time, yet he led His team in home runs for 18 years in a row.

Some believed that unlike the more ill-tempered McGraw, Ott wasn't mean enough to be a winning manager. It has been attributed to Leo Durocher, even if some minor editing applied, that he said, "Nice guys finish last." It was also believed he was referring to Mel Ott with the Giants. The rivalry between the Dodgers and Giants was as intense as they come, later even being transported 3,000 miles to California. Yet once a rowdy Brooklyn fan making noise about the enemy bellowed, "You're a nice guy, Mel! But the rest of those guys are bums."[10]

It was the Cardinals, not the Giants or Dodgers, who captured the pennant in 1942. The Billy Southworth Cardinals were on the rise and kept climbing the standings, going 106–48 and beating the New York Yankees in the World Series. Mize was on the outside, left behind.

The Giants finished 85–67, in third place. The hated Dodgers also had a terrific season, going 104–50. So the Giants did all right, but were still eating the dust of the two runaway teams, 20 games out of first place. The Chicago Cubs finished fourth at 76–76.

There was a gap to be considered, but the Giants loomed as potential threats for 1943 with a little beefing up. Only 1943 turned out to be nothing like 1942. By then, the United States was deep into World War II, fighting on two fronts, Japan in the South Pacific and Germany in Europe. Manpower was thin for baseball. Baseball only continued in 1942 because President Franklin D. Roosevelt deemed it to be worthy entertainment for the hardworking masses and factory workers on the home front.

No special exemptions were granted to baseball players to play the game. Some of the sport's biggest stars enlisted or were drafted and joined up for military service in the prime years of their career. In the early war years, before the tide shifted toward victory, there was much to worry about on a grander scale than who was going to win the pennant. Ted Williams, Bob Feller, Joe DiMaggio, and such future stars as Warren Spahn and Yogi Berra wore different kinds of uniforms in the 1940s. So did Johnny Mize. He had swapped out Cardinals garb for Giants garb in 1942. In 1943, and through the 1944 and 1945 seasons, he belonged to the U.S. Navy, and that outfit issued its own clothing.

The hints were strong that Mize would be drafted before he departed for service. In February of 1943, it was reported that Mize was called for a draft physical and then was reclassified as 1-A by his draft board from his previous 3A status as a married man. By March, it was being suggested that he would be called up within a month. "It's bad news for us," said Giants owner Horace Stoneham. "But it's also bad news for the Hitler league. John really will make a good soldier."[11]

Stoneham admitted that his team was in the market for another first baseman, particularly Babe Dahlgren. Dahlgren had done some good hitting for the New York Yankees in the 1930s, originally behind Lou Gehrig, and then taking over first when Gehrig abruptly retired due to his illness. But by 1943, Dahlgren was 31 and seemed to be on the downside. No deal was consummated with the Giants, and Dahlgren showed up with the Philadelphia Phillies instead, where he did regain his hitting stroke.

Mize's status changed more quickly than that. Before the end of March, he had been inducted into the Navy, and the Giants embarked on a search for another first baseman. "Naturally, we are disappointed," Stoneham said, "but I hope Mize proves as valuable as a fighting man for Uncle Sam as he was a ballplayer for us."[12] To say anything less would be deemed unpatriotic.

Mize was assigned to the Great Lakes Naval Station on the outskirts of Chicago, and he was also assigned to the base's baseball team. This military installation was known for its powerful sports teams. Among Mize's teammates there were future Hall of Fame shortstops Phil Rizzuto of the Yankees and Pee Wee Reese of the Dodgers, star outfielder Dom DiMaggio of the Boston Red Sox, and other big leaguers like Sam Chapman, Johnny Lipon, and Barney McCoskey. Mize batted .417 for his service team. Mize did not go to war but provided entertainment for fellow troops.

At the very end of World War II, in 1945, Mize was shipped to the island of Tinian in the Pacific. It was near the end of his three-year service.

There were a few Sundays when we were off duty, my buddies and I, and we would get us one of those big canned hams, two or three loaves of bread, some mayonnaise and pickles, and a case of beer and go drive up on the hill and spend the day relaxing. One time, we noticed some Marines sitting on top of a hill overlooking the whole area below. Mostly, they watched everything like hawks. Heck, we'd just sit there, eating sandwiches and drinking a few beers and having a good time, never really asking our selves what those Marines were guarding over there.[13]

On July 26, 1945, some of the final segments to complete assembly of the Atomic bomb arrived on Tinian via the Naval ship the USS *Indianapolis*. Only four days later, the *Indianapolis* was sunk with the deaths of 879 crew members. The ship had delivered uranium isotope U-235 that was required to complete the bomb that soon after was dropped on Hiroshima and led to the end of the war.

"We found out later, that's what they were sitting up there for,"

Extraordinary screwball artist Carl Hubbell, the Hall of Fame hurler, was rated one of the best Mize ever saw and worked in the team's front office when Mize was acquired from St. Louis.

Mize said of the group of Marines. "They told us later it wasn't really armed until they got it on the plane, but if I'd known we were picnicking a few yards away from that thing, I would've asked for a transfer."[14]

Hiroshima was bombed on August 6 and Nagasaki on August 9. No specific number of dead were totaled, but it was estimated about 140,000 people lost their lives in Hiroshima, immediately and gradually over time, and another 70,000 from the bombing of Nagasaki. Japan promptly surrendered.

By then, the baseball season of 1945 was concluding. Mize was released from the Navy after three years in the service, and in the spring of 1946 he rejoined the New York Giants to resume his big-league career. He was 33 years old during that campaign, basically at the tail end of his prime athletic years after the three-season intermission.

The Cardinals kept winning, also grabbing pennants in 1944 and 1945, to make it a three-peat in the National League. St. Louis won 105 games in each of those seasons, adding on to the stupendous record of 1943. At 67–87 in 1944, the Giants were about 20 games worse than they had been in 1943. In 1945, the Giants went 78–74, an improvement. Mel Ott was still the manager when Mize returned.

Everyone in the nation was ready for a fresh start, not only in baseball, but in every aspect of life.

11

Getting Back in the Swing
with the Giants

Baseball played on during World War II, though with numerous differences and at less than full strength. Hundreds of professional players from minor-league clubs and big-league teams served in the Army, Marines, Navy, and what would become the U.S. Air Force. Some volunteered. Some were drafted.

Some fought and were killed. Some fought and were wounded. Some, like Johnny Mize, mostly were used on the home front, as morale builders. It was estimated that 420,000 Americans were killed during the war, including civilians. Worldwide, it was estimated that somewhere between 70 million and 90 million people died during the conflict. While more than 500 major leaguers were in uniform, just two perished, and neither were stars.

Come 1946, the country was relieved and exhausted, optimistic and hopeful, yet adjusting to peacetime. Baseball, with its reunited rosters, its return to action and stature as the National Pastime, was something that people could enjoy, embrace, and welcome back as a sign of normalcy.

The team that experienced the greatest wartime success was the St. Louis Cardinals. As a bonus, during that period, in 1944, the long-suffering St. Louis Browns won their only pennant in a half-century of competing in the American League.

Some players were wounded and were no longer able to play ball. Some players returned to their homes with rusty skills and never quite shook the rust off. Some players grew old during their absence from the game.

Mize lost three full seasons to the war, and when he came back to the New York Giants' fold, he was a 33-year-old first baseman. But he was one who could still hit. It was headline news for baseball fans in New York that Mize was shedding his military uniform and pulling on his Giants duds again, even if the headlines were not bold, big ones, but merely informative. "Sailor Mize Is Back, Returns to Giant Deck," read one.[1]

It being October, the Giants were done for the year. The Chicago Cubs won the 1945 National League pennant. Although Mize was not dressed to play ball, he was back near baseball for a visit after being shipped back to the United States from the South Pacific. Mize was visiting with some friends on the Cubs in his street clothes during the World Series against the Detroit Tigers.

It was a convenient stopping place for him, and he chatted with players Bill Nicholson, Phil Cavarretta, and Roy Hughes. Hughes, clearly an admirer of Mize's hitting, made Mize feel welcome enough. "I wish that big guy was with us today," said Hughes, a back-up middle infielder.[2]

Mize described his street duds as an in-between-uniforms wardrobe.

"I was discharged from the Navy Tuesday at 9:30 o'clock in the morning and inside of an hour was in this suit," Mize told his audience. "Look at this vest. It is two or three inches too large for me. I'm lighter now than when I was playing ball in the bushes."[3]

Since they did not have to worry about him doing them any harm with his bat for some months, it was more in the nature of idle conversation when the Cubs quizzed Mize about his conditioning and recent baseball practice. Nicholson asked Mize if he did any running in his hot weather stopovers. "Did you keep in shape running?" Nicholson injected. "You know, twice around the park?" Mize said he had not. "No, I didn't run much this summer, but I played badminton every day with the officers and that kept my pins in good shape for quick action around first base.

"I haven't played any serious ball in the Navy for four months, but before that I got into some games. I was on Guam this summer. We had some pick-up games around camp and I pitched most of the time."[4] An unlikely role for the slugger.

These fellow players had not forgotten how good Mize was, though an inquiry came about whether or not Mize was still with the New York Giants. The query was quickly answered by someone else in the huddle in this manner: "Is he still a Giant? He is THE Giant."[5]

It was a little bit of a surprise that Mize was free and clear of the Navy at that point. Only a couple of weeks earlier, he was slated to go on leave for a visit to St. Louis and planned his World Series excursion then. In late September, there was no mention of Mize being discharged. But by Series time, he was home for good. There had been rumors Mize had gained too much weight in the service, but more recently he had endured an illness that sent him to a hospital in Maryland. When he saw the Cubs players, Mize was thinner than he had been, and he insisted it wasn't because he had been sick. Maybe it was the badminton that trimmed the pounds.

None of that October evaluation meant a thing once Mize returned to the Giants for spring training later. He was ready to go and resume his status as one of the game's premier hitters. When he was healthy, Mize was still a very tough out. He appeared in 101 games in 1946, slugging 22 home runs with 70 runs batted in and a .337 batting average. His on-base percentage was .437. When he was as good as new, Mize hit like the Mize of old.

Yet two injuries slowed Mize in his first year back, though neither was attributable directly to old age. He missed a third of the games with first a broken hand and then a broken toe, the latter the kind of injury that mostly comes under the fluke category, not in the body-is-breaking-down category. It was frustrating to miss those years in the Navy, come back refreshed, and be sidelined for big chunks of the schedule with such niggling injuries.

Maybe there was a bit of karma involved. Mize had had an easy ride during his absence from the majors compared to most other soldiers. He received celebrity treatment, played baseball, his favorite pastime, just as in peacetime dodging baseballs, not flying bullets. At times during his deployment, especially in the tropics, Mize and his teammates were playing a sport in the sunshine while being fed steaks and drinking Scotch. They didn't have to think too hard to realize they had it good since often their audience consisted of wounded soldiers grateful to watch their favorite sport and absorb a taste of home. It was soft duty being in the Navy and playing baseball, but his benefactors wanted Mize wearing that kind of uniform.

It didn't take a heap of swatting to lead the NL in home runs in 1946. The individual crown was captured by Ralph Kiner, the first of seven straight home run championships the Pittsburgh Pirates star earned. Kiner's winning total was 23 home runs, a low lead-the-league figure. Mize's 22 was totaled in 43 fewer games.

Probably because he stayed sharp competing for the Great Lakes team, it was not a big adjustment for Mize to return to the top level of the sport. His gaudy batting average indicated a limited re-entry period needed. Of course, this was a player who had a battle plan to fight off slumps etched in his head and later transferred to paper.

"A slump is the worst thing that can happen to a hitter," Mize said. "But it happens to every player. There are no exceptions. Nobody knows what causes a slump, but everyone has ideas. My explanation is that a slump always seems to follow a hitting splurge."[6]

That stands to reason. Someone who is on a 6-for-10 tear isn't going to keep it up forever, so hitting is bound to tail off.

"When a player is hitting everything, thrown by everyone, he relaxes too much and takes his eye off the ball to watch where it is going," Mize said. "Everything bad seems to happen when you are a victim of this hitter's disease."[7]

Sure, Mize was not immune to slumps, but he stuck with what he believed in and followed his own rules. New Yorkers were hungry for baseball after the war, and the Giants' lineup was dotted with some well-known and enduring names. However, the pitching staff was a black hole. In a season when the Giants drew more than 1.2 million fans to home games, resurrecting the baseball-rooting gene in the post-war crowd, they finished 61–93, last in the league.

There really was no staff ace. There weren't even any staff winners to take note of, unless 2–1 registers big points. Dave Koslo went 14–19 with an okay earned run average of 3.63, and no other hurler recorded double-figure victories. Monty Kennedy was 9–10, Bill Voiselle 9–15, and Ken Trinkle, 7–14.

Righty Hal Schumacher was the Giants' most reliable arm for a decade, until he went into the service in 1943. Schumacher 10 times won 10 or more games for New York before leaving town for the war, one year collecting 23 victories and two other seasons amassing 19 wins. He was 31 when he went into the Navy and 35 in 1946 when he came back to the mound. He went 4–4 that year.

Schumacher, who was born in 1910, was pitching for St. Lawrence University in upstate New York when John J. McGraw first got wind of the 6-foot, 190-pound hurler, signing him at 21. Schumacher's entire minor-league apprenticeship, the opposite of Mize's, lasted eight whole games. McGraw was enamored of the guy, and the boss said he saw traits in Schumacher that reminded him of Christy Mathewson. That might have been hyperbole, though when those big-victory seasons came around early in his career, Schumacher quickly became a two-time All-Star, including being selected for the first one contested. Although he did win 158 games in his career (less than half the amount "Matty" won), Schumacher was a big-league success.

Schumacher's nickname (Prince Hal) was a worthy one. His chief pitching weapon was a sinker. On that first Giants post-war team, the club could have gleaned a little bit more value from Schumacher, but he was out of gas by then. He mustered 96 2/3 innings and then he was done, his career over.

Soon after retirement, Schumacher, who had personal ties to upper New York State, hooked on with the makers of Adirondack Bats, a competitor of Louisville Slugger, in Dolgeville, New York. After retirement, when the pitcher who compiled a lifetime 3.36 earned run average became a bat salesman, his conversion was met with some humor. "Although Hal Schumacher is a pleasant, gentlemanly, good-looking, pure-hearted and friendly fellow," a story about his post-playing days began, "for many years he was a bitterly hated man. Hundreds of National League hitters detested the very sight of him. But now, less than four years after his last appearance in a New York Giant uniform, Hal is the batter's best friend, and it is his former colleagues, the pitchers, who bitterly resent his appearance. For Prince Hal has turned traitor. He sells bats."[8]

Schumacher was vice president of the company in his hometown of some 3,000 people. "When I was playing, I used to take sticks for granted," he said, not imagining he would help convince such players as Larry Doby and Gil Hodges to wield his favorite brand. "But now that I know the business from the inside, the process of making them fascinates me."[9]

In a slightly different way, that could have been Mize speaking. He always took extraordinary care of his bats, made sure he had enough of them, and was clued into their workmanship and how they fit the moment and the pitcher he was facing. He could have been both Schumacher's and Louisville Slugger's best customer. He was like a wine connoisseur, only with bats. He knew good lumber when he saw it.

Just as young players today often choose the bat they swing because they are enamored of a current player, Mize actually did the same. His early bat of choice was that Rogers Hornsby model. Except for Ty Cobb, Hornsby compiled the highest lifetime batting average in history at .358. Even Hall of Famers can follow other Hall of Famers. As Mize said,

My own experience with different weight bats has also proved that during spring training and the early part of the season there is a tendency of overswinging. Using a heavier bat cures this fault quickly. Immediately after signing my contract each year, I would ask the ball club to order a dozen 40-ounce bats which I would use during spring training and the same amount of 36-ounce bats for the regular season.

If I were using the lighter bats near the end of spring training, I would switch back to the heavier ones when we broke camp and headed north. I would do this because the weather would be much cooler, and by using the heavy bat I would protect my hands from the stinging that comes with cold weather.[10]

Despite his toe woes and the Giants' woes as a team, Mize was again selected for the National League All-Star team in 1946. Baseball itself was back to full strength with all of its available players, and its stars, renewed in their return to the game after their hiatus in military service, definitely enjoyed a warm reception from the public in 1946. Even though the Giants played poorly and sank to the bottom of the standings, their home games at the Polo Grounds attracted 1,219,873 fans. And that was only third-highest in the eight-team National League. The Cardinals were on their way to still another World Series championship and drew more than 1 million fans, too, but were just fourth in the league in attendance. Fan turnout was exploding all over. The Dodgers' turnstile count was 1,796,824. Of course, some of those other teams were actually in a pennant race, not something that helped the Giants put fannies in the seats.

The Giants' pitching was like a double Achilles heel that season. When it came to hitting, Mize was by far the big batsman, so his injury was costly. There were some other fascinating players passing through that season, but some of them too early in their careers to make a difference and others too late.

Catcher Walker Cooper had also been exiled by the Cardinals, and his loss, along with Mize's, was coupled together by Stan Musial as a departure that may well have cost St. Louis another pennant. In 1946, Cooper was 31 and appeared in just 87 games for New York with a .268 batting average. But he was also an All-Star, as he repeatedly was for the Giants from then on.

Sid Gordon, a solid hitter wherever he played, held down one outfield spot and batted .293. Willard Marshall manned another outfield position and hit .282 An illustration of New York's lack of power without Mize in the everyday lineup was that Marshall's 13 home runs were the second-most on the team. Second baseman Buddy Blattner hit 11, and he was the only other player in double figures.

The sad story was the fadeout of Mel Ott on the field. An All-Star with 21 home runs only the season before at age 36, Ott was a non-factor in 1946, appearing in just 31 games with 74 plate appearances. His average was a depressing .074. This was pretty much it for the future Hall of Famer as a player, though Ott briefly took the field in 1947, if only to affirm he didn't have it anymore. He played in only four games that year, making four plate appearances, and he didn't get a hit.

The 1946 season was Ott's lowliest as manager, as well, but he thought he could restore Giants glory and remained in the dugout.

Mize missed Opening Day on April 16, 1946, and started slowly at the plate, as if he was still on Guam swinging a badminton racquet. When he recorded a two-hit game against Brooklyn in New York's fifth game, it only brought his average to .167. But that got him going, and a three-hit appearance the next game against the Phillies showed the true Johnny. At the end of April, Mize was batting .361. It was as if he had never been away from the big leagues, never aged.

By the end of June. Mize was hitting .333 and had 15 homers with a .433 on-base percentage. Those National League pitchers still feared the damage he could do and pitched him carefully. Just like the weather, Mize was even hotter at the end of July, with his average at .347, his on-base percentage up to .442, and his slugging percentage at .601. All that was with no one in the batting order to protect him. Mize's last fully healthy day in the Giants' lineup was August 4, in the second game of a double-header against the Pittsburgh Pirates. He went one-for-three with two walks, one of them the 12th intentional base on balls he received that season.

On August 5, the Giants played in an exhibition game against the New York Yankees in what was called the Mayor's Trophy Game. Yankees reliever Joe Page broke Mize's hand with a pitch. No such exhibition appearances are required of million-dollar player these days for these types of reasons. Although the games were played for charity purposes most times, nowadays with interleague play, American League and National League teams located in the same cities, and geographic rivals, play only games against one another that count in the standings.

That errant pitch knocked Mize out of the lineup until September 13. The Giants had been no great shakes with Mize, and they didn't fare particularly well without him, so those weeks later it was a welcome sight when the Big Cat showed up on the field.

However, that didn't last long at all. Mize made three plate appearances, went oh-for-two, and broke a toe, sidelining him for the rest of the year. Mize suffered no war wounds in military service, yet broke two bones in his first season back in the majors. He could only look forward to another fresh start in 1947. The Giants desperately needed one, and they needed Mize in first-class condition to rejuvenate the team.

12

Johnny Mize's Greatest Year

Cured of his broken bones, back in rhythm following his return to big-league baseball after his intermission in the Navy, Mize was itching to go with the New York Giants for the 1947 season.

The Giants needed Mize to be Mize at his best. Mize needed to stay healthy and return to his thrilling days of yesteryear. Even though Mize was not especially old, he was creeping up in years, playing the 1947 season at age 34. The preceding season had not been a waste, but for a good player who was trying to come back from a three-year absence, the 1946 campaign was not completely satisfying.

Mize very much wanted 1947 to be better, to demonstrate that his bat was as scary as ever. After what had to feel like an interminable break and then extra, unwanted rest away from the sport, this was an important season for Mize. Mize wanted to justify his gradually built reputation as one of the smartest and hardest-hitting players in the game.

Due to the recent backdrop of uncertainty based on his injuries and his lost time in the game because of World War II, the 1947 season was an important one for Mize's future. He came through. The 1947 baseball season was the showiest and the best of his career. Needing to step up, Mize did a lot of hitting the ball where the fielders weren't: on the other side of the ballpark wall. Mize slugged balls to parts unknown; he was the Giants' big gun in the middle of the order, and circled the bases more frequently than any other player in the National League. If there had been thoughts that Mize might be turning fragile, they were benched.

The key stats Mize recorded in 1947 read this way: 51 home runs, 138 runs batted in, 137 runs scored. All three of those numbers ranked first in the league. He also batted .302 with a .614 slugging percentage, and for those who might have felt he was falling apart, Mize created all that magic while playing in all 154 Giants games. Mize also walked 74 times and was picked for yet another National League All-Star team.

Things began well and remained mighty good throughout this season. Forgotten were the injuries of 1946. Freshly implanted in the minds of New York fans was what Mize could do when healthy. It had become a specialty of his to homer in clusters, particularly those three-homer performances that caused everyone's eyeballs to bulge.

It was on April 24 that Mize brought his habit over from the Cardinals to show off for the Giants. New York had an afternoon game against Boston at Braves Field. Johnny Sain, the excellent right-hander, was on the mound for the hosts. This was not the finest pitching showing of Sain's career, but it might have been one of the luckiest. He gave up five earned runs, and Mize hit three home runs off of him, in the third, sixth, and eighth innings, yet Sain got the win in a 14–5 decision.

Mize had otherwise not been in a groove, but this day he scored three runs and knocked in four with his blasts.

This was one of those years when Mize provided evidence suggesting he was in the elite ranks of the wise men of hitting. Sometimes those discussions broke out spontaneously, such as on the occasion of batting practice before the Giants were to duel with the Cincinnati Reds. Someone spoke up, asking, "John, what's the most important thing in hitting?" Mize sensed he was not being invited into a serious conversation about one of his favorite topics and responded succinctly: "Swinging."[1]

This was like asking a grand master what was the secret road to checkmate. The questioner was serious about learning more about hitting and requested more elaboration from Mize, and the batsman then obliged.

"Get good balls to hit and then hit them as hard as you can," Mize said. It was still an answer on the simplistic side.

> Anyway, that's the way I hit. You hear about fellows being great bad ball hitters—how they reach up like this and hit the tar out of the ball. Sure they do, sometimes. But they miss a lot, too. You only notice the ones they hit and forget about the ones they miss.
>
> Generally, I want that ball to be in there where I can hit it. What's the use of chasing a ball or swinging up here at it when you know a pitcher has got to come in there with it sooner or later?[2]

It took a lot to satisfy Mize when it came to hitting. He never did warm up to the Polo Grounds as a good ballpark for a home run man, and that was even when he was ripping homers more frequently than ever. "This is a tough park to hit in," Mize said even in the midst of his primo season. "They pitch different to you here and play different for you. They are trying to keep you from pulling the ball. They don't play you along the lines as much as they do in other parks."[3]

Mize had to make do. The Polo Grounds was his home grounds

with the Giants, and that meant half of the regular season for him, 77 games, would be played in this stadium. Even if he realized they were inevitable, Mize seemed to take any slump as a personal affront. He didn't do much slumping in 1947.

The Giants lost, 4–3, on Opening Day and so did Mize, going 0-for-four against the Philadelphia Phillies. Mize hung up another 0-fer the next day, and the Giants lost that one to Philadelphia, too. The Giants won their third game and Mize went two-for-three. He was starting to come out of it. Another win over the Brooklyn Dodgers produced a Mize hit, two runs scored, and two runs batted in. Overall, though, the Giants kept losing, and Mize was stuck with an average under .200.

Despite his electric showing on April 24, Mize finished April with a .244 batting average, and New York was 4–7. It was very much a running-in-place month. Looking back, it seems odd that Mize would be able to build on such a slow start so well. By May 15, Mize had lifted his batting average to .316, and the Giants surpassed the .500 mark for the first time all season. After besting the Chicago Cubs, 8–3, that day, they were at 11–10.

The Giants surged through the rest of May and concluded the month at 21–14. Mize was tearing the cover off the ball, with 14 homers and a .354 average. To show how frequently he was bashing the ball, as of May 31, Mize's slugging percentage was .717. Also, his on-base percentage was .457. Pitchers didn't want to have anything to do with him.

Nobody was running away with the pennant. The Giants slipped into a first-place tie on May 20 after a 9–1 victory over Cincinnati. Although it was hardly a stranglehold, New York was in first place for 13 days between then and June 4.

It may have all been kindling false hope because once again the pitching was thin. Baseball is the sport of the long run, and the very long season is the great equalizer. It felt fine to be in first place in the early stages of June, but the pitching staff was not built for the long haul. Mize had overcome his own slow hitting start quickly enough to become an All-Star selection again.

The pitching remained rough around the edges. There really was no depth at all in the mound corps. Just five pitchers won as many as eight games. Ken Trinkle, at 8–4, was one of them, but in an era when there were few showcase relief specialists, Trinkle did not start any of his 62 appearances. He finished 38 games.

Clint Hartung (9–7) and Monty Kennedy (9–12) each won nine times, but they had shaky earned run averages in the mid-to-high 4.00s. Starter Dave Koslo's ERA of 4.39 wasn't any better, but he was luckier and his record was 15–10. The one hurler who seemed to know what he was doing in every outing was starter Larry Jansen.

Jansen, a 26-year-old rookie, went 21–5 with a 3.16 earned run average. He did not overpower hitters, collecting just 104 strikeouts in 248 innings, but he was the undisputed mainstay of the operation. Jansen won 122 games in his career, and a few years later, in one of his two All-Star seasons, he upped his win total. Jansen went 23–11 with a 3.04 ERA for New York in 1951.

The pitcher was a latecomer to the majors. While pitching semi-pro and minor-league ball in Oregon, his home state, Jansen also operated a dairy farm for his wife and 10 children. Earlier in the 1940s, when he may have been a prospect for the majors, Jansen accepted a deferment rather than be drafted, to stay with his family and help with wartime food production through his farm.

Immediately after the end of the war, Jansen turned to baseball full-time with the San Francisco Seals in the Pacific Coast League, and in 1946 he was a huge winner, finishing 30–6 with a 1.57 earned run average. When he was with the Giants in spring training in 1947, Jansen was smashed in the face by a line drive hit by Cleveland Indians pitcher Bob Feller. The impact broke a cheekbone, and it took Jansen a few weeks to recover. He feared he had lost out on his big chance at the majors. But after Jansen recovered, he was superb and was runner-up for the Rookie of the Year Award in 1947, losing out to barrier-breaking Brooklyn Dodgers star Jackie Robinson.

Jackie Robinson, formerly of UCLA, formerly of the United States Army, formerly of the Montreal Royals, was the biggest story in sports in 1947, and one of the biggest in sports history, because of the color of his skin.

In an era of strong bigotry, Robinson was the man who broke baseball's color barrier, the first Black player allowed into this major league club in the 20th century. By then, Branch Rickey had shifted his employment allegiance from the St. Louis Cardinals to the Brooklyn Dodgers. History has credited Rickey with being foresighted enough, courageous enough, and smart enough to plunge forward against prejudice and to recruit the right man for a job that was of phenomenal importance, but one that carried a great burden and included trying times.

The hiring of Robinson, easing him around the landmines that were exploding around him, and building a winner out of the Dodgers simultaneously, did add up to remarkable achievement. Robinson fought through society's and the sport's barriers and went on to become a member of the National Baseball Hall of Fame.

The year of 1947 and the season of 1947 were all about Robinson and the Dodgers, about players and managers who performed shamefully, and others who acted heroically simply by acting as human beings.

Some 82 years after the Civil War concluded, many backwards-thinking Americans were still fighting the bloody conflagration, at least in their heads. Robinson received hate mail. On the field, he was the object of nasty invective. Above all, he persevered, created an enormous number of new fans for the Dodgers and the majors, and opened the floodgates of opportunity to generations of players of color. It is no accident that his No. 42 is retired by all big-league baseball teams.

The Giants felt they were live wires in a pennant race, and for the first part of the season they were right. Robinson was a tremendous help to the Dodgers, and they were challenging. So were the Cardinals, who had already put their stamp on the 1940s. No one had expected big things from the Giants, especially with that mediocre pitching staff. Of course, no one saw Jansen coming, and he was a tremendous gift.

In addition to Mize, the Giants had some pop in their order. If the pitchers were going to surrender four runs a game, the hitters had to score five. After his All-Star years in St. Louis, catcher Walker Cooper rejuvenated his play with the Giants. As good as 1947 was to Mize, it was equally good for Cooper. This was his greatest year as well, batting .305 with 35 home runs and 122 RBI. It was no wonder Stan Musial said the exiling of Mize and Cooper from the Cardinals cost the team a dynasty.

The combination of Mize, Cooper, and their friends produced 221 home runs for the Giants, setting a record. The power swingers made up for the arm deficiency and kept New York in the race. It may not be well remembered so much later, but Cooper was an eight-time All-Star. He had a more accomplished career than pitching brother Mort.

Although Walker Cooper put this notable slugging season together, he was as highly regarded as a fielder as a hitter. At 6-foot-3 and 220 pounds, he was bigger than most catchers of the era and was reputed to possess big-league strength, as well as big-league catching prowess. He could be ornery, spitting tobacco juice on the spikes of opposition players when they stepped into the batter's box if he was in a bad mood. If the player replied testily, Cooper was prepared to challenge him to a fistfight.

Cooper was a winning player and an essential cog for the Cardinals, though like Joe Medwick and Johnny Mize, Walker and brother Mort had perpetual salary squabbles with Branch Rickey. Even when Walker had a good year, he did not get a raise, once going three straight seasons making $12,000 per. This got on his nerves. Eventually, soon after players returned to their teams following World War II (but with

Walker Cooper still in the Navy), the Cardinals sold him to the Giants for $175,000.

The last time the Giants squeezed into first place in 1947 was on June 18, after a win over the Pittsburgh Pirates. Not long after that, Cooper went on a tear when he hit seven home runs in six games, at the time a National League record. In the midst of all that, Mort rejoined Walker as a teammate when he joined the Giants. Mort won the game when Walker set his home run mark. It should be noted that after Walker's stupendous season, the Giants gave him a raise to $30,000. Money flowed more freely in New York.

The 1947 campaign was also Willard Marshall's finest. Selected for one of his two career All-Star teams, the outfielder bashed 36 home runs as a major contributor to the team record and drove in 107 runs. That was the only season Marshall hit more than 20 home runs and the only time he knocked in more than 100 runs. That season, Marshall hit three home runs in one game and also scored 102 runs.

Marshall broke into the majors with the Giants at 21 in 1942 and then went into military service for three seasons. While he put together eight seasons with double-figure homers, he hit by far the most in 1947 with those 36 blasts. The Giants were kings of the long ball that year, but Marshall never could put his finger on why the team set a record and why he hit his most ever. "I have no idea," Marshall said. "It was just one of those years when everything worked out perfectly. But I couldn't get it back anymore."[4]

One of the young players in the Giants' lineup, 23-year-old Bobby Thomson, who gained tremendous baseball notoriety for hitting one of the most famous homers in baseball history a few years later, slammed 29 home runs in 1947. Opposing pitchers had to be very careful while trying to set down this lineup. Thomson, who played in 18 games the year before while showing promise with a .315 average, of course hit the Giants' pennant-winning home run in a playoff against the Dodgers in 1951 after they made a grand charge in the standings. Thomson hit 264 regular-season home runs in a 15-year career. Sid Gordon was also with this team and struck 13 homers as part of his career total of 202.

The Giants could bludgeon you. Except for Jansen, they might not win many pitchers' duels, and they were not well-balanced. That's the kind of thing that normally catches up with a team over the long season. The Giants kept hitting, especially Mize, but the team began to fade in the pennant chase. The Giants never held down first place after June 18, but they clung to the race with their fingernails.

On July 4, the traditional mental halfway mark of the season, New York lost to Brooklyn, 5–4, leaving the Dodgers 2½ games ahead of the

Giants. The Giants never got hot enough to make up that difference, but always seemed to hover with the threat that they might.

Mize and the Giants did provoke enough excitement to lure the fans into the Polo Grounds, however. New York drew more than 1.6 million paid spectators that season. On July 5, in a 4–0 shutout of the Philadelphia Phillies, Mize hit two home runs off Schoolboy Rowe, giving the slugger 24 homers for the season.

Mize was not going to set a single-season home run mark, topping Babe Ruth's record 60, but smashing 50 home runs, then, as now, is a notable feat no matter the generation of baseball. As of the 2021 big-league season, there were 46 occasions when a player hit at least 50 homers. Everything pretty much must go right for a player to conclude the season with at least 50 bombs.

The National League began play in 1876, and the American League did so in 1901. It took until 1920, when Babe Ruth moved from the Boston Red Sox to the New York Yankees and began revolutionizing the game with his power, for anyone to crack the 50-homer mark. The Bambino did so that year with his record-setting 54 homers, a total that astounded and excited fans and baseball observers and was a numerical example of the possible.

If anyone did not receive that message, Ruth went out and slugged 59 home runs in 1921, and in 1927 he mashed 60 homers, the record that remained at the top of the list for 34 years. Ruth also hit 54 homers in 1928, although that is not as well-remembered because it was not a new record.

While Ruth put the pop in the game, few players put as much pop into their swings as he did, even if they were power hitters in his style who were part of that first generation of bashers. The great Lou Gehrig, who finished just shy of 500 career homers only because of the illness that forced him into premature retirement and took his life, never hit 50 in a year.

Rogers Hornsby, the brilliant all-around batsman, hit 42 once, in the same season he batted .401. In 1940, when Mize struck 43 homers, it was Hornsby's St. Louis Cardinals team record he broke.

The first person not named Babe Ruth to top 50 home runs in a season was the Chicago Cubs' Hack Wilson, when he smacked 56 in 1930. That stood as the National League record until 1998, when the Cubs' Sammy Sosa and the Cardinals' Mack McGwire unleashed their famous dual chase of Roger Maris' record of 61 homers. Maris had taken over the top spot from Ruth in 1961. That 1930 season, Wilson knocked in 191 runs, a mark that more than 90 years later remains the all-time record.

After Wilson came Jimmie Foxx. Foxx twice topped 50 homers, with 58 homers for the 1932 Philadelphia Athletics, when it appeared for a time he would break Ruth's record, and then with 50 even in 1938 for the Boston Red Sox. That same season, Hank Greenberg gave it a go, accumulating 58 homers for the Detroit Tigers.

Even in the Ruth era and the post–Ruth era, it was clear to base-ball people that any slugger who hit at least 50 dingers in a season was in an elite class. By the time Mize made his move in 1947, no player had reached that milestone in nine years, since Foxx and Greenberg.

However, Mize did not even lead the National League decisively in 1947. The Pittsburgh Pirates' Ralph Kiner, the steadiest power hit-ter of his generation, also hit 51 homers in the same season as Mize, marking the first fifty-plus tie for league leadership. This was particu-larly unusual because over the decades it was more likely a fair number of years would pass between sluggers reaching 50 than there would be two in one season.

Kiner hit 54 in 1949, two years later, and in the 1950s, Willie Mays (51 in 1955) and Mickey Mantle (52 in 1956) were the only ones hitting that target. Maris did his thing in 1961, but Mantle hit 54 home runs that same season. Mays reached the milestone a second time in 1965 with 52 homers, but then nobody did it again until 1977, when George Foster of the Cincinnati Reds stroked 52. It took until 1990, when Cecil Fielder of the Detroit Tigers slammed 51, for anyone else to put his name on the list of 50-homer kings.

After that it was the Wild West, with McGwire setting the record with 70 homers in one year (and hitting at least 50 four times) and Sosa four times hitting at least 50 and topping out at 66. Ken Griffey, Jr., belted tons of deep balls and such others as Alex Rodriguez, Albert Belle, Greg Vaughn, Brady Anderson, David Ortiz, Jose Bautista, Ryan Howard, Luis Gonzalez, Jim Thome, Chris Davis, Andrew Jones, and Prince Fielder (Cecil's son), joined the 50-homer club.

Many of those hitters reached their heights and highs in hom-ers during a period of time Major League Baseball has referred to as the "steroids era," with many stars facing allegations of using perfor-mance-enhancing drugs. Ultimately, the single-season and career home run records came to rest in the possession of Barry Bonds, a lin-ear descendant of Mize's with the San Francisco Giants. Bonds estab-lished the still-standing mark of 73 in one season in 2001. That broke McGwire's record. Bonds is also the career homer leader with 762 home runs. That broke Hank Aaron's record of 755 homers, which had toppled Ruth's old 714 record. Bonds retired after the 2007 season.

More recently, the Yankees' Aaron Judge hit 52 homers in 2017,

Giancarlo Stanton, then with the Miami Marlins, hit 59 the same season and the New York Mets' Pete Alonso hit 53 in 2019, setting the rookie home run record, previously set by Judge.

For such a long list of seasons, it is a short list of big boppers, and Mize is on it. He could always hit the ball a long way. There were two ironies about 1947. For one, Mize's home field was the Polo Grounds, where he said he didn't like to hit. The second was the lurking Ralph Kiner. No one expected two players in the same league to hit more than 50 homers in the same season and tie for the league lead.

In his own way, despite not having a lengthy career, Kiner was one of the most formidable home-run hitters of all time. He broke in with the Pirates in 1946 as a 23-year-old. He played just 10 years in the majors, retiring young because of back problems, but led the NL in homers the first seven years of his career.

A six-time All-Star, he led the league in runs batted in once, once in runs scored, three times in walks, and three times in slugging percentage. He went on to a long broadcasting career with the New York Mets and was elected to the Hall of Fame.

Although it is iffy that Mize and Kiner discussed this, Kiner was still another star who ran afoul of Branch Rickey over money. Rickey had gone from the Cardinals to the Dodgers to the Pirates. His assignment was to rebuild the woeful Pirates of the late 1940s and early 1950s that featured Kiner as its main jewel. Inevitably, they bickered over money.

"I try to hit the ball as hard as I can every time I swing," said Kiner, who averaged just about 36.9 homers a year in his decade-long career.[5]

As a broadcaster, Kiner was the king of the malapropism, but capably sprinkled his observations of baseball with wisdom and humor. He was credited with first uttering a phrase that became a cliché, yet even in this era when baseball's salary structure is vastly different than when Kiner played, still seems appropriate. "Singles hitters drive Fords, home-run hitters drive Cadillacs," Kiner said. The comment might not still reverberate if he had included Studebakers.

Although Kiner did not say that until later, during his broadcast days, a budding superstar actually took note of that notion by watching him and Mize bash homers in 1946 and all season long in 1947. The Cardinals' Stan Musial, Mize's old teammate, said he adapted to hitting the long ball more (he ended up with 475 homers) realizing those guys were getting more financial remuneration for their slugging. Musial studied the way pitchers approached him and switched his own approach in order to hit more homers. "Pitchers had generally thrown high and tight to me," Musial said. "But now they were throwing low and away, a tough pitch to pull."[6] Already an All-Star and a two-time Most Valuable Player, Musial increased his home runs from 19 in 1947 to 39 in 1948.

In 1947, Kiner hit his first home run on April 29 in a 6–2 win over the Philadelphia Phillies. In the same game, teammate and future Hall of Famer Hank Greenberg hit his third. Greenberg was a refugee from the Detroit Tigers, where he had starred for years. Kiner was still a young player and later said he was greatly influenced by and learned much from Greenberg's proximity. Given the way Kiner's home run production ratcheted up so swiftly, it didn't take long to absorb the lessons.

Kiner had five home runs by June 1 but was up to 17 by June 29. By the end of a July 4 doubleheader, he had 19 blasts. They were mounting up. During the heat and humidity of summer, Kiner erupted. By the conclusion of an August 16 drubbing of the Cardinals, Kiner had 35 homers after a three-homer performance. His mentor, Greenberg, had 23 homers for Pittsburgh, but the Pirates couldn't beat anybody. They kept sinking in the standings, lower than the Giants. They were on their way to a 62–92 finish, in seventh place out of the eight National League teams.

Mize was running a little bit ahead of Kiner in the home race. The Big Cat slugged his 36th on August 10. The only thing keeping the Pirates out of the cellar was the Phillies. The Giants were running out of steam, essentially running in place, futilely trying to catch the eventual pennant-winning Dodgers.

At least during September, the New York fans could root for Mize to best Kiner, even if it became increasingly clear that the Giants were unlikely to gain a pennant. Might as well cheer for Mize and his bat. Kiner poled his 40th homer on September 1 in a loss to the Cardinals. However, Mize belted his 44th on August 28, so he was still in command.

Mize reached the 50-homer mark on September 20 in a 5–3 win over the Phillies, slugging the notable shot off Ken Heintzelman. At that point, he trailed Kiner for the National League crown. Kiner got his 50th on September 18 in an 8–7 victory over the Dodgers. Kiner took the lead with his 51st homer on September 23 in an 8–4 loss to St. Louis. Could Mize answer? He did so on September 25 in a 3–1 Giants win over the Boston Braves, taking Si Johnson deep.

As the days of the season were running short, neither man was on fire. Kiner did not hit another home run, failing to loft one out of play in his final four games after September 23. Once Mize ripped his 51st, he also could not take any other hurler deep. On the last day of the season, September 28, he played in both games of a doubleheader. Manager Mel Ott even batted Mize leadoff in one of those contests, getting him an extra at-bat to try and make the difference.

But there the race rested, 51 homers apiece for both Mize and Kiner. There have been several times sluggers have equaled one another's production for most homers in a season. The most recent time prior to the Mize-Kiner tie occurred in 1937, when Mize's boss Ott tied for the NL crown with Joe Medwick, each hitting 31 home runs. In the other league, Greenberg and Foxx had done the same thing once, and even Ruth and Gehrig tied for home run leadership with 46 each in 1931.

Various sportswriters gave Mize his due in 1947, some probing back in time to the early days of his stellar minor-league career, when he was marooned in the Cardinals system, some referring back to his leg surgery that nearly cost him the at-last beginning of his big-league career.

With Ruth being a distant relative, as well as being the king of

Like many of his fellow players, once the Japanese bombed Pearl Harbor, triggering the involvement of the United States in World War II, Johnny Mize gave up his baseball uniform for a military one, serving in the Navy.

the home run swing, there was a certain amount of glee among sports reporters when it was learned that Ruth encouraged Mize with a photograph of himself and 60 baseballs representing the Sultan of Swat's single-season record and inscribed, "I hope you try to break this record." There was also mention that the familial pal Ruth once gave Mize a souvenir bat that the younger slugger never used in a game but admitted to sometimes swinging "just for inspiration."[7]

While both Mize and Kiner exceeded the 50-homer mark, it cannot be said that either of them threatened Ruth's 60 in 1947. However, early in that season Mize did set a National League record by scoring in 16 straight games.

Many ballplayers are superstitious. Many follow carefully planned routines quietly. Some respond poorly to minor injuries. Some slough them off. By 1947, Mize figured he had been around the game long enough that he had seen and experienced almost everything. Not that he had many bad moments on the field, while still admitting everyone has slumps, but he seemed to take this especially good season in stride.

"If you're gonna have a good year, you're gonna," Mize said. "And there's not much you can do about it either way. Most ballplayers' troubles aren't in their arms or legs. They're in here [pointing to his head]. Nothin' bothers me anymore, sore arms, batting slumps, or baseball writers. Nothin'. You gotta have an unworried mind to play good ball."[8]

Mize played great ball in 1947. He was the leader of the hitters for the Giants, the most productive of seven players who reached double figures in home runs. But none of them pitched, and New York finished just 81–73 after its promising start. That was only good for fourth place in the National League standings.

13

Last Call with the Giants

Mel Ott was one of the greatest of Giants players. He desperately wanted to follow in the tradition of his mentor, John J. McGraw, and win a championship for the club. When Johnny Mize was made available by the St. Louis Cardinals, Ott lobbied hard for New York to obtain him.

Mize produced and produced big in 1947, those 51 home runs serving as a desperately appreciated weapon in the lineup. Mize, who had received a good raise to $20,000 a year, was worth what he was paid. Yet still the Giants were not close to a pennant. Ott had not been able to lead his favorite team to the promised land. He had another chance in 1948, and Mize loomed as formidable as ever with his big stick.

When the season began, Mize was a three-time National League home run champ. The Giants wielded as many big bats as anyone in the league, with only shortstop Buddy Kerr the one non–power hitter in the starting lineup. Yet the overall circumstances seemed unchanged for New York. Once again, pitching appeared to be the primary weakness.

Larry Jansen was back following his sterling rookie year, and he finished 18–12 as a sophomore. Not quite as good as his debut campaign, but good enough to lead the staff. The problem—again—was that there wasn't much of a staff behind him. Who was going to fill out the rotation? Who else was going to start? It was a mystery to Ott and the fans alike. Dave Koslo had been looked to for help, but he wasn't much help in 1948, finishing 8–10. There was hope invested in Ray Poat, who had appeared in seven games with a 4–3 record the preceding season. Poat did indeed step up to fill a role, but he was not the second coming of Christy Mathewson, either. It was not sufficient that his 11–10 mark was the second-best record on the team.

There was a sameness with the Giants, a stagnant quo, if not a status quo, with one major exception. For the first time since 1926, there was no chance that Ott would appear on the field. He retired as a player following his few appearances in 1947. He made it official on September

20 of that season, so it was well-known well before the next spring training that Ott was returning solely as manager.

As always, the player himself knew his days were numbered, and when he was asked directly when he knew it was over, Ott did not hesitate in pinpointing this awareness. "Last summer, for sure," he said. "The ball was starting to play tricks. It would jump on me in flight." When sportswriters wrote flattering passages about his playing days, he thanked them. To one, he said, "Thanks for the kind word. I mailed your piece home to my wife and I told her this was my obituary notice and I hoped she liked it. Funny thing, my eyes went before my legs. I knew what to do, but I just couldn't do it."[1]

All Ott had done was make his retirement from the field official. It was obvious to observers that he no longer counted on himself since he came to bat just four times as a pinch-hitter in 1947. As good as Ott was as a Hall of Fame outfielder, the Giants' need was all about arms.

The Giants held spring training in Phoenix in 1948, and Ott was as popular as ever with the fans, especially the kids, who were wide-eyed at meeting any ballplayer. He mingled with the youngsters and signed autographs, a one-man ambassador for the New York franchise. Eddie Brannick, secretary of the Giants, watched it all unfold with a sportswriter and said, "That's the way it's always been. They all love him, from the old-timers to the kids. Here or anywhere he goes."[2]

The Giants had made no major off-season trades to obtain frontline pitching. It was only during spring training that they held what amounted to open tryouts for pitchers nearing the end of their careers, or who were already there. Not a one of them was going to pay dividends for the Giants that season.

The one holdover with no track record of note who did come through, making reality of some of his potential, was right-hander Sheldon Jones. He had played sparingly for two seasons, but in 1948 Jones showed off new dimensions. He emerged behind Jansen as the next-most important pitcher on the staff. Starting 21 games but also relieving, Jones made 55 appearances, went 16–8, and compiled an earned run average of 3.35. It proved to be the best season of his career.

Everyone is optimistic in spring training, when every team is 0–0, so the Giants began the season with hope blinding close scrutiny. For all the angst and uncertainty, the Giants did begin the season fairly well. After losing on Opening Day, April 20, New York won seven of its next eight games, and even after dropping the last two games of the month stood at 7–4. They were in first place.

Coming off his big 1947 season, Mize started hitless in the opener but bashed his first homer of the new year in the second game, a 9–5 win over the Dodgers. The rivalry was as feisty as ever. At the end of the month, Mize was batting .300 and had two home runs. He was very much still the feared slugger, whether or not he or anyone else in the league really expected him to smack 51 homers again.

Continuing on till mid–June, the Giants played good overall baseball. They were capable of lighting up the scoreboard like Christmas on occasion, such as scoring 16 runs one day against the Boston Braves and scoring 16 more against the Pittsburgh Pirates on another. That season, seven of the everyday starters belted at least 10 homers. Sid Gordon knocked 30, and Bobby Thomson and Walker Cooper had 16 apiece.

And then there was Mize. It was a long way from April to October, but Mize ended up in another home run competition with the Pirates' Ralph Kiner. It was almost as if the previous season's contest had never ended, only returned after a winter intermission.

As late as June 10, the Giants were in first place, an unlikely contender to the pre-season prognosticators. Although Mize's average was down to .264, he went three-for-three that afternoon. But he had just nine home runs at the moment. He had not quite revved up yet, but he and Kiner resumed their duel.

A week later, the Giants began a slide in the close National League. Their record of 27–21, good for a first-place tie on the 10th, began declining. It took only days to drop to fourth place, and by mid–July, with a record of 37–38, Ott was ousted as manager. The Giants' winning percentage of .493 had them 8½ games behind the Braves in the standings, tied for fourth.

Owner Horace Stoneham had run out of patience with John McGraw's protégé. He had spent a couple of weeks exploring a change, first investigating whether Burt Shotton was available to take over the Giants, but upon discovering that he wasn't, he kept looking around. Although Ott lasted a few more games, by the time of the All-Star break, his departure was assured.

His replacement was a shocker. Brooklyn won the 1947 pennant with two fill-in managers, Clyde Sukeforth (2–0) and Shotton (92–60). But they were placeholders for manager Leo Durocher, who won 96 games in 1946 but was suspended for a year by Commissioner A. B. "Happy" Chandler. The cause was a litany of alleged immoral behaviors.

In 1948, "The Lip" regained his seat in the dugout, but the Dodgers bore faint resemblance to the pennant winners of the previous year, sitting at 35–37 when Brooklyn, too, decided change was warranted. For a guy who had dissed nice guy Mel Ott, for a guy who was the face of the enemy, to turn up as the new manager of the Giants was halfway between unbelievable and bizarre.

This was true not only because Durocher was probably the most hated of the Dodgers to the Giants' way of thinking, but also because Ott was still under a long-term contract that paid him through the 1950 season and was going to be around in some capacity. Complicating matters was that Hall of Fame hurler Carl Hubbell was still in the front office, too, as director of player development, and he was no particular pal of Durocher's. Baseball fans looked at this administrative development and shook their heads as violently as dogs seeking to dry off after a dip in the lake.

The press conference introducing Durocher to the New York sportswriters put some pressure on the man who often was too blunt for his own good to say the right thing. "I feel the change will do me a lot of good," Durocher said politically, "because I have always liked Ott and Stoneham and their organization. Of course, I was also very happy in Brooklyn and I definitely was never asked to resign."[3] There were reports that this statement was not true, however. It also came out that when Stoneham told Ott he was going to be dropped as manager, he asked who he thought should succeed him. And Ott said Durocher. That was not quite the same thing as selecting one's own executioner, but it wasn't so dissimilar, either.

Durocher was not so thrilled that the Dodgers were prepared to let him go (while at the same time refusing to say he was fired), but when he was told the Dodgers were giving permission for the Giants to talk to him, he figured he should listen. To negotiate the details of a contract, Horace Stoneham was supposed to meet his new employee at Durocher's apartment so they could converse out of the limelight. Stoneham arrived a half-hour before Durocher, and he was the one who informed Laraine Day, Durocher's new wife, that her man was switching jobs within the New York boroughs. Day, who was listening to Red Barber's call of the Dodgers game on WHN 1050, said, "Then what am I listening to this for?"[4] And she promptly shut the radio off. Day then asked Stoneham if he preferred Scotch or bourbon as a refreshment.

This managerial change was big news in the baseball world and huge news in New York. Ott was regarded as mild-mannered. Durocher was rough around the edges and could be louder than a subway car. In his first team meeting with the Giants, Durocher went around the clubhouse, speaking to each man, occasionally praising, but often needling, always repeating that he wanted to see more energy and liveliness from the players on the field.

"Mize," Durocher said, critiquing his fielding, "you're no Hal Chase out there, but you're a good ballplayer and a wonderful hitter. I want you to show some life out there."[5] This was Durocher's version of a pep talk to the players, but deep down he really didn't think that much of the talent he had inherited. He wanted to see some major changes made to the roster.

When he concluded his one-by-one little chats, Durocher was asked by Stoneham what he really thought about the Giants. He responded, "Back up the truck."[6] The translation was a request to the owner to trade away a bunch of the guys and start all over again.

The shake-up was supposed to lead to instant victory, though Durocher had the same problem as Ott did when it came to starting pitchers. The Giants were not instant winners. They fluctuated between fourth place and fifth place, and although Durocher led New York to a winning mark on his watch, it was only 41–38, just slightly better than Ott.

Durocher did benefit from Mize's improved hitting. His average climbed into the .280s from the .260s, though that was far from his usual .300-plus territory. Right about the time of the managerial switch, the Giants engaged in a three-game series with the Pirates. The teams played a doubleheader on July 15 and a single game on July 16. Pittsburgh won the first game, 4–3, with Mize going 0-for-three and Kiner going two-for-four with two runs batted in, including notching his 24th home run. In the second game of the doubleheader, won by New York, 10–3, Mize knocked in four runs and recorded his 19th homer of the year. Kiner went one-for-four without a home run. After a day off, the teams met again. The Giants won, 6–5, but both sluggers slugged away. Mize collected his 20th homer and Kiner his 25th.

They were at it again. Both men, two of the premier sluggers in National League history, were again on a parallel track. Mize needed to catch up, but he would, heating up with the weather, heating up a bit for Durocher. On October 3, the last day of the regular season, the Pirates, who finished with an 83–71 mark, lost 1–0 to the Reds in Cincinnati. Kiner had a single official at-bat and went 0-for-1. He also received three bases on balls. The Giants hosted the Boston Braves at the Polo Grounds, losing 11–1 and finishing at 78–76. Mize came to bat just once and smashed a solo home run.

That blow gave Mize his 40th homer of the season, matching Kiner for the NL lead. For the second year in a row, both men shared the leadership in the National League home run category, 40 homers apiece. It is the only time in Major League history that the same players tied for the home run title twice.

The Giants slammed 164 home runs in 1948, still the most in the league, but 58 fewer than the year before. Mize was 35 and slowing down. Cooper was a catcher and was never a threat to Jesse Owens in the 50-yard dash, even when he was younger. Durocher, who admired the way Jackie Robinson played the game, wanted to see speed on the base paths and running savvy.

When the season ended, New York hadn't made much progress, and Durocher had spent a half-season watching the lineup up close. He was asked about his thoughts for the off-season and the next season of 1949. He spoke only in generalities, but it was obvious that the original "back up the truck" comment to Stoneham was no idle observation. "I got plans," Durocher said. "You can damn well bet on that. I'm gonna put a better ball club in the Polo Grounds. I'll tell you what, my kind of team."[7]

The Leo Durocher moving van did back up to the Giants' front office. The team was not showing much improvement in 1949, and Durocher did not like relying on the power game. He wanted that speed. In June, the Giants dumped perennial All-Star catcher Walker Cooper for a back-up catcher named Ray Mueller in a deal with Cincinnati.

Soon after departing, Cooper made it clear that he was not sad to be splitting up with Durocher. "We never had words," Cooper said, "but I always felt he never wanted me around and it was just a question of time when he would get rid of me." He did not give Durocher a rave Broadway review, either. "I don't think he uses the right tactics in handling players. You can get on some fellows and help them. You get on others and you hurt them. Durocher jumps on everyone."[8]

It was somewhat surprising that Mize was still around. He was 36 and he wasn't hitting homers with nearly the same frequency as he recently had. However, he did belt a milestone homer on May 5 in a 3–2 victory over the Pirates that went 10 innings. It was just Mize's third homer of the young season, but it was the 300th home run of his career. The blow won the game over his rival Kiner's team, and it was Mize's third hit of the day.

In 1949, the Big Cat played in 119 games for the Giants, periodically mashing the ball as he always had and periodically being benched. He cracked 18 home runs with 62 runs batted in, but his average dipped to .263.

While half of his teammates in the clubhouse by late season might have been strangers, Mize was still a Giant—for the moment. Things were about to change much more dramatically soon after the season ended. In December, with Durocher orchestrating the deal, the Giants shipped power hitters Willard Marshall and Sid Gordon, shortstop Buddy Kerr, and rarely used pitcher Red Webb to the Boston Braves for a couple of Durocher favorites, infielders Eddie Stanky and Alvin Dark. "It wasn't a great thrill to be with him at the time," Marshall said of playing for Durocher. "But he was a good manager. He needed a double-play combination and he got it."[9]

However, between the exile of Cooper and the swap of those other mainstays, Mize, too, hit the road. His departure was the by-product of a spontaneous conversation with New York Yankees manager Casey Stengel. The two New York teams were playing a mid-season exhibition game. Stengel sidled up to Mize and in way of greeting asked, "How do you feel?" Mize responded, "All right. But I'm not playing much." Stengel said, "If you were over here, you'd play." Mize quipped, "Well, make a deal."[10]

These days, Stengel would be fined $50,000 or so and charged with

During the last stages of his career, the 10-time All-Star was sold to the New York Yankees. It was great timing and of great benefit to Mize, who played on five straight World Series championship teams with the American League club.

tampering for such a risqué chat with an opposing player. No such punishment was meted out at the time. "I was only kidding," Mize said, "but then late in August they did just that [make a deal]."[11]

Mize learned that the Boston Red Sox, who had tied with the Cleveland Indians for first place in the American League before losing a one-game playoff for the pennant the preceding season, had been scouting Mize as a 1949 pennant-run pickup. The Yankees heard about that and, after thinking it over, decided that if they could grab Mize, it would be a double whammy on Boston. The Yankees gave the Giants $40,000 for Mize's services, and he became a Yankee on August 22.

Mize did not need much reimbursement for moving expenses. The Polo Grounds was situated less than two miles from Yankee Stadium. Different subway lines ran to each ballpark, but the trade was less about geography than circumstances. Overnight, Mize went from being phased out by what would end up as a 73–81, fifth-place National League club to playing a critical role for a pennant-contending (and ultimately pennant-winning) American League team.

It was a quick same-season turnaround. For the first time in his big-league career, Johnny Mize was on his way to the World Series. "It was a good trade for me, going from the Giants to the Yankees," Mize said.[12]

At the tail end of his career, Mize was about to experience what it felt like to be a world champion.

14

A Winner in No Time

Thank you, Casey Stengel. Johnny Mize's card to his new manager could have been in the mail before Columbus Day. No doubt as an off-shoot of Mize's casual summer conversation with the Yankees manager, Mize was purchased by the American League club. He became a Yankee on August 22, and by October 9 he was a World Series champion for the first time in his career.

After all of those years with the St. Louis Cardinals and the New York Giants, Mize won a championship less than two months after join-ing the Yankees. This was a good time to be a Yankee. The team was about to embark on the greatest run in baseball history. Mize was going into his late 30s, inching out of his prime as a hitter supreme, but was still a player who could do some damage with a bat, especially if he was not a full-time starter. Yet he was still a key component on a first-rate team.

During the first two decades of the 20th century, the Yankees were an also-ran club. In fact, they weren't even always the Yankees, but orig-inally the Highlanders. Less than a decade after they became Yankee Doodle Dandies, they really became Dandies. Babe Ruth was stolen from the Boston Red Sox in a slick player transaction, and his acqui-sition, popularization of the home run as an offensive weapon, and his phenomenal all-around hitting ability served as the cornerstone of the first great Yankees teams.

Yankees dominance and dynasty did not stop with the end of Ruth's reign and Lou Gehrig's death, however. Sometimes overshadowed is the franchise's brilliance immediately post–Ruth (though some of the suc-cess overlapped with Gehrig). Between 1936 and 1943, while Mize was toiling in the National League hoping for just one taste of pennant glory with the Cardinals or the Giants, the Yankees won the AL crown seven times in eight seasons. Six of those seasons, they won the World Series.

The only lull for the Yankees occurred during, and immediately after, World War II. The front office was so spoiled that any time the season ended without a Yankees championship, there was disappointment and the threat of a manager being fired. Stengel was in his first season as field boss of the Yankees in 1949, but he knew Mize from the National League. Stengel had a solid and colorful playing career between 1912 and 1925, with a lifetime .284 batting average. Until Stengel took over the Yankees and was proclaimed a genius, his early managerial records were not as stellar.

Stengel began managing in the majors in 1934, and between then and his New York gig, with time aside for additional work in the minors, the "Old Perfesser" handled the Brooklyn Dodgers and Boston Braves (or Bees) without terrific success. Due to Stengel's iffy results with those National League clubs, which never contended for a pennant and only once even finished above .500 in nine seasons, many believed he was a peculiar hire to lead the demanding, elite Yankees. Stengel clearly showed that all that stood between him and managerial fame was talent on the roster, but nobody knew that in 1949.

On August 21, the Yankees beat the Philadelphia Athletics, 8–7, to raise the team's record to 73–42. Yet that phenomenal record gave New York just a 2½-game lead over the Boston Red Sox, who were 72–46. The Yankees were clearly a terrific team, but there was reason for their insecurity. August 22 was an off-day, and the Yankees spent it investing in Johnny Mize. Horace Stoneham welcomed the cash, and while Leo Durocher didn't care about the owner's money, he was likely relieved to be rid of Mize, a player who did not figure into his long-term plans. He wanted speedsters, and Mize was a plodder at this stage of his career.

At 36, Mize had a new uniform, even if it also read New York on one side. The season was winding down, and he appeared in just 13 games, with one home run, while batting .261 for the Yankees. He did not play much as the Yankees hurtled towards the pennant and fended off the Red Sox. That was partially because of a shoulder injury that limited his throwing.

Although the $40,000 price tag later came out, it was originally reported in newspapers that the deal was for an undisclosed sum of money. As an aside, Mize was waived out of the National League for the deal to be consummated, meaning the rest of the circuit thought he was washed up, or was just being accommodating to the Giants to let them complete the deal.

There was a dash of irony about the timing of the sale. Even though Mize was only barely moving down the road, he had to catch a train to catch up to the Yankees because they were on a road trip against the Detroit Tigers. Mize caught a midnight train to Detroit out of Grand

Central Station, and a hustling sportswriter caught up to him there for comment.

Mize said it was a "surprise" the Giants parted with him. "I received word of the deal at dinner time," he said. "Since I've played in the National League all my life, I never thought I'd ever land in the American League. It's too hard to get waived out. It looks like the Yanks are headed to a pennant and I'm going to do all I can to help out."[1]

At that point in his career, Mize had 315 career homers, a batting average higher than .320, and although he was more than a full season away, he had 2,000 hits in his sights. Yet Leo Durocher had benched him for not hitting well more than once to that point in the 1949 season.

Stengel also chimed in with comments. Whether his previous talk with Mize was a significant element in the purchase, Stengel made no mention of that. When a reporter asked what his plans were for using Mize, Stengel equivocated. That was something he was good at, though usually by expressing himself in "Stengelese," a language all his own. This time he commented in English, meaning he said a fair amount without saying much of anything, another of his specialties.

> With the exception of our one exhibition game with the Giants this season, I haven't seen Mize play since the spring training season of 1948 when I watched him briefly on the Coast. Naturally, I know what Mize was in the past. But just how much of his old form he still retains is something I couldn't know anything about until I've had a chance to see him. So until I've seen him work out in batting practice and have had a talk with him, I can't say how we'll use him.[2]

Stengel said an injury to hurler Bob Porterfield played a part in the Yankees seeking Mize. The fact that Porterfield was sent to the minors, to AAA Newark, for recovery, meant New York had roster space, Stengel said. "Had a worthwhile pitcher been available, I certainly would have grabbed him, so with the chance to add possibly a little extra punch, we took Mize," he said.[3]

When Mize disembarked in Detroit to join his new team, Stengel had to ponder the options for his lineup. Joe DiMaggio, who was hurt in several different ways that season, had given it a go in batting practice the day before, but a shoulder problem was holding him back. That affected Stengel's thinking. "After Joe had two turns in batting practice yesterday I asked him how his shoulder felt," Stengel said, "and he said, 'Not so good, but better than it was yesterday when I could not have swung a bat.' I told Joe to take a rest and he agreed that this was the wisest move. With DiMaggio missing, I may try Mize at first base, with [Tommy] Henrich in right, Charlie Keller in left, and Cliff Mapes in center."[4]

Those were the choices Stengel made for the Briggs Stadium game of August 24, but the results were not very satisfying. Mize made his first appearance for the Yankees at first and went one-for-four at the plate. The other three guys also had one hit apiece. However, Detroit won the game, 13–2, battering starter Tommy Byrne at the front end of the game and reliever Cuddles Marshall (seven runs) at the tail end.

DiMaggio was back in center field the next day for the opener of a series against the Cleveland Indians, but he went 0-for-5. Mize cracked two hits, including his first home run for the Yankees, and it came off Bob Feller. New York won this game, 6–3.

New York's biggest challenge in fending off the Red Sox, though, was keeping the players healthy. It had been that type of injury-marred year for the Yankees, and it showed how Stengel's reliance on depth and platooning could be valuable. The scenario had gotten so bad by the end of August that famed sportswriter Dan Daniel, who authored a column in the *New York World-Telegram* called "Daniel's Dope," poured out some words of parody that were close to the mark.

Life with the Yankees has depended largely on penicillin and X-rays and has reeked with the peculiar attar of iodoform. In the daily lives of the players, Dr. Sidney Gaynor has been a more important contact than Casey Stengel. Gus Mauch, the trainer, has been more vital to them than coaches Frankie Crossetti, Bill Dickey and Jim Turner. Back in April, the New York club engaged a room in the Lenox Hill Hospital for the year. It has been occupied constantly by someone connected with the Bombers. Not so long ago, [owner] Dan Topping discovered that the facilities were not being used for the day—so he climbed into bed there and had his appendix removed. This preserved the room's record of unbroken use. Today, Tommy Henrich was there.[5]

Maybe Mize walked into a Yankees seasonal jinx because soon after that, his shoulder began aching and he needed more rest than at-bats. Perhaps his shoulder problem was transmitted from DiMaggio, like the common cold.

This type of thing was a season-long plague, or else Daniel would not have taken such a writing tactic. He reported that Mauch reported daily to Stengel on how many of his players would be available for use in that day's game. "There are three hay fever knockouts, three sinus patients, a busted thumb, four sacroiliac miseries, two sore arms, and four bruises," Mauch supposedly said. To which Stengel allegedly replied, "When I was a player, the trainer used to report on the hangovers. Incidentally, Mauch, can you pitch?"[6]

The acquisition of Mize made for five future Hall of Famers together by the end of the season. There were Mize and Stengel, Yogi

Berra, Phil Rizzuto, and Joe DiMaggio, who only played half of the schedule because of injury. However, the roster was not really top-heavy. The rest of the fielders were very solid characters who could be counted on in the clutch and whom Stengel platooned to optimize their lefty-righty hitting skills and their specialties given their ages and athleticism. The Yankees filled in around the Hall of Famers with such notable players as Tommy Henrich, Bobby Brown, Gene Woodling, Jerry Coleman, Hank Bauer, Charlie Silvera, and Charlie Keller.

While none of the top pitchers did reach the Hall of Fame, the staff was well-stocked with high-caliber winners the likes of which Mize had not teamed up with in more than a decade. That season, Vic Raschi went 21–10, Allie Reynolds, 17–6, Eddie Lopat, 15–10, and Tommy Byrne, 15–7. Reliever Joe Page was ahead of his time as a bullpen guy, going 13–8, and under today's rules would have earned 24 saves.

For all of that talent under one dugout roof, the Yankees and Stengel needed every bit of it. They barely eked out that pennant over the Red Sox by one game. New York ended up 97–57, Boston 96–58. There was much joy in the Bronx. Surprise, as well, among those who had not highly rated the Stengel hire.

Stengel was a smart baseball man, a savvy guy, but he was a showman who told jokes, enjoyed the nightlife, and had a reputation as more of a fun-lover than a buttoned-down Yankee. Lee MacPhail, who spent 45 years as a major league executive, eventually was president of the American League and was elected to the Hall of Fame, at the time was a minor-league official with the Yankees. "The general consensus was that Stengel simply didn't fit in with the Yankees, that image of dignity, class, refinement. Everybody knew Casey Stengel. He talked a lot, he was loud, and he drank publicly. When we heard it [of his hire] there were a lot of people around the Yankees who said in one way, 'My God, we've hired a clown.'"[7]

Those sarcastic observations were both right and wrong. Stengel was a clown—and he enjoyed the role. But he was also an astute manager, proving the jobs were not mutually exclusive, except perhaps to stuffed shirts.

The transformation of Stengel in the baseball snob's eye this season was remarkable not only because he steered the Yankees to a pennant through rough seas against a sturdy challenger from Boston, but he also he did so with only part-time help from DiMaggio. Everyone else, it would have been thought, was expendable, but not DiMaggio. Even if the lineups were sometimes patchwork, you take DiMaggio out of the center and you get a doughnut hole, not a cupcake.

The year before, 1948, DiMaggio, nursing neither his Achilles tendon nor sour shoulder, played in 153 games, led the American League with 39 home runs and 155 runs batted in while batting .320—and the Yankees did not win a pennant. Now, here they were, as Daniel put it, a human hospital ward, with DiMaggio's assistance only half the time, and they were being led by a guy some may have described as the anti–DiMaggio. Stengel came off as rumpled, DiMaggio as doing everything first class. How could the Yankees pull this out with him sidelined? It should be noted that in 1948, DiMaggio was being paid $100,000 to play baseball for the Yankees, more than Babe Ruth ever made in a season.

The Yankees could add Johnny Mize, a potent bat, for the stretch run, but fans and observers knew victory would not be the same, and might not even happen, if DiMaggio could not play.

The day after DiMaggio took the collar in five at-bats against Cleveland, and only a couple of days after he said he couldn't have swung the wood if he had to, he ripped a couple of hits and brought his average to .330. By September 4, his average was at .355.

On September 10, DiMaggio became a sportswriter for the time being, accepting an offer from the *New York World-Telegram* to write a column on the pennant race. This was a time-honored tradition, dating back at least to the days of Ty Cobb, though it was more often employed as a gimmick during the World Series. Most often, the star player in question did not actually write the words that appeared under his name, but worked with a sportswriter whom he knew with the paper that hired him.

DiMaggio's debut column was headlined, "Read Joe DiMaggio ... on the Pennant Race" and was accompanied by a boasting little box of type explaining to readers that this feature would appear "Exclusively in the World-Telegram" and DiMaggio "will give his expert opinions."[8]

Of course, DiMaggio was not going to write anything controversial, might not reveal his true opinions, and was going to say his team was going to win. Was that worth the few cents copy of a paper? Near the beginning of his first column, DiMaggio wrote, "First, let me tell what kind of team I will write about. The Yankees are a club with tremendous spirit. I want to make that strong because there was a point where we might have been discouraged. It may have been close. Something wonderful happened. We didn't crack. That is the secret of our season."[9]

DiMaggio did highlight, or lowlight, the rash of injuries, and said a realization there was someone capable who could step in and do the job, kicked in around mid–August. "There is always a man ready," DiMaggio wrote. "I think we can win. That's the way we all feel. We do not believe it is in the bag. There is no cockiness on this team. There is no slacking. We go out every day to show ourselves we can win."[10]

Later in the month, though, the hurting DiMaggio went back to resting. He did not even play in a critical series against the Red Sox that began with a 3–0 loss on September 24. Mize did, though, pinch-hitting and delivering a hit. The Yankees lost all three games to the surging Red Sox, and their lead in the standings was reduced to one game.

That didn't hold up, either. The Yankees were in first place in the AL from opening day on April 19 until September 26, the end of that Boston sweep. The third game, a 7–6 Boston victory, included a rhubarb that drew the attention of Will Harridge, president of the American League, and he chastised some Yankees by penalizing them through their pocketbook. Cliff Mapes was hit with a $200 fine, Stengel and Ralph Houk, then a back-up catcher, with $150 fines. Nasty talk to the umpire and a claim Stengel pushed one of the arbiters were cited as reasons.

The Yankees had to stay cool to recoup the lost lead. Five games remained. Although New York won four of them, on September 30, they were in second place, one game behind Boston. On October 1, the next-to-last-day of the regular season, the Yankees beat the Red Sox, 5–4, in Yankee Stadium. DiMaggio played and collected two hits.

The race came down to the last day, October 2, and the Yankees won, 5–3, scoring four runs in the bottom of the eighth inning. Tommy Henrich's home run and Jerry Coleman's double were the big blows. DiMaggio did play, had a hit, but he personally did not win it in the clutch. Nor did Mize factor into that triumph.

The World Series was still ahead. The opponent was almost as much of a rival to the Yankees as it had been to Mize's Giants: The Brooklyn Dodgers.

15

Getting Set
for a World Series

The World Series was still one of the most important events in the United States corner of the world in the late 1940s. The country paused as much of its labor as it could to stay abreast of developments. Fans of the specific two teams involved could barely regulate their heartbeats in October. The leaves on the ground could remain there until the games were over. The ears were glued to radios where they were turned on and wherever sound could be heard over the noise of traffic.

Baseball owned the nation, and during this era, for most of a decade, New York owned baseball, as the New York Yankees unleashed some of the most powerful and consistent winners in history, and regularly their opponent was one of two National League flavors, the Brooklyn Dodgers or the New York Giants.

For his entire career to this point, Johnny Mize had been on the outside looking in, a runner-up for a pennant at best, a player longing to play on the biggest stage, in the stadium where the fencing was decorated with red, white and blue bunting and where, six times in the past, the president of the United States threw out the first pitch right before an umpire shouted, "Play ball!"

This is what little boys dreamed of when they pretended to be big leaguers. They imagined themselves on the field in front of roaring throngs, and just about every single sandlot kid invented a scenario in his head where he struck the winning hit to win the World Series.

Finally, for Mize, who was 36 years old and had been paid to play baseball for half of his life, in the minors and the majors combined, this was reality. It was his turn in the limelight. It was a late-season turnabout moving him along from the out-of-contention Giants to the American League pennant-winning Yankees. He was not the slugger he had once been, the beefy hitter who four times led the National League in home runs and who had been a perennial All-Star. But he was a Yankee at the right time, a respected player whose manager would not be afraid to count on him in the clutch, to give him a shot when the situation called for it.

The Yankees' starting lineup was set, at least when everybody was healthy, so Mize was not going to get the call to hit four times per game. But he had to be ready because Casey Stengel liked to juggle things, called on his bench players in strategic moments, and expected them to come in cold and make things happen.

Of course, given the rivalry with Brooklyn and Mize's extended stay with the Giants, he was very familiar with the Dodgers' personnel. He even knew them personally. The Dodgers, under the mentorship of Burt Shotton, who inherited the club after Leo Durocher shocked the world and ended up in the Giants dugout, finished 97–57, to win the pennant. Brooklyn won 63 percent of its regular-season games, yet only edged the St. Louis Cardinals out by one game in the final standings. Stan Musial was probably right, that by dumping Mize and Walker Cooper, the Cardinals cost themselves a pennant or two. This may have been one of those years if there had been a do-over.

This was a loaded Dodgers team. Catcher Roy Campanella, second baseman Jackie Robinson, shortstop Pee Wee Reese, and center fielder Duke Snider all became Hall of Famers. Recently, after decades of delay, the late Gil Hodges, that team's first baseman, was elected to the Hall. And outfielder Carl Furillo, the man with the golden arm throwing to home plate, batted .322 that season. Those "Boys of Summer," as they were later called, could hit.

Much like the Yankees, the Dodgers had balanced starting pitching. It was not that they had four aces like a deck of cards, but in 1949, Brooklyn fielded a quartet in the rotation that could win on any given day against any given opponent. Don Newcombe won 17 games, Preacher Roe 15, Ralph Branca 13 and Joe Hatten 10. Jack Banta, who had a very limited career, won 10 games that season, most of his career output of 14. Young Carl Erskine, just 22 and soon to become a major factor in the rotation, went 8–1. Not that they were likely to run out of options, but the Dodgers could also summon Rex Barney, 9–8, who started 20 of his 38 appearances, if they needed another arm. This was a formidable outfit as an aggregate.

The Dodgers attracted 1,633,747 fans to Ebbets Field that season. The Yankees lured 2,283,676 spectators to Yankee Stadium. This meant that New Yorkers' line to buy tickets should have been long enough to stretch between the ballparks. If you had New York in your blood and cared at all about baseball, you wanted to see these games.

In spring training, before the season began and before Stengel could tell how things would play out, he was excited. He had only managed mediocre (or worse) major league ballclubs. This time he made the comment, "I never had a ball club like this. Imagine having a fellow like Joe DiMaggio on your side."[1]

If there was a Mount Rushmore of Yankees, Babe Ruth, Lou Gehrig, Mickey Mantle and DiMaggio would have their faces carved on it, though there might be a few other nominees. As DiMaggio's injury-plagued regular season ended with the New Yorkers beating out the Red Sox for the pennant, the fans showed their love for him by bestowing gifts on him on October 1. His presents included two cars, a motorboat, three watches, two television sets, a deer rifle, three sets of luggage, a dog (cocker spaniel), a golf bag, and even rosary beads. In a brief chat with sportswriter Red Smith, who asked DiMaggio how he was feeling, no doubt seeking to solicit an emotional response, he said, "I'm kind of worried." Smith thought he meant about the outcome of the game. Typical of DiMaggio's coolness on the diamond, that wasn't on his mind, but also typical of his general shyness, he was fretting over the speech he had to make to say thank you to the fans. DiMaggio did take the microphone and issued appropriate words and emotion, saying, "This is one of the few times in my career that I've choked up. Believe me, ladies and gentlemen, right now there's a big lump in my throat."[2]

Never really considered during that time was that DiMaggio was earning $100,000 to play ball, and the gifts came from an adoring public in the working world where the average annual salary of an American family was $3,100. This was one year when DiMaggio earned his money in blood, sweat and tears with all his injuries. Those fans could not have known how much he was hurting, nor how he put himself on the line for the Series when he probably should have been recuperating. But if you're going to play with pain, it might as well be in the World Series.

In the 1940s, there were no divisional playoffs or American League or National League Championship Series. Pennant winners proceeded directly to the World Series. There also wasn't much of a gap between the end of the regular season and the start of Series competition. The Yankees won their pennant on October 2. The Dodgers won their pennant on October 2. Almost before they could recover from the champagne hangovers, they had to be ready to go for Game 1 of the Series on October 5 at Yankee Stadium. First pitch was at 1 p.m. World Series night games lay years in the future. At least no serious travel was required.

There was barely enough time to hype up the annual greatest show in American sports, though a multitude of New York newspapers tried. *Newsday*, the Long Island–based paper, did not feature the home address of either club, even if both operated nearby. Before the games began, the paper did man-in-the-street interviews, asking who the Long Island residents thought would win it all. A police officer picked the Yanks in five. A high school football player chose the Yankees. A high school cheerleader picked the Dodgers, saying they were both loves of her life, but now that it was down to the nitty-gritty, she had to choose Brooklyn because "the Yankees are overconfident." The owner of a luncheonette said, "I think the Dodgers will win quicker than you can fry a hamburger." A professional cartoonist Dodgers fan volunteered that he had bet a Yankee fan friend the cost of a no-limit dinner for the protagonists and their wives. "I'll be eating at the Waldorf. But I think the Series will be a letdown. The pennant races were so hot anything else is bound to be mild." The newspaper folk also checked in with a dog named Butch II, whose answer they interpreted as "Us bums stick together. Them Yankees? Grrr."[3]

Leading up to game time, Guy Lombardo and his orchestra played songs to entertain the early arrivals. It was noted in one sports story that Lombardo played "tunes from 'South Pacific,' the Broadway show based on the stories written by a young writer named James Michener, probably because tickets to that hit and to the Series are equally hard to get."[4]

Mize had been an All-Star for years. He played in baseball-crazy St. Louis for the Cardinals, and he played in baseball-hungry New York for the Giants. He was nationally known. But he discovered that with the Yankees, a pennant-winner in the middle of a city series World Series, the attention increased even more.

A happily married man, Mize played in an era when newspapers often referred to wives as "Mrs. Mize," as opposed to by their first names. Occasionally, a newspaper would seek out "the little homemaker" for perspective on what it was like to be wedded to a ballplayer. Of course, when she wasn't cooking, cleaning, or doing the dishes. One story from Mize's days with the Giants was labeled "From the Feminine Viewpoint," and her first-person account carried the byline of "Mrs. Johnny Mize," no doubt just in case readers might be confused by the name of Jene Mize.

The account began:

I don't know why it is, but the first thing a new girl acquaintance asks me is: "Are you jealous of your husband?" This question probably is a natural one in view of the fact that a ball player is in the public eye. His friendship is much-sought-after, not only by the female of the species, but men, as well. It is an environment that is different from all others. Yes, from football, which is of short-seasonal duration, and from hockey, racing and all other sports. A certain adulation that comes to a ball player makes him in demand.

People want to fraternize with him, especially if he happens to hit home runs, or in any other way becomes a heroic figure to sports-loving people.

Perhaps [that isn't why] people ask me, "Are you jealous of your husband?" It may be predicated more on the fact that the average player must run the gauntlet of feminine fans outside the clubhouse after a big game. They stand around in groups, lots of them pretty young things. They want autographs, maybe a close-up view of their hero. They usually get both while we wives stand back in a corner under the grandstand making ourselves as inconspicuous as possible, waiting for the big fellow who won the game with a homer to come out.[5]

Jene Mize said she got angry when fans yelled to pitchers to hit her husband in the head with a pitched ball. The most egregious beaning of Mize's career happened in 1947, when with the Giants he was hit in the head with a pitch thrown by the Cardinals' Harry "The Cat" Breechen. Maybe Breechen did not want to share a similar nickname with "The Big Cat," but some believed the fastball that conked Mize was thrown with a bit more purpose than necessary.

Mize was felled in the batter's box of Sportsman's Park. The scene looked bleak, and fellow Giants hovered around him as if he might be roadkill. Stunned, but awake, Mize had the presence of mind and wit to ask for a message to be sent to his wife to allay her fears. "Call Jene and tell her I'm all right," Mize told teammates. "Tell her I'm taking the rest of the night off."[6]

Jene Mize did say that sometimes it hurt when they booed her husband, too. That she recognized as part of the game. While Brooklyn fans had a reputation for being perhaps more vociferous than others, she said she did not find them to be so when Mize joined the Giants.

Now, with Mize aligned with the Yankees against Brooklyn in the World Series, it remained to be seen how much animosity carried over from his affiliation with the Giants. This was a whole 'nother level of stakes involved than in those regular-season games.

Although Mize was hardly the main reason, and only a small percentage of why the Yankees won the 1949 American League pennant and were in this World Series, the gathering of sportswriters for the sport's biggest conclave did spill some ink speculating on how he happened to become a Yankee in the first place. If Mize was still a hot commodity, they reasoned, how was it that he cleared waivers right out of the National League? Who was colluding with the Yankees to pass him up when he could have provided a still-valuable bat to an NL club?

Did the entire National League believe that Mize was washed up? Casey Stengel did not. "He's a slugger who hits like a leadoff man," the Yankees manager said.[7]

Many years later, in a biography of Stengel, one-time Yankees public relations man Marty Appel said that at the time, it appeared that Mize seemed to have lost his gifts and that he seemed older than his 36 on the field. Then he was rejuvenated with the Yankees, played out the sunset of his career and proved remarkably valuable. Mize, Appel wrote, "became the poster boy for smart late-season pickups by the already talent-rich Yankees."[8]

When baseball people talk of Stengel being a genius, this is the kind of thing they mean—his creative and timely use of personnel to supplement the stars on the roster. Of course, if they had only asked Stengel directly, he would have been pleased to tell them he was always smart, even when managing the Dodgers and Braves to lousy finishes. Then he just did not have the talent needed to win. Now with the Yankees, he did. Stengel may have had the mindset of a Depression-era survivor who could never have too much money or security later in life. The addition of Mize to the Yankees' championship roster might not have been necessary for New York to win, but it was an insurance policy.

16

The 1949 World Series

There was plenty of hoopla for the World Series in the late 1940s, but it was just packed into a shorter lead-up time to first pitch. The first of a possible seven games between the Yankees and Dodgers, what they called a "subway series" since fans could travel on public transportation between the two ballparks, took place at Yankee Stadium on October 5 and drew 66,224 fans.

Brooklyn started Don Newcombe, whose nickname was "Newk," but whose name seemed prefaced at all times by the word "Big." Newcombe stood 6-foot-4 and weighed 220 pounds. His specialty was a blinding fastball. Newcombe was a rookie in 1949, technically, anyway, though he was an African American player held back by his skin color and not given a chance at the majors until he competed for the Newark Eagles in the Negro National League.

Effa Manley, who owned that club with her husband Abe, and who later was elected as a Hall of Fame executive, always complained that the Dodgers stole Newcombe from her team without any compensation. She did not stand in the way of one of the first Black players to advance to the big leagues, but she wanted something in return.

Newcombe was among a handful of the first Black ballplayers to break into the majors, along with Jackie Robinson, Roy Campanella (all with the Dodgers), the less-successful Dan Bankhead and also Larry Doby, the first Black player in the American League, with the Cleveland Indians. Newcombe was 23 that season and finished 17–8 with a 3.17 earned run average for the flag winners.

In Game 1, Newcombe kept company in the Brooklyn starting lineup with Campanella at catcher, Gil Hodges at first, Jackie Robinson at second, Pee Wee Reese at shortstop, Spider Jorgensen at third, Gene Hermanski in left field, Duke Snider in center, and Carl Furillo in right.

Newcombe, who in 1956 won the Most Valuable Player Award and the first Cy Young Award when it was given to just one pitcher instead of one pitcher in each league, when he compiled a 27–7 record, was

120

brilliant in this outing. He threw a complete game, allowed just five hits and one run with 11 strikeouts—and he still lost.

That's how good right-hander Allie Reynolds was that day. Stengel started Yogi Berra at catcher, Tommy Henrich at first base, Jerry Coleman at second base, Phil Rizzuto at shortstop, Billy Johnson at third base, Johnny Lindell in left field, Joe DiMaggio in center field, and Cliff Mapes in right field.

On a day when Newcombe was so sharp, surprisingly, Reynolds, who also won 17 games during the regular season, got two of the hits, a double and a single. Reynolds struck out nine men, though he did walk four to balance out the base runners a bit since Brooklyn collected just two hits, a single by Reese and a double by Jorgensen.

Stengel never hesitated to shift his lineup, depending on who was pitching, or favoring lefty--righty matchups, but he made no changes this day. Johnny Mize's name was never mentioned, and if there was any thought to his being given the starting nod over Henrich, Stengel looked smart for leaving Henrich in there. Henrich swatted a solo home run to right field leading off the bottom of the ninth inning to win the game, 1–0.

Henrich put the period on an enthralling game, a memorable pitchers' duel, that gave the Yankees a 1–0 lead in the best-four-out-of-seven Series, though not by any dominating margin.

The teams were back on the same field the next day—there were no days off during a Subway Series. Much of the cast in Yankee Stadium remained the same on October 6, though not all. Naturally, the two starting pitchers had different identities. The Yankees started Vic Raschi, one of New York's big three starters along with Reynolds and Ed Lopat. Raschi, 30 at the time, had actually been the Yankees' biggest winner of the regular season with 21 victories. Brooklyn went with Preacher Roe.

This was the first of four straight All-Star seasons for Roe, who was 15–6 with a 2.79 earned run average. Even though he was already into his 30s, Roe's biggest seasons lay just ahead for the career 127-game winner. Roe's given first name was Elwin, but he had carried the nickname of "Preacher" since he was three years old. An uncle teased the youngster, asking him what his name was, and the little guy said "Preacher," apparently because a minister took him horseback riding and he had heard others call the man that.

Some other players said Roe threw some of the slowest fastballs extant, but after he retired, Roe admitted he got by with the illegal spitter, something he discussed in a national magazine article when it was too late for a do-over and for anyone to take back any of his strikeouts.

Game 2 in many ways resembled Game 1, and Brooklyn tossed a platoon of outfielders into the mix at various times as substitutes and pinch-hitters. Mike McCormick, the old Cincinnati Reds star, Luis Olmo, and Marv Rackley all made appearances for the Dodgers.

Stengel, too, did some finagling in his efforts to reach Roe. His Yankees, supposedly known for their hitting prowess, had not exactly battered Newcombe, and as the afternoon wore on, it was clear they were not taming Roe, either.

Stengel went with Hank Bauer in right from the get-go, and the old Marine was good for one hit. Charlie Silvera stood in for Yogi Berra at catcher before Gus Niarhos took over. Stuffy Stirnweiss came in as a pinch-runner. Bobby Brown, later the president of the American League, not merely a member of it, pinch-hit late. And Johnny Mize got his first chance on the World Series stage.

It was the bottom of the eighth inning when Mize lumbered off the Yankees' bench, carrying his lumber to pinch-swing for Silvera. Silvera, a right-handed hitter, was no easy out. In 58 games that year, he batted .315. But Mize was a lefty hitter, and Stengel wanted the percentages on his side, like a poker player weighing the odds in a Las Vegas gambling establishment.

The score was 1–0 Brooklyn, the Dodgers touching Lopat for that run in the second inning for a slender lead. Jackie Robinson started things in the inning with a double, and Gil Hodges' single three batters later brought him home. The early lead held and held as the pitchers twirled with devastating effectiveness.

The Yankees were running out of time to catch up when their turn at bat arrived in the eighth inning. Roe still ruled on the mound when Mize stepped into the batter's box instead of Silvera. Yankees supporters would have been happy if Mize cracked a home run, but his job was to get on base and start something. Mize did smack a single to right field, but no rally followed.

Next up was Raschi, and although he had been pitching superbly, the Yankees needed to get on the scoreboard more than they needed him to take an at-bat. Waiting in the background was reliever Joe Page, a rare relief specialist of the time and available to fill in.

Mize's single gave New York a man on and the hope it could pile up some runs. Less of a Big Cat than a Slow Cat at this point in his career, Mize was not expected to leg it from first to third on an outfield hit, so Stengel pinch-ran Stirnweiss for him. Bobby Brown pinch-hit for Raschi, but Roe foiled the maneuver with a strikeout. Phil Rizzuto reached base on an error, moving Stirnweiss to second, but Roe retired Henrich and Bauer, pitching out of trouble.

Joe DiMaggio did get on with a single in the bottom of the ninth, but the Yankees could not produce, and the Dodgers made that solo run hold up. After two games, the Series was tied 1–1, both final scores 1–0. The beat writers, and probably some of the fans, were surprised that the Yankees were even here, battling it out in the Series after their ridiculous ill fortunes health-wise. People did not really know Stengel yet, but this may have been one of his greatest managing jobs, shepherding the 1949 Yankees to the pennant, a championship so coveted by him, but which few expected from this new manager in charge. Then to have the situation compounded by injury after injury, it was good to remember that the Yankees had little business being in this situation, even in the Series.

The trainer, whom Stengel relied on so heavily for reports on the status of the bandaged, had a close-up view of the information hidden from the spectators and understood better than most how remarkable it was that Stengel's next-man-up strategy (a phrase later applied to the National Football League's high casualty rate) was so significant. "It was hard to believe, but Casey would take a guy out of the lineup and the substitute would do better than the original," said Gus Mauch. "He moved players around. He switched positions. He did everything and everything seemed to work."[1]

Even some old-time Yankees watched and marveled at how the Yankees hung in there during the pennant race but didn't envision them fending off the Red Sox. "If Casey pulls this one out, he's a Houdini," said Bill Dickey, a Hall of Fame catcher, who was a coach on Stengel's staff.[2]

After his siege of injuries and a bout with pneumonia, there was much conversation about DiMaggio not being at full strength and how he probably should not even be playing because his health was so fragile. DiMaggio was not going to take the easy way out with a championship on the line. His health was only speculation because he stayed the course, and Stengel was not about to yank him unless he gave his blessing. If DiMaggio had to sit out, the new Yankees lineup might well have placed Henrich in the outfield and Mize starting at first base. It never came to that, however. It was even casually reported that Commissioner Chandler took DiMaggio aside and urged him to take care of himself. But these are not the circumstances championship athletes walk away from, even when their body is shy of 100 percent.

It may be that DiMaggio sensed his own mortality for the first time that season, two years before his retirement, with the near-constant and increasing pain in his heel, his illness, and other aches, but the warning signals were there after being sidelined so frequently. DiMaggio, one of his biographers noted about him in that World Series, "played in that Series by force of will and nothing else. He was weak at the plate, 2-for-18."[3]

Roe allowed just six hits that afternoon, and when quizzed afterwards by sportswriters, he said he didn't have his best speed, but his off-speed pitches worked better than usual. When he mentioned the exceptional value he got out of his forkball, one writer who had seen him pitch for some time noted that he was unaware Roe had a forkball to throw. "Sure do," Roe said. "I struck out DiMaggio with my forkball."[4] It was no forkball at all, but a spitter, though Roe was not about to admit it and employed "forkball" as a euphemism.

The Series shifted to Ebbets Field for Game 3, which was, of course, only a subway ride from Yankee Stadium, not exactly a heavy-duty road trip. Travel days were minimized in the scheduling anyway when all of Major League Baseball was located between the Northeast and bounded by Chicago and St. Louis in the West and South. There was no day off between games, and the next chapter took place on October 7.

New York put Tommy Byrne on the mound, and Brooklyn pushed out Ralph Branca. There was a bit more scoring in Game 3, though no one would describe the events as a slugfest. For a change of pace, Stengel started Gene Woodling in left field (he went one-for-three), and Burt Shotton employed Eddie Miskis at third base. The rest of the starting lineups were familiar.

Byrne was 15–7 with a 3.72 ERA that season, less renowned than the big three of Reynolds, Raschi, and Lopat, but just as important in the context of the rotation. He was 29 that year and recorded one of his top performances. Byrne spent parts of 13 years in the majors and had some glittering numbers a few times, but he was never quite a true star.

His main problem was that he walked way too many batters. He often pitched out of trouble, but too often he put himself into trouble. It was definitely in the back of Stengel's mind that if Byrne showed signs of weakness, the patience line would be drawn thinly.

"Don't watch Byrne pitch," Stengel once told Ralph Houk, a Yankees player, then coach, and eventually manager. "Just turn away and listen to the crowd. It's easier on your stomach. If you watch him you won't last long."[5]

Byrne led the American League in bases on balls in 1949, 1950, and 1951. Later in life, he made jokes about himself, even if he didn't have very much fun at the time when batters figured out their best offense was to stand in the box with the bat on their shoulders. He once walked 16 men in a 13-inning, 3–1 loss. "I did more to keep Yogi Berra's weight down than anyone," Byrne said. "When he caught me he caught a game-and-a-half."[6]

Byrne was one of those players who greeted Stengel's appointment as manager and his early days in the role with some skepticism.

> In '49 Casey did everything against the book and the older players thought he was crazy. Despite all our injuries and DiMaggio being out, we won on the last day. I remember Tommy Henrich saying, 'Well, hell, we're going to win in spite of Casey." Casey was sending up left-handed pinch-hitters to bat against left-handed pitchers and all that. It was unreal, but we had fun. We wanted to win and that was the key.[7]

The Yankees took a 1–0 lead in the top of the third inning. Cliff Mapes worked Branca for a walk to lead off the inning, and after Jerry Coleman struck out, Byrne hit a single, sending Mapes to third. Phil Rizzuto hit a fly ball to right field for a sacrifice fly that scored Mapes.

Brooklyn tied the game with a lone run in the fourth inning when Pee Wee Reese led off with a homer, knocking the ball out between left and center. After Byrne obtained one out, however, the Dodgers began working him over. He surrendered a single to Carl Furillo and walked Jackie Robinson and Gil Hodges, loading the bases. Stengel did not like the trend and yanked Byrne from the game after 3 1/3 innings, going with Joe Page.

Page, a southpaw who did not break into the majors until he was 26 in 1944, was an ahead-of-his-time relief specialist. He was a crisis manager before the phrase was in vogue. Later, relievers who came into games to put down rallies were referred to as firemen in general. In Page's case, "Fireman" was his nickname in particular.

Three years in a row, 1947, 1948 and 1949, Page led the AL in games finished. Two of those seasons, 1948 and 1949, he led the league in appearances, in 1948 with 55 games and in 1949 with 60. Although the save was not a statistic kept at the time, retroactively, when historians pieced together numbers, Page was credited with leading the league with 17 saves in 1947 and 27 in 1949. He was a pitcher who could come in cold out of the bullpen and excel. By 1949, he was a three-time All-Star. This day would be a highlight in Page's career, when poor Byrne got the quick hook.

Except for the lack of faith in the Yankees starter, Game 3 resembled Game 1 and Game 2. The score was 1–1 through eight innings, and neither team was tearing the cover off the ball. Hits were precious. The Yankees accumulated only four and the Dodgers three. As this game proceeded as a third straight pitchers' duel, fans had to wonder what happened to all the solid hitters on both clubs. Some 26 innings into the World Series, each team had scored two runs total.

Top of the ninth inning, and Ralph Branca was cruising. Until he was not. This Yankees rally was a slow boil on the stovetop. Henrich grounded out for the first out. Yogi Berra walked, but DiMaggio hit a pop out to third base. Not even a low simmer yet. Bobby Brown singled Berra to second, and Gene Woodling walked. The bases were loaded, but no harm done.

Mapes was up seventh in the order, but now it became Mize Time. Stengel motioned Mize to grab a stick and pinch-hit for Mapes. The count was 1–2 on Mize when the tipping-point moment arrived. This was what Mize was acquired to do late in the 1949 season. He twitched the bat and smacked a single to right field. Berra scored. Brown scored. Woodling came around to third base. Mize drove in two runs, the go-ahead runs, before Hank Bauer pinch-ran for him. It was a short workday, but an incredibly important workday.

While Mize was trotting back to the dugout, Shotton was waving in his own reliever, Jack Banta, to replace Branca. But Jerry Coleman singled to center to keep the surge going, sending Woodling to third. The Yankees had three runs in and led, 4–1. It stayed that way as Banta struck out Page.

Nowadays, a manager would never have let Page hit for himself in that circumstance, especially because he would have had two more relievers warming up, ready to replace him. Stengel did not have anyone else handy he trusted as much as Page, though, so he left him in. That almost backfired.

In the bottom of the ninth, Hodges led off for the Dodgers with a groundout to second base. But the 32,788 Ebbets Field fans were stirred to life when Luis Olmo, one of the most unheralded of Dodgers hitters, hit the ball out of the park for a home run. Olmo was in the majors for parts of six seasons, and in three of them, all but one as a back-up, he did hit over .300. This was one of the biggest hits of his career.

Duke Snider struck out, but when Roy Campanella powered another solo home run, Yankees fans got worried and Dodgers fans got loud. Catcher Bruce Edwards came off the bench to pinch-hit for Banta, but Page came through with the big pitches and struck him out. The Yankees survived, 4–3, the third one-run game of the Series, now with New York leading 2–1 in games.

Mize was the hero. One newspaper employed the headline "Yanks Spell Mize-ry For Flock, 4–3" to describe the action. "A storybook hero named Johnny Mize was responsible."[8]

One of the light-hearted pre–Series moments that basically came to life with Mize's swing was Joe DiMaggio's prose. After the opponents were determined and it was clear the Yankees and Dodgers would meet, DiMaggio wrote one of his opinion columns. He was carrying on from the pennant race as a scribe for the Series and took note of Mize's National League background (along with pitcher Hugh Casey's) as providing familiarity. "Mize studies pitchers," DiMaggio said. "All good hitters watch every move pitchers make. He has batted against all the Dodger staff and can tip us off from the hitting angle. Casey and Mize can fill us in on the sketchy book we have on Brooklyn. Casey and Mize have been through that [the player impression] with the Dodgers on the same field."[9]

Mize did not spend a long time on the field with the Dodgers this day, but it was long enough to ruin their hopes. When Mize was removed for the pinch-runner and returned to the dugout, he was enthusiastically greeted by his teammates shaking his hand and slapping him on the back.

The reception and celebrating around Mize was at least as enthusiastic in the clubhouse, as well, when the game ended. He had waited seemingly forever to play in a World Series, and now he was the toast of the Series, feted by Yankees fans near and far. "Tickled? I'll say I'm tickled," Mize said. "Say, it's one of the happiest moments of my life."[10]

It was a highlight moment of his career, for sure, one to be savored. The student of hitting, who would soon become an instructor on the topic as a coach and with the written word, gave an impromptu lecture to sportswriters who very much wanted to hear his thoughts on this long-awaited sparkling occasion. "I like to hit where you can see those fences all around," Mize said. "At the Polo Grounds you have that big gap in center where the clubhouse is. It does something to you. Here, you see nothing but fence. Your target is unbroken, and when you swing, something generally happens. I'm glad it happened today—the way it did."[11]

On the two occasions Stengel had utilized him as a pinch-hitter, Mize produced hits. This went down merely as a single, but it was such a shot, and so deep, it nearly climbed the right-field wall. It did not miss by much traveling out of the park for a home run. This counted just about equally, though.

Mr. Scientific Hitter was pretty scientific in his analysis of what transpired in the battle between pitcher and hitter, between the mound and the plate. "I hit a fastball just about belt-high," Mize said. "Or maybe a little bit lower. You know, though, for a fraction of a second, I didn't know whether I'd get the chance to hit. His first pitch was in close and in the split second you get to think about it I was planning to let it hit me and get on. That would have forced in a run. But it was too close to my right elbow. That's my sore shoulder side."[12]

It would have been interesting to sacrifice his body for the cause in that manner against Branca, and Mize would have driven in a run since the bases were loaded. But it turned out the Yankees needed both of the runs he drove in with the single. Mize said he would have taken a walk, still driving in a run, if less risky than having the ball bounce off him. "I looked at a strike because it wasn't my kind of pitch," Mize said. "I was going to make him give me a good one or walk me. Either way it was all right. But he gave me one with the count one-and-two and it was the one I was waiting for. They tell me it would have been a home run in the Stadium, bouncing off the screen out there as high as it did. Maybe so, but it got us a couple of runs and that's what counts."[13]

Supporting the notion, as espoused by Byrne, that Stengel managed more by his gut than what was supposed to be conventional wisdom, the manager said he was going to stick with Mize as his pinch-hitter even if the Dodgers swapped pitchers. "No, I never gave a thought to taking Mize out if they changed pitchers," Stengel said. "He's a pro. He hits right-handers or lefties. He's proved that often. Say, that big guy came through, didn't he?"[14]

It was a day of glory for the Yankees—and for Mize. The Series, however, was just halfway to a conclusion. It was a pivotal victory, but no one would say the Yankees appeared to have wrapped things up. Not after three one-run games and still needing two more wins to capture the trophy.

Once again there was no rest between games and Game 4 followed, at Ebbets Field, on October 8, less than 24 hours after Game 3 ended. Stengel finally got around to using Eddie Lopat, with his 21 wins in the bank from the regular season. The Dodgers countered with Newcombe for a second whirl. The Yankees may have had the lead, but as sharp as Newcombe had been in losing the opener, the Yankees were glad to see him ready to go for a second start.

Mize's rear end remained glued to the bench in Game 4, and although this also started out as a pitchers' duel, that changed after a few innings. The Yankees scored three runs in the fourth inning and three runs in the fifth inning to go ahead, 6–0. Newcombe was not nearly as untouchable and was replaced after 3 2/3 innings. Lopat hung tough into the bottom of the sixth.

The Dodgers put together a strong inning, collecting four runs to close the gap to two runs, driving Lopat to the showers in favor of Allie Reynolds. Stengel was looking for someone well-rested who could be a factor and had used Page for some long innings. Reynolds stepped in and quieted the Brooklyn bats. Neither team scored again, the Yankees prevailing, 6–4. Now the Yanks were on the brink, ahead 3–1 in games with the Series staying at the home of the National League champs for a third straight game and a third straight day. The philosophy had to be to sleep when you were dead, as the old joke goes, with no day off and the teams playing their fifth day in a row.

This situation gave the advantage to the team with the most pitching depth, and that was the Yankees. Having used up a second try by Newcombe with nothing gained, the Dodgers were reeling. Game 5 was a must-win showdown, and in a situation that might be faced in a poker game, Brooklyn was out of aces. The starter was Rex Barney, whose 9–8 regular-season mark was sixth-best on the staff.

Barney was 24 that season, but his big-league career was over one year later. This seemed to be a surprising fizzle. At a time before radar guns provided accurate ratings of the velocity fastballs traveled, Barney's speed pitch had a remarkable reputation. People talked as if he might be as fast as anyone, someone who could be in the Walter Johnson or Bob Feller category. Although he was still young, Barney had also seen some bright-lights World Series activity. Two years earlier, Barney struck out Joe DiMaggio with the bases loaded in the Series. He had also pitched a no-hitter against the New York Giants. So perhaps he was not so callow as it seemed on the surface.

Sought after as a smoking pitcher, Barney provoked interest from various major league teams, but signed with the Dodgers. He had good stuff, but he was wild, and that was a problem that needed fixing. Barney made his big-league debut at 18, before entering military service for three years, and fell in love with the organization and atmosphere. "The Brooklyn Dodgers, Ebbets Field and baseball were the greatest triple play God ever executed on this planet," Barney said.[15]

Barney, who received two Purple Hearts for his wounds suffered in World War II, pitched the last no-hitter in the Polo Grounds, but never quite reached his potential. When he was dropped out of the majors at 25, he later revealed, he contemplated suicide. He quelled the impulse and became a long-time, popular sportscaster in Baltimore.

At this very moment, however, when manager Burt Shotton, whom he did not get along with as well as he had with Shotton's predecessor, Leo Durocher, anointed him as the starter, a performance turning around the Series may have changed his own fate. Instead, Barney was hit hard and was wild, too, giving up five hits and six walks in 2 2/3 innings in a game when the Yankees' bats were resurrected.

Although Vic Raschi was not in prime form that day, allowing six runs, New York triumphed, 10–6, and he received the win. New York took the Series, four games to one. Bobby Brown and Gene Woodling stroked three hits apiece. Mize was not needed as a pinch-hitter. One of the most notable aspects of the game for posterity, other than that it kicked off a fresh Yankees dynasty, was that a contest that lasted three hours and four minutes took so long to play that lights had to be turned on for a day game at Yankee Stadium.

Mize was thrilled at how his season ended. He was a member of a pennant-winning team in New York, and a World Series champion. Neither would have occurred if he had not been traded from New York to New York after spending his entire career in the National League. It might be said that at that stage of his career, when many felt he was finished, he was playing less, but enjoying it more. He had earned a great many individual accolades. Finally, at last, he was part of a team that earned accolades. "After all those years in the National League I finally get into a World Series and find myself getting the base hit that helps win for the American League," Mize said.[16]

For anyone who believed Mize was sated, that now having contributed to a championship team he was satisfied to hang up the spikes, they were mistaken. Mize felt he could still hit, and so did the Yankees. They wanted to keep him around and he was willing, and most importantly, able.

17

Let's Do It Again

After the New York Yankees won the pennant and World Series in 1949, manager Casey Stengel said it was his greatest thrill in his long baseball career. That was understandable. After managing teams at the bottom of the standings looking up, it had to be exciting, satisfying, and vindicating to be the leader of the team at the top of the standings looking down.

Likewise, Johnny Mize, the late-arriving player, had spent years with two other teams regarded as a star who was never in the right place at the right time. Some of his teams came close to winning pennants, but until he was traded to the Yankees near the end of the 1949 season, he never sipped the champagne emblematic of victory.

What neither man could know was that they had arrived, had their first seasons in pinstripes together for what was a fresh beginning, as key links in a reborn club that was just inaugurating a new dynasty. They had so much fun winning one year they decided to keep on winning, winning almost every year.

Mize gradually won over the American League scribes who hadn't studied his hitting quite so closely in the National League. When one writer went so far as to ask Stengel why he even chose Mize to pinch-hit in the World Series against Ralph Branca, Stengel made it clear that he knew more about the topic than the journalist. "They tell me he always hit Branca hard," Stengel said, "which I didn't actually see because I wasn't in the other league, but what I do know is that he is one of the great hitters in baseball, and in that spot, tied in the ninth in the World Series, I want to have one of the great hitters in baseball at the plate for my team."[1]

Even before the Internet age, when everyone could watch everything, Mize did have a good reputation with the bat. Word got around not only through the force of his numbers, but from word of mouth, that when Johnny Mize talked about hitting, it was smart to listen.

Yankees shortstop Phil Rizzuto, ultimately a Hall of Famer,

though he was always prized more for his glove than his bat, first met Mize during World War II, when they played service ball. Rizzuto found himself in Hawaii, sometimes near the front, but also as part of a morale-building crew of baseball players. He was part of a support group of soldiers that always seemed just behind General Douglas MacArthur's forces in the Pacific as the war went on.

> I was in the first landing at New Guinea. Later, as the invasion moved north-ward from Australia, we moved to the Philippines. But they still managed to hold a World Series baseball tournament in Hawaii every year between the Army and the Navy. They pulled players from all over the world. For exam-ple, Dom DiMaggio [of the Red Sox] and I came from Australia and Johnny Mize came from the Great Lakes. We won seven of the nine games. The admirals won a lot of money from the generals in that series.[2]

So although Rizzuto had always been an American Leaguer, he was acquainted with Mize when they became teammates in New York. Rizzuto had played a couple of seasons in the majors in his early 20s before spending three years in the Navy. He was 28 when he came back to the Yankees in 1946.

Rizzuto batted .275 in 1949, not far from his lifetime average of .273. But he began following Mize's advice during spring training in 1950, and his batting average exploded for a while. Mize had not been present with the Yankees most of 1949. This was his first time around. As a teammate who saw Rizzuto each day, he noticed the way he took his stance and swings and thought he could help out his friend. Rizzuto was receptive, and he was on his way to the finest hitting season of his 13-year career, batting a robust .324.

When Rizzuto was asked for an explanation for this sudden batting explosion, he credited Mize.

> Johnny Mize started it all. Johnny and his bat. I used to grip my bat too hard. I was so anxious to get hits that I was too tense. It made me commit myself and sock at balls that I should have let go by. Mize noticed that at batting practice one day in Florida and suggested that I loosen up my grip and relax. At Mize's suggestion I adopted a spread stance at the plate, wid-ening the distance between my feet. It's the same stance I used to use in the minors when I hit with more power than I have in the American League. My hitting seemed to improve in the exhibitions and I figured I was on the right track.[3]

Rizzuto did his best to implant the memory of how he used to do things, but then his hitting dropped off again, going 0-for-11 at a stretch. Mize kept watch and still felt Rizzuto could produce more pop. "Try my bat," Mize said.[4]

Mize was well-equipped with bats for every occasion, and,

apparently, he was well-equipped with bats handy even for guys who were much smaller and built nothing like him. Rizzuto was 5-foot-6 and 150 pounds, seemingly half of Mize's size. But the magic transferred. "Mize's bat started me off," Rizzuto said. "I'm not saying that I just took John's bat and held it out and the base hits bounced off. But it was almost like that the first time I used it. We were playing Washington and I tried to duck away from a pitch. The ball hit the bat and went into center field for a line drive single. I said to myself, 'This is it.'"[5]

Nobody would have bet that "Scooter" Rizzuto would lead the Yankees in batting in 1950, not on that star-laden team. He cranked out 200 hits. Catcher Yogi Berra, at 25, was beginning to come into his own as a superstar. Berra batted .322 with 28 home runs with 124 runs batted in. Hank Bauer, who was edging aside Tommy Henrich and Cliff Mapes for playing time, showed why Stengel was liking him more each day. Bauer hit .320. Even Joe DiMaggio, healthy enough to play in 139 games, couldn't match averages with Rizzuto that season, notching a .301 mark. DiMaggio was still able to provide the big power numbers Rizzuto never would, of course, slugging 32 home runs with 122 RBI. DiMaggio was 35, and some days he felt as if he was 50, but at least he wasn't being rushed to hospitals on a stretcher or forced to the bench for weeks at a time.

The Yankees had survived the suspense in 1949 by winning their last two games over the Boston Red Sox. Just because New York won that AL pennant and capped the season with a world championship did not mean that other American League teams played scared against them. The Red Sox were still good, but there were other challenges in a deep league, each club thinking the Yankees were ripe to be had. This was a serious pennant race.

New York beat the Red Sox, 15–10, on Opening Day of 1950, April 18, and between them the teams pounded out 30 hits. DiMaggio and Berra collected three hits apiece. Mize, reprising his Fall Classic role, was sent in as a pinch-hitter by Stengel, and sure enough got a hit. But except for that day, the Yankees spent zero time in first place in April and only one other day in first over the season's first month.

The Yankees put together a 17–3 hot streak between May 9–30 and seemed accustomed to residing in the penthouse. They maintained that first-place status through June 11, when they were 19 wins above .500. But in a stratified league, other clubs were turning in mighty fine work, too, so there was no cruising for the Yankees.

Other teams were not fading. Rather, they were digging in for the long run. Let the Yankees own the spring; they would take them down in the summer heat. Upon exiting first place after taking life's stresses out on the St. Louis Browns, New York did not again reinhabit first between June 12 and July 30, and then the Yankees only gripped that status for a day. It was not until August 29 that the Yankees slipped back into first place. If they hadn't taken the hint by then, they were in a fight for their lives, a darned serious pennant race.

Enemies lurked over hills, behind trees, and maybe even underwater snorkeling. New York could not shed its unwanted company for long. The Yankees tightened their hold on first place a little bit, but then, between September 10–15, they found themselves located in second place once more.

What Stengel could always count on was his solid core of starting pitchers. The same four men, just as they did in 1949, kept coming to the rescue, turning back assaults. Vic Raschi was on his way to 21 wins, Ed Lopat to 18, and Allie Reynolds to 16. Tommy Byrne was right there with 15 wins. There were two other major changes in the staff. Joe Page seemed to lose his stuff almost completely and finished 3–7 with a 5.04 earned run average, a lack that could have been fatal. The other development was more positive.

A new face, another left-hander, Whitey Ford, worked his way into the equation. The 21-year-old rookie went 9–1 with a 2.81 ERA, the beginning of what would become a Hall of Fame career. As prominent and essential as the Raschi-Lopat-Reynolds trio was, in the end Ford would eclipse all of them.

Stengel could see Ford coming, but he was still quite young. Ford was not on the team's 40-man roster and was not invited to early spring training. Stengel recognized Ford as a comer but didn't put a date on it. The date turned out to be July 1. Ford won his first nine decisions and was an elixir for the staff. "I knew Whitey could pitch," Stengel said. "I told you that as far back as March. But I did not look for the amazing poise and the veteran's know-how, which he showed me right from the start in July. It's the thrill of a lifetime in a manager's career."[6]

It should never be forgotten, though, in those first Stengel seasons on the Yankees bench, that the Raschi-Lopat-Reynolds triumvirate represented the cornerstone of the championships. Not only were they winners, they threw complete games.

Right-hander Raschi didn't pitch in the majors until he was 26 in 1946, after World War II. His lifetime record was 132–66, meaning he won two-thirds of his decisions, including four seasons in a row for New York when he won 19, 21, 21, and 21 games, one of those lucky 21 seasons being 1950. A combination of attending college and serving in the Army delayed Raschi's career, but when he and Reynolds and Lopat played together, they were called "The Big Three." Raschi was the first member of his Italian-American family to attend college when he enrolled at the College of William & Mary.

Raschi was known as a genial, pleasant man in daily life—except on the days he was scheduled to pitch. He sought out a private corner of the clubhouse to think, and Reynolds and Lopat acted as de facto bodyguards, keeping interlopers away, especially members of the press, so Raschi could withdraw into himself. "Vic was the gentlest man in the world, but on the day of a game you didn't want to be near him," catcher Yogi Berra said.[7] Every athlete has a different, personal way of relaxing and preparing himself for competition. Raschi went from Dr. Jekyll to Mr. Hyde.

The hurler raised in West Springfield, Massachusetts, was brought up to take his responsibilities seriously. Even though he coped with an aching shoulder during the 1950 season, Raschi never asked out of the rotation. He did not miss his turn for five seasons. Raschi, who won the first World Series game in manager Casey Stengel's Yankees career, was deeply appreciated by the boss. He saw in Raschi the estimable qualities to rely on within a starting pitcher. "He had it here, here, and here," Stengel said of Raschi's arm, head, and heart.[8]

Lopat, at 32, went 18–8 that year. He did not make his major league debut until 1944,when he was also already 26. Eleven times he won at least 10 games in a season, and he totaled 166 over the course of his career. Only one of those was a 20-victory season, however, 1951. Born in New York City, Lopat was not originally signed by the Yankees. His first big-league games came with the Chicago White Sox. The Yankees picked him up in a trade when he was 30, for Fred Bradley, Aaron Robinson, and Bill Wight. Bradley never won a game in the majors. Robinson did some so-so hitting. Only Wight gave the White Sox some true value with a 15-win campaign in one of his seasons with Chicago.

Lopat's real last name, of Polish origin, was Lopatynski, and his nickname was "The Junk Man" because of the assortment of slow stuff he dished up to the plate. He remained in baseball long after his playing days, as a coach and then a manager.

Reynolds came from Oklahoma and was of Native American origin, of Muscogee Creek heritage. Because of that Indian connection, he was sometimes called "Super Chief" as a compliment to this throwing ability. Reynolds, who won 182 games over 13 seasons, likewise with his partners got a late start in the big leagues. He did not pitch at the top level until he was 25. Even then, in 1942 with the Cleveland Indians, he only got into two games with a 0–0 record.

Reynolds won as many as 18 games in a season with Cleveland, but truly blossomed at 30 when he had those Yankees sluggers backing him up. He recorded his only 20-win season with New York, but eight times won at least 13 games in a year. A six-time All-Star, Reynolds' earned run average of 2.06 led the American League in 1952, and he also led the circuit in strikeouts that season.

Not even trying baseball when he was young, Reynolds was attending Oklahoma A&M, later Oklahoma State, showing off a strong arm as a javelin thrower. Henry Iba, far more renowned for winning 751 college basketball games, was doubling as the baseball coach at the time and wooed Reynolds onto that team, first as a batting practice pitcher, changing his life. Reynolds made a huge first impression by striking out four batters without even warming up. Reynolds was such a good athlete he was also drafted by the New York Giants of the National Football League, but he calculated that he would have a more profitable career in baseball. In 1951, Reynolds was chosen as the winner of the Hickock Belt, emblematic of being the top professional athlete in the United States.

One of the grander achievements associated with Reynolds' history, besides playing for six World Series title winners, was his pitching two no-hitters in 1951. There was a certain irony that on a team full of Hall of Fame batsmen (plus Whitey Ford), the Yankees would have been nowhere without the trio of Raschi, Lopat, and Reynolds, possessors of great arms, but none of whom reached the Hall of Fame despite their success and notoriety.

As good as the Yankees were in 1950, on their way to a 98–56 record, they were hounded all the way to the finish line in the pennant race once again, just as they had been by the Red Sox in 1949. It took a serious hot streak during the second half of September for New York to quell all threats. In a rarity, four teams in the American League finished with at least 92 wins. Besides the Yankees, the Detroit Tigers were the eventual second-place squad at 95–59. The Red Sox were next at 94–50, and the Indians could do no better than fourth at 92–62. Those four teams finished within six games of one another in the standings.

The flip side was that quartet feasted on the bottom half of the league. The Washington Senators were 67–87, 31 games behind the Yankees. Then came the White Sox at 60–94, the St. Louis Browns at 58–96, and in last place were the Philadelphia Athletics at 52–102. There were races for first and last. On October 1, the Yankees went to bed as pennant winners, and they didn't even have to win the last game of the season again as they did in 1949.

Mize was viewed as a welcome beefing up of the lineup at the start of the 1950 season. He had only been around for a short time at the end of the 1949 regular season, though he played a significant role in the

World Series. Now the Yankees had him for a full year. There were two problems, though. He had slowed down in the field, almost to the point that he was no longer referred to as the Big Cat at all. The other was his perpetually aching shoulder, which was slow to heal completely over the winter.

He was still an important player, a keen threat with the bat, when available. But the Yankees' front office was thinning the herd among some of the back-ups. Johnny Lindell, Stuffy Stirnweiss, and Gus Niarhos were traded away. That is the kind of thing that can do morale damage in a clubhouse, but the Yankees were exceptional at coming up with the proper fill-ins and key new team members from the farm system.

A fiery fresh face that season was infielder Billy Martin, then 22, and eventually an accomplished if controversial manager. Initially, he was like a son to Stengel, and Martin desperately loved being a Yankee. He was not going to be a superstar player, but he had a super work ethic. "Hustle" might as well have been his middle name, although later it would probably be suggested that "Trouble" would have fit better. Martin made it into 34 games and batted .250 that season, so his full worth as a player had not yet been exploited.

Late in the pennant race, when the Yankees were on the cusp of making their move, Phil Rizzuto received a threatening letter in the mail that caused some consternation. "I'll never forget September 6, 1950," Rizzuto said later.

> I got a letter threatening me, Hank Bauer, Yogi Berra and Johnny Mize. It said if I showed up in uniform against the Red Sox, I'd be shot. [New York was preparing for a two-game series at Fenway Park, September 6–7].
>
> I turned the letter over to the FBI and told my manager Casey Stengel about it. You know what Casey did? He gave me a different uniform and he gave mine to Billy Martin. Can you imagine that? Casey thought it'd be better if Billy got shot.[9]

Although he was crushed when the Yankees traded him a few years later, maybe Martin should not have been so surprised.

Once Mize was fully healthy, Stengel gave him plenty of opportunity to hit. He caught fire. After his slow start and infrequent play, Mize became an everyday guy who ignited the team from the cleanup spot in the batting order. In all, he batted just .277, but during the latter part of the season he went on a rampage, belting 25 home runs and knocking in 72 runs. Mize was a gorilla at the plate, able to do whatever he wanted, hit the ball as far as he wished, it seemed, almost any time he wanted. It could be said that in 1949 Mize rode his teammates' coattails to a world championship. This year he put them in position to win another one.

For decades, Mize held the record by his lonesome for the most times hitting three home runs in a game with six. Sammy Sosa of the Chicago Cubs eventually tied him, and then the comparatively unlikely Mookie Betts hurried into the picture in 2020 when he was only 27. The final time Mize accomplished the impressive power feat was during the 1950 season with the Yankees.

On September 15, 1950, Mize had one of those special slugging days that helped burnish his reputation. It was the sixth time he bashed three homers in a single game. The slugger excelled in a slugfest, going three-for-four with six runs batted in, yet the Yankees lost to the Tigers, the team they were in a Texas Death Match with and were just about to catch in the standings.

This was the best season of right-hander Art Houtteman's 12-year career, with a 19–12 record, but this was the worst roughing up he ever took from a single batter. He was tagged for all three of Mize's blasts, in the first, fourth, and fifth innings. All of the balls soared out the right-field side. Houtteman was removed after pitching five innings and allowing seven earned runs. Yet he didn't take the loss. Indeed, Detroit didn't lose. Despite Mize's fireworks, the Tigers won, 9–7. A day later, New York did move into first place and stayed there.

The Brooklyn Dodgers, who at this time in their history seemed to believe they had first dibs on National League pennants, were disappointed in 1950 when they won 89 games, but finished two games behind the Philadelphia Phillies, also known as "The Whiz Kids." Philadelphia was a lot happier than jaded Brooklyn would have been because the last time the Phillies won a pennant was 1915, a lifetime ago for many.

This was a team that captivated the sport. That was partially because the Phillies had been so awful for so long before this abrupt improvement. The team had a losing record every season between 1933 and 1948, though the club also fielded a large number of young, appealing players. The average age of the 1950 team was barely over 26 and included two future Hall of Famers, pitcher Robin Roberts and center fielder Richie Ashburn. Plus, there were notables like Curt Simmons, Granny Hammer, and Del Ennis.

Roberts won 20 games, and Ashburn batted .303, but the heart and soul of the team that year was Jim Konstanty. The bespectacled right-hander, who did not reach the majors until he was 27 in 1944, was already 33 when he enjoyed the season of a lifetime. Konstanty was a full-time reliever who finished 16–7 with an earned run average of 2.66. He appeared in 74 games, just about half of the Phillies' games, made his only All-Star team, and was chosen as the National League's Most

Valuable Player. He saved 22 games and pitched 152 innings, way more than modern-day relievers ever accumulate in the closer role. Konstanty did not specialize in throwing to a couple of batters and then taking a seat. When he came into a game, he stayed for innings. He was a specialized weapon at the time and was someone the Yankees would have to contend with to win the Series.

Years later, Curt Simmons, who won 17 games that season as he turned from 20 to 21, reflected on how special that Phillies team was. "We played hard and we had guys come through in the clutch all year long," Simmons said. "It seemed like every game went down to the wire and we won more than our fair share."[10]

The Phillies almost put together a runaway season in the NL, but Simmons was called up for military duty before it ended, and some injuries kicked in, leaving the door ajar for the Dodgers, who could not quite capitalize down the stretch. A grateful City of Brotherly Love did not get jilted after months of a taste of success.

In 1950, the Phillies were managed by Eddie Sawyer and were still playing in old Shibe Park, where they drew 1,217,035 fans, the most of any team in the league and a fitting turnout given the years of doom and gloom that preceded it. Shibe Park opened in 1909 and was the first concrete and steel ballpark structure. That was innovative at the time, but four decades later the park was a bit dated. Its name changed in 1953 to honor Hall of Famer and long-time Philadelphia Athletics owner Connie Mack, and it remained in use until 1970. Ashburn, who spent the prime of his playing career with the Phillies with Shibe as his home stadium, and then became a long-term Phillies broadcaster, was a generous salesman for the place. "It looked like a ballpark. It seemed like a ballpark. It had a feeling and a heartbeat, a personality that was all baseball," he said.[11]

The Yankees, playing in much larger Yankee Stadium, drew 2,081,380 fans, leading the American League in attendance. During this era of baseball, the three New York teams seemed to have a monopoly on the pennants with the World Series games all being played a subway ride apart. At the least, Philadelphia was out of that orbit, even if it was only 100 miles from New York.

Game 1 took place on October 4, at Shibe Park, which held 30,746 fans that day, less than half of Yankee Stadium. For the most part, this would be a pitchers' Series, with the arms outfoxing the bats. This was not to Philadelphia's advantage since the Phils were without Curt Simmons, absent in the Army because of his call-up during the Korean War. Although Simmons was able to obtain leave as a spectator, he did not play in the World Series and missed the entire 1951 season as well.

Raschi got the start for New York and twirled a two-hit shutout, going the distance in a 1–0 victory. Philadelphia went with Konstanty, who went eight innings, surrendered four hits and just one run, though it wasn't good enough. The only run came for the Yankees in the top of the fourth inning. Bobby Brown, the future president of the American League, led off with a double and went to third on a Hank Bauer fly out. He scored the same way, on a fly out by second baseman Jerry Coleman, the future long-time broadcaster. That was the game's only run. Unlike in the previous World Series, when he was a late-comer to the roster, and coming off his scathing late-season hitting stretch, Mize started at first base. But he went 0-for-four.

Shibe Park handled a few more people, 32,660, the next day, who witnessed another pitchers' showdown between Robin Roberts for Philadelphia and Allie Reynolds for New York. The game went 10 innings, with the Yankees prevailing, 2–1, this time.

New York scored a run in the second inning when Gene Woodling drove home Coleman, who had reached base on a walk. The Phillies tied the game in the home half of the fifth when Ashburn brought Mike Goliat across home plate with a fly ball. Goliat started the inning with a single. Reynolds allowed seven hits with four walks and Roberts 10 hits with three bases on balls, so it wasn't as if the bases were lonely. It was just that the hitters could never connect in a timely way. Mize went one-for-four, just a single. The game was decided in the top of the 10th. Leading off, Joe DiMaggio lofted the ball out of the park for a solo home run and the triumph.

The teams motored the short distance to New York and resumed activities the next day at Yankee Stadium, this time with attendance counted at 64,505. It was no surprise on the Bronx Bombers' side that Ed Lopat started, the third of the Big Three, and while he permitted nine hits, he regularly squashed rallies, allowing only two runs. The Phillies, who were running short of reliable starters, sent out veteran Ken Heintzelman. Expectations had to be low since the lefty's record was only 3–9 that season. But Heintzelman came through. He tossed 7 2/3 innings, allowing only four hits and two runs, just one earned. You wouldn't hear a complaint out of Sawyer about such a performance.

The Yankees took a 1–0 lead in the bottom of the third inning, Coleman's single the key blow, scoring Phil Rizzuto, even if the inning did end on the same play when Coleman tried to stretch his luck to second base. Philadelphia tied the game in the top of the sixth inning when Dick Sisler followed a Del Ennis double with a single. Then the Phillies edged ahead, 2–1, when a Hammer single was followed by an Andy Seminick sacrifice bunt and a Goliat single.

New York obtained three straight walks in the bottom of the eighth inning, and the tying run scored on an error by Hammer on a grounder hit by Brown. Mize came in as a pinch-hitter and faced Konstanty, but he hit a pop foul-out. The Yanks brought in a new pitcher in Lopat's stead, Tom Ferrick, who got through the ninth inning, and then rallied in the bottom of the ninth against Russ Meyer. Coleman, who was everywhere this day, singled in the game-winner after Woodling and Rizzuto both singled, and the Yanks won, 3–2, to put the Phillies on the brink.

Game 4, also at Yankee Stadium and with no days off between encounters, was set for October 7, the stage set for a Yankees sweep. Mize started again and got one more hit, but he was not a factor in the critical offensive action.

Casey Stengel went with his young lefty, Whitey Ford, for the start, counting on the fabulous way Ford had come along in late summer to

One of Johnny Mize's teammates with New York was the young Mickey Mantle (left), the future Hall of Famer just breaking into the majors. And Mize's mentor was the venerable Casey Stengel (right), who had great faith in Mize's pinch-hitting talents.

wrap things up. During the course of his long career, with 236 wins, and a winner of almost 70 percent of his decisions, Ford was very much a money pitcher, a luminary in World Series lore. That reputation was established this day.

New York scored two runs in the first inning to stake Ford to the lead, the run-scoring hits provided by Yogi Berra and Joe DiMaggio. The Yankees added three more runs in the sixth inning, a home run by Berra and a triple by Brown delivering the most damage.

The Phillies threw not-completely-rested Konstanty into the game and then Robin Roberts, too, but they couldn't save Philadelphia. Ford was masterful. He was still mowing them down until the ninth inning, when the Phillies managed two unearned runs through errors and Stengel waved in Reynolds for the last out.

In the fourth inning, Mize was in the midst of a seemingly controversial fielding play that was costly to the Phils, yet once it was sorted out proved no controversy whatsoever. Del Ennis singled for the Phillies, Sisler flied out to right, and then Hammer hammered a single to right, sending Ennis to third. Seminick came to the plate and whistled a hard shot towards Mize at first base. Mize plucked the ball on the bounce, stepped on first for one out, and fired home to Berra, who tagged Ennis for a double play. Berra rolled the ball to the mound, signifying the conclusion of the inning. But not everyone realized the facts of the case besides Mize, Berra, and the first base and home plate umpires. Yankees feared there were only two outs. Phillies wanted to believe there were only two outs and ran to inhabit bases. Berra and Mize turned to the arbiters for confirmation, and they ruled as they had from the start—the Yankees had collected two outs on the play, and the inning was over.

It was a four-game sweep. The Yankees were World Series champs for the second year in a row. They were dream-busters for a hungry National League team again.

That was Rizzuto's greatest season, concluded with a World Series victory and the AL Most Valuable Player Award sparked by the highest average of his career, and that in turn emanating from his conversations on hitting with Mize and switching bats.

At times, Mize referred to Rizzuto as "The Flea" because he was so much smaller. Mize said when he first suggested the little guy use one of Mize's bats, Rizzuto thought he was joking. He tried it out, and the results were good. Slumps still occurred, but after the 1950 season, when Rizzuto first made the bat change and needed to stop a bad trend, he always revisited Mize's advice.

"In 1950, when Phil had his greatest year at the plate, and in addition received the Most Valuable Player Award, he had switched to my bat almost exclusively," Mize said. Rizzuto borrowed Mize's bat again after some frustration at making too many outs. Mize said, "he asked to try my bat again, and with a great deal of satisfaction, I watched Phil spray hits to all fields. That was all the convincing he needed."[12]

18

Legends Crossing

Until they knew how sweet it tasted, guys like Casey Stengel and Johnny Mize did not completely understand what they were missing by living long careers in baseball without World Series victories on their resumes. But once they began winning, it was like extra trips to the buffet table: Give me more.

After the first victory, a vindication of Stengel following his seasons of managing teams at, or near, the cellar, Jerry Coleman thanked him for having confidence in him and playing him more. "You're thanking me?" Stengel said. "I gotta thank you. You made me a manager of the world champions. Nobody ever did that kind of favor for me before."[1]

Stengel always looked back on the first title as the most exciting moment of his career. His wife, Edna, his sounding board and advisor as well as partner, said the same. "No thrill in our entire lives will ever equal that first World Series win," she said.[2]

By 1951, the New York Yankees had won two American League pennants and two World Series in a row. They had entered one of those periodic stretches in franchise history where they, and almost everyone around baseball, expected them to win it all again.

This did indeed turn out to be yet another Yankees triumphant tour of the Bronx and the nation. But the year also proved to represent a confluence of Yankees and baseball history that went beyond the average season. This would be the end of Joe DiMaggio's storied career, him finally shuffling off into the sunset with a limp because of a nagging Achilles heel, and what no one imagined in his wake, another young, superstar center fielder who would equal his legend and performance starting out in the same season.

The season ended, as it did during this streak, with Yankees superiority proclaimed, but not before some of the most suspenseful and memorable baseball ever played right down the street in the Polo Grounds and in Brooklyn.

Stengel was no longer described as a clown, even though he had a great talent for making people laugh. But after two straight titles, his reputation had soared. He had made many personnel moves that were considered somewhat controversial (sometimes by the players involved in them), but which supported the idea that he knew what he was doing. Mize was certainly not one to question Stengel. Stengel was behind his acquisition by the team and showed great belief in him as a hitter, using him as often as possible at first base and deploying him judiciously as a pinch-hitter in big situations.

One Yankee who always seemed uneasy over Stengel's authority was DiMaggio. DiMaggio had been told he was Yankees royalty so often that he came to think everyone should bow to him as the king. He was beloved by the fans of the Bronx, and he was worthy of the adulation based on his ability. He did not understand what to make of Stengel at first, though Stengel, understanding the popularity pecking order initially, was deferential and was not foolish enough to think he did not need DiMaggio in the lineup.

However, with all of his injuries and illnesses, DiMaggio grew frustrated. His body was starting to let him down, so it was natural for him to have moments of despondency. Stengel said the right things about needing DiMaggio, about DiMaggio setting his own pace for recovery, about how important DiMaggio was to the team. When Stengel kvetched at home about DiMaggio playing when he wanted to play, not necessarily when the manager needed him, Edna told him to shut up and let him play whenever he could.

However, three years into this awkward partnership, with DiMaggio beginning to yield to the inevitability of athletic old age, the politeness of their connection was fraying. DiMaggio bristled over some of Stengel's team rules, and he did not react well when Stengel experimented with putting him at first base for a game. Many an outfielder has made the shift from the green pastures to the first base bag in the latter stages of his career (some, like Mize, even earlier), but to DiMaggio, first base might as well have been Brooklyn. This was a one-game deal after DiMaggio pointedly said that the time for learning a new position was spring training.

At 36, in 1951, DiMaggio was fading, though. He appeared in 116 games, hitting 12 home runs, driving in 71, and being chosen for his last All-Star Game. But he batted just .263, very un–DiMaggio-like. Interestingly, Mize's statistics were similar, at 38, and without the flare-ups of injuries. He played in 113 games, hit 10 home runs, drove in 49, and batted .259.

There were other mainstays in the lineup in Coleman, Phil Rizzuto, Hank Bauer, and above all Yogi Berra, who at 26 had blossomed into a team leader and won his first Most Valuable Player Award that season. Including the seasons when Major League Baseball staged two All-Star Games, Berra was chosen for All-Star play 18 times. Between playing, managing, and coaching, he was part of 13 World Series championships.

At only 5-foot-7 and weighing 185 pounds, Berra did not have the chiseled physique of a bodybuilder, and given his verbal quirks, this left him not much different in the public eye from Stengel. All Berra did was produce, year after year, as a handler of pitchers and a producer of runs. He could bash the ball far, and he did it in the clutch.

As extraordinary a player as Berra was, he was considered the equal as a man and human being, although it took time for both reputations to ripen in a parallel way. Maybe it was because of his loose name connection to Yogi the Bear, but it took time for Berra to be taken seriously. Berra quips, or off-hand comments, morphed into pearls of wisdom over the years. Some stuck to him like flypaper, such as his famous phrase, "Nobody goes there anymore. It's too crowded."[3] That was said about an old-time favorite restaurant in his hometown of St. Louis. Later, when he was managing, Berra was quoted as exhorting his troops with such observations as "It's not over until it's over."[4] That has been repeated in the sports world countless times, including by sandlot competitors on playgrounds, and not only in baseball.

Just how much truth and how much fiction followed Berra around was a topic of discussion during his playing days and for the rest of his life. Once, *The Sporting News* noted, "If Yogi had been nearly as funny and as clever as an amused press made him, he would have put the wittiest Hollywood and television gag writers to shame and out of business."[5]

The remarkable thing was how much Berra was underrated as a player coming out of St. Louis when he was poor enough to eat banana sandwiches for meals. He and Joe Garagiola, who made the majors, too, but was more prominent in the sport later as a broadcaster, were good friends growing up. Berra was stubborn enough in the 1940s to demand that any team that wanted to sign him should ante up $500, something Garagiola was able to garner from the home St. Louis Cardinals. Neither the Cardinals nor the American League St. Louis Browns were smart enough to grab Berra at the bargain price, to their eternal regret.

"I wanted $500," Berra said many years later. "And I had to have it, that's all. I told any and all of the scouts who talked to me, 'I don't care what the salary is I get later, but I have to have that $500.'" Berra had more self-respect than the teams had for him until the Yankees took a flyer.[6]

One important new face for the Yankees in 1951 was Gil McDougald, who came out of San Francisco and became the American League

Rookie of the Year. An all-purpose infielder, McDougald played just 10 years in the majors, but was part of eight pennant-winners and was chosen for six All-Star squads. At a time when the Yankees were aging at some positions, he was one of the new-blood guys who helped replenish the roster.

New York always had depth, which gave manager Casey Stengel choices when moving around his chess pieces. Not everyone was an All-Star, although sometimes it seemed as if was so. Outfielder Hank Bauer, known for his Marine service in World War II, during which he won two bronze stars and two Purple Hearts, did not break into the majors until 1948 at age 25. He first fought for playing time, but he made himself into an All-Star. In 1950, Bauer batted .320. In 1951, he hit .296. He did make three All-Star squads and was a starter when the Yankees were winning World Series titles, even if there was barely enough publicity available after coverage of other outfield luminaries like Joe DiMaggio and Mickey Mantle. "In '49, Casey Stengel carried seven outfielders," Bauer said. "Eventually, [Johnny] Lindell and [Gene] Woodling platooned in left and I platooned in right with [Cliff] Mapes. Charlie Keller had a bad disc in his back, so actually there were six outfielders. I didn't like being platooned, but we won every year, so what can you say?"[7]

Stengel appreciated the hard-nosed approach Bauer brought to the team, and he appeared in nine World Series for New York before later managing the Baltimore Orioles to a World Series title. Neither Bauer, nor others, claimed he was a natural talent whose skills leapt out at the casual observer. Bauer was a player who gave his all and never skipped on the hustle.

"When Hank came down the base path, the whole earth trembled," said Boston Red Sox infielder Johnny Pesky. Bauer said he couldn't have fun playing if "you don't make somebody else unhappy. I do everything hard."[8]

Nineteen-fifty-one was the year Mickey Mantle met the majors. He was 19 years old, discovered by a Yankees scout on the fields in his home state of Oklahoma, a perfectly built athletic specimen of muscle and speed who became a legend. He and DiMaggio were ships passing in center field, the past and future briefly crossing paths.

Mantle got into 96 games and was very raw, but he showed hints of the enormous potential that led to 536 career home runs, three Most Valuable Player Awards, and enshrinement in the Baseball Hall of Fame. Mantle was not completely ready-made for the majors, but when speculation arose about Mantle going to AAA for 1951 or staying with the big club, Stengel, who recognized potential, said something about planning to keep this young man right by his side to learn. By coincidence, the other New York City team was introducing its own phenom in center field. Willie Mays, who was 20 that year, played more, in 121 games, hit 20 homers, batted .274 and was voted the National League's Rookie of the Year.

The 1951 Yankees had to fend off their share of challenges. Once again, the Big Three on the pitching staff was dominant, with Vic Raschi and Ed Lopat each winning 21 games and Allie Reynolds 17, though some of his victories were more spectacular. However, the Big Four envisioned did not come to pass. Whitey Ford was drafted and did not play again until 1953. This lack of rotation depth gave opponents openings. New York was in fourth place three weeks into April before catching a spark and moving into first place.

The Yankees spent all of June in second place before inching back into first again on July 1. But in the heart of that steamy month, they dropped to third place for a time. They also spent much of August and half of September in second place before they wrangled first place for good on September 16, when they beat the Cleveland Indians, 5–1. Reynolds got the big win that day in a match-up with future Hall of Famer Bob Feller.

Even though he was only third on the team in wins, it had really been Reynolds' summer. He was the headline grabber for pitching two no-hitters in the same season. Only Johnny Vander Meer of the Cincinnati Reds has ever thrown no-hitters in consecutive starts. Any no-hitter is rare. Throwing two in one season is even more uncommon.

On July 11, the Yankees were in Cleveland, with Reynolds hurling for New York and Feller for the Indians. Just 11 days earlier, Feller had twirled a no-hitter, the third of his career. On this day, Reynolds was a little bit sharper, prevailing 1–0. It was a double shutout until the top of the seventh inning, when the Yankees scored the game's only run. Gene Woodling cracked a solo homer for the score. "I don't think it was the best game of my career, but I'll take it," Reynolds said after the game as he sat by his locker in the visitors' clubhouse.[9] The odd thing about the outing was that Reynolds didn't feel right before it began, thinking he might be hit hard by the Indians. Instead, they didn't hit him at all.

Reynolds jokingly explained how if anyone on the Yankees was jinxing him by breaking the taboo of mentioning a no-hitter in progress, it was himself. "When we went into the dugout after the eighth inning," Reynolds said, "we figured that Bob Lemon would bat for Feller, so Yogi Berra asked me how I wanted to pitch to him. 'I'm going for a no-hitter, so I'll stand or fall with my fastball.' Yogi gulped and looked at me kind of funny, I had to laugh. I'm not the least bit superstitious."[10]

Reynolds was just being forthright when he noted that kind of self-analysis, which has been occasionally heard from a zoned-in pitcher. "It would have been silly for me to have made believe I did not know I was pitching a no-hitter," he said.[11]

The Yankees only touched Feller, who did pitch a complete game, for four hits, off the bats of four different players. Mize was not one of them. He did not get into the game, but he was hitting well enough at that point of the season to attract attention, even if the point of most stories about him discussed his age.

One article began by observing in July of 1951, he was "a year and 10 months older than his veteran Yankee teammate Joseph Paul DiMaggio." There were some less-than flattering descriptions of how the Big Cat had ballooned in weight "and it requires quite an effort to haul his 242 pounds around the base paths and to bend for ground balls."[12]

The day before, Mize banged out two hits, including a home run, in a 3–2 Yankees win over the Indians—it seemed just about all the important games for New York that season involved Cleveland. The homer provided the winning run for Vic Raschi off future Hall of Famer Early Wynn. Mize was wearing a wide grin, but nothing else, when a sportswriter appeared to chat, though also smoking one of his favorite cigars. "I'll play as long as I can help win games and they keep paying me enough," Mize said. The writer emphasized his Southern accent.

> Don't know if this team'll want to pay me for pinch hitting and such next year, but I'd be willin'. Yes, m'legs've slowed. And I'm not getting the distance I used to into my hits.
>
> Used to be able to whack 'em way out of the park. Now I just barely make it—just into the front row. My eyes still are OK, though. This winter I tried buying a pair of glasses for reading and driving. Wanted to rest my eyes. But the doc said I didn't need 'em. Biggest trouble is m'weight. I was 210 when I first made the majors with the Cardinals in 1936. Can't seem to lose any poundage, though.[13]

As the Yankees revved up, flexing the muscles provided by their mix of weapons, and began to take control of the pennant race, albeit if a little bit later than made everyone involved comfortable, the baseball world was treated to Allie Reynolds Deux, or Allie Reynolds II. A second no-hitter in the same season.

By September 28, only days before the end of the regular season, New York, barring a last-minute collapse, had deflected the challenges of the Indians and the Red Sox. Scheduled for a doubleheader that day at Yankee Stadium, the Yanks held first place by 2½ games. Stengel sent Reynolds to the mound in the opener to face Boston's estimable southpaw, Mel Parnell. The Red Sox had tumbled to third place, and first place was pretty much out of reach no matter what they did.

They didn't do much in that game. The Yankees pummeled Parnell. New York scored two runs in the first inning, two in the third, one in the fourth, and were piling it on. Parnell was lifted after three innings, though the Yankees still scored against his replacements. Eight different Yankees hit safely. Woodling and Joe Collins, who played first base instead of Mize that day, each had two hits. The only Yankee in the lineup who did not get a hit was Reynolds. But that amounted to symmetry since he didn't allow any either.

Although those defeated were the Red Sox, the victory actually clinched a tie for the AL pennant for the Yankees with the Indians, who ended up tailing off to five games behind the 98-win Yankees.

In winning his 17th game of the season, Reynolds walked four batters and struck out nine. Future Hall of Famer Ted Williams, the most feared swinger in the Boston lineup, got on once with a base on balls, but did no damage with the wood. Indeed, he made the last out of the game and had two chances to break up the no-hitter in the ninth inning. Just when Reynolds thought he had Williams safely retired, catcher Yogi Berra dropped a foul popup for an error that gave Williams a fresh swing. So everyone dug in again, and a near-instant replay broke out. Reynolds threw the ball, Williams swung, and he hit another foul popup. This time Berra caught the ball, squeezed it, and the game was over, the Yankees winning 8–0. A couple of weeks later, *The Sporting News* ran a photograph of Reynolds kissing a baseball, presumably the same baseball since he was in the clubhouse, still in uniform.

Fussbudget that he was, Reynolds said his sharpness was so good in the game that he never should have walked four men.

> I should have done better with my control. This game was easier, and yet, not easier than the July 12 affair [his first no-hitter]. In Cleveland, I not only had to pitch the no-hitter, once I got into the seventh and saw the feat within reach, but I had to win the game. In the Stadium, the boys gave me plenty of support with their bats.
> In the Cleveland game, I was relaxed and kidded around with Yogi and Lopat about having a no-hitter and they were scandalized. I got a lot of letters from fans giving me hell for violating a tradition of the game and flaunting the whammy. So against the Red Sox, it was all serious business. No quips. In fact, no conversation. After Yogi had dropped that Williams foul, I said, "Don't let it bother you. Let's get that guy now."[14]

Even though Reynolds was recording fantastic accomplishments, when discussion focuses on the pennant races of 1951, it invariably halts in place with the National League. That was the year the Brooklyn Dodgers had things sewed up before Labor Day, somehow blew the flag in September, and the New York Giants' Bobby Thomson hit one of the most famous home runs in baseball history to propel his team into the World Series against the Yankees.

Brooklyn held a whopping 13½-game lead over second-place New York on August 11 when things began to unravel. It took the rest of the season, the Giants on fire, the Dodgers fizzling, for the Giants to catch up, and the teams ended the regular season tied, necessitating a best-two-out-of-three playoff.

The games were set for October 1–3, an extra Subway Series, so to speak, and the results and the statistics counted in the regular-season totals. The first game took place at Ebbets Field, but the Giants won, 3–1. Yankees coach Bill Dickey slipped into the stands to scout. The pent-up Dodgers ripped the Giants, 10–0, a day later at the Polo Grounds, with Clem Labine throwing a two-hitter. Several Yankees turned out to see the next team they were scheduled to play. For the deciding game, New York started Sal Maglie and Brooklyn Don Newcombe, though neither was around at the end.

The Dodgers took a 1–0 lead in the first inning, and the Giants tied it in the seventh. When Brooklyn scored three runs in the top of the eighth, the Dodgers seemed poised to place a punctuation mark on the long, exhausting race. But the Giants retaliated in the bottom of the ninth. Their four-run rally, capped by Thomson's walk-off homer off Ralph Branca, won the game and the pennant for New York. It set off delirium among fans and came to be nicknamed "The Shot Heard 'Round the World." It was both climax and anti-climax, a home run talked about forever, yet only leading New York into an all–New York World Series to try and win it all.

As was typical of the time, there was virtually no break before the start of the Series, with Game 1 going off on October 4 in the Polo Grounds. This was one time New York sportswriters could have used a pause to assimilate what they had just seen, realize that chapter was over, and adjust to a whole new ballgame. Famed columnist Jimmy Cannon still felt that way even after the Giants had salted away the first game, 5–1, acting almost as if Thomson's home run hadn't landed yet. "Anyone who witnesses an authentic miracle isn't going to be rolled in the aisle by card tricks," Cannon wrote. "Guys who see visions don't bite their nails at suspense movies. If you've watched an atom bomb explode, you're not thrilled by Fourth of July fireworks. I feel like a guy who finished his ninth martini. I can't get numb-er."[15]

They decided to play the 1951 World Series anyway. The Yankees were two-time defending champions, and suspense aside, whether it had been the Dodgers or Giants triumphant, they were happy to take on anybody the National League put forth.

The Giants started Dave Koslo, and he was the gritty guy on the mound this day, limiting the Yankees to seven hits and one run while his teammates roughed up Reynolds. Reynolds was not himself, giving up eight hits and five runs, all earned, with seven walks in six innings. Nothing compared to the no-hitter days of summer.

Joe DiMaggio, still anchoring center field, and Mickey Mantle, in right, played together, though combined they were 0-for-seven at the plate. Mize was called on to pinch-hit but didn't jumpstart anything either, making an out. The Giants won, 5–1, as if they were playing the Dodgers again. Monte Irvin, late of the Negro Leagues, and later of the commissioner's office and the Hall of Fame, swatted four hits.

Game 2 was played at Yankee Stadium, and as a good host, the Yankees won, 3–1, with Ed Lopat allowing just five hits in a complete game and besting Giants 23-game-winner Larry Jansen. The Yankees pieced together three single-run innings, with no player managing more than one hit. Joe Collins' hit was a home run, though.

The most enduring aspect of the game, and with 20–20 hindsight the most memorable, was Mantle's famous injury. In the fifth inning, Willie Mays hit a fly ball to right-center. Mantle and DiMaggio began chasing the ball. When DiMaggio yelled, "I got it," Mantle veered off. But in a fluke, when he pulled up short, he stepped on the cover of a storm drain, catching a spike, and fell to the ground in shock. The misstep tore ligaments in his right knee. As Mantle lay on the grass, DiMaggio said, "You OK, kid?"[16] Mantle was not OK. In fact, he would never be truly OK again, this being a cruel blow affecting his running when he was so young, though not the only damage his knees took. He was carried off the field on a stretcher.

As the games switched locales, transferring the short distance between Yankee Stadium and the Polo Grounds, the Giants took the lead with a 6–2 victory in Game 3 at home. Vic Raschi gave up all the runs for the Yankees, but only one was earned. Rookie Gil McDougald was the only Yankee with two hits. DiMaggio was still hitless three games in. Mize pinch-hit, but he didn't advance the cause either.

Reynolds regained his good stuff in Game 4 when the Yankees needed him most, and DiMaggio contributed a home run as the American Leaguers thrust themselves back into the picture at a critical moment, winning, 6–2. They beat Sal Maglie, who won 23 games for the Giants in the regular season.

Game 5 was pivotal with the Series knotted, 2–2. The Polo Grounds was the scene again, but this time the Yankees played as if they were in their own backyard. Lopat won for a second time, permitting just five hits, and it was an everybody-hits-day holiday for the position players. It took five Giants pitchers, including Jansen, to get out of the building alive, with the Yankees running away with a 13–1 win. The previously somnambulant DiMaggio cracked three hits, Mize started at first base and had one hit plus an intentional walk, and McDougald smashed a grand slam. Most of the Yankees mobbed McDougald after the blast when he returned to the dugout, practically smothering him with affection.

"I just can't tell you how I felt when I hit that one," said McDougald, who was being coaxed into doing just that by sportswriters after the game. "It is a great thrill, make no mistake about that. Guess I'll never forget it. I only wish my wife could have been here to see it. She's been after me to hit a homer. So have my mother and dad. My wife would have been there, but for the fact it's hard to get a baby sitter for three children. It was a fastball I hit, letter-high. I didn't know it was going into the seats when I struck. You never can tell that. But I knew it was a good smack."[17]

Gene Woodling and Phil Rizzuto had walked, and Joe DiMaggio singled in a run, going to second on an error. This is where Mize played a part in the strategy. Rather than risk coping with Mize's slugging prowess, Giants manager Leo Durocher looked at open first base and pondered rookie McDougald being in a pressure situation. So he had Larry Jansen give up the walk to Mize.

Manager Casey Stengel did not criticize Durocher for what turned into catastrophe for his club. "I don't think Durocher was wrong to pass Mize to get at McDougald in the third inning," Stengel said. "I would have done the same thing. It was a wise move. Happily for us, the move backfired on them. Which goes to prove you never can tell. Maybe Mize would have hit one. Maybe Johnny would have knocked in only one run. But I would have done the same thing in a similar situation."[18]

It was still a one-game Series lead, but the atmospheric conditions favored the Yankees as Game 6 began, and they did end it then, 4–3, on the afternoon of October 10 in front of 61,711 of their fans. Giant Dave Koslo wasn't as effective the second time around. Raschi got the win, but the relief was a bit shaky, with Johnny Sain allowing two runs in two innings. Hank Bauer's three-run triple was the biggest blow, Yogi Berra had two hits, and Mize added another hit and walk for a .286 Series average and a .444 on-base percentage. DiMaggio gathered a hit and two walks in the final game of his career. He limped off into the sunset, and Mantle limped off into a long career.

Mize, who was older, decided to stick around. This winning stuff was fun and addictive. And his jewelry collection was expanding by the season, year after year being part of new championships with the spoils they brought.

19

1952

Johnny Mize knew his career was winding down. He turned 39 before the start of spring training for the 1952 season. But he was getting so much darned pleasure out of winning championships with the New York Yankees that he was in no hurry for this joy ride to end. Besides, he was playing for a manager in Casey Stengel who not only appreciated him but was the master manipulator of the pieces that could make up a stronger whole.

If Mize could win him five games over the course of a season as a pinch-hitter, as a late-inning strategy payoff, as an insurance policy, then Stengel felt he was worth keeping around. For Mize, whose best years gained him renown as a hitter but who couldn't win a single pennant in the National League with two teams, winning pennants and World Series titles every year with the Yankees was not something to be dismissed casually. Who wouldn't want to be part of the winningest, most-feared, most-famous organization in sports?

Glamor by association is what the Yankees were, not only in the world's most vibrant city, but all over the country, anywhere they cared about baseball, being linked to the Yankees meant something special. Everyone knew they were the best around, and if you were on the roster it rubbed off on you. The 1952 season would be different, if only due to the absence of Joe DiMaggio, no longer connected to the club for the first time since 1935. His legend lived on, but his smooth stride did not. Members of some of those contending AL teams were getting sick of Yankees success, the Red Sox, Indians and Tigers harboring starry-eyed goals of stealing a pennant, and those cries of "Break up the Yankees" that endured as a cliché, were sneaking into the lexicon.

But if you were Mize, Yogi Berra, Phil Rizzuto, Gene Woodling (a .309 hitter that year), Hank Bauer, Allie Reynolds, Ed Lopat, or Vic Raschi, you just shrugged and responded to the umpire's cry of "Play ball!" and kept on winning. Stengel added some fresh weapons, too. Johnny Sain, formerly of the Boston Braves and his partnership in winning with

Warren Spahn, won 10 games. Bobby Brown still could come in and give the team a spark. Gil McDougald followed his rookie year by holding on to a full-time slot at third base. Joe Collins pretty much edged Mize out of the picture as a starter at first base, and Billy Martin was a semi-regular at second.

Oh, and a guy named Mickey Mantle was recovered sufficiently to bat .311 and hit 23 home runs with 87 runs batted in as a 20-year-old. The youngster might make something of himself yet.

Bobby Brown would, too, although in another field. Brown was a solid ballplayer who studied to become a doctor in the off-season in the late 1940s and early 1950s. He made it into just 27 games in 1952 because he was busy serving in the military during the Korean War. Jerry Coleman batted .405 that season, but the reason why people never hear about him among those high-average hitters was because he only got into 11 games before he, too, was taken into the service. Stengel had numerous talented veterans to work with, but the Korean War did interrupt baseball service for some Yankees who missed out on regular play in 1952 and 1953. To defend the club's three World Series championships, Stengel had to resort to patchwork with available guys at different times. It may be that the missing players' situations contributed to Mize being able to extend his career.

Brown was a winner as long as he stayed with the Yankees, but unlike so many American boys who dreamed of growing up to be a major league baseball player, his dream was to become a doctor. He spent years of part-time schooling achieving the necessary education to fulfill that goal, and then he gave up professional baseball in 1954. Much later, he became the president of the American League. Brown was part of five world championship teams and then became a heart surgeon, one profession that might have provided more pressure, if less of it under bright lights on a public stage. It was more life and death duty, though. Brown's lifetime batting average was .279 when he walked away from the field at 29.

As a Yankee, Brown played for Bucky Harris and Casey Stengel as managers, two men with different philosophies in deploying their personnel. "They were different kinds of managers and they had different types of teams," said Brown, who turned 96 in 2020. "Bucky essentially was a manager who stuck with eight people in the lineup. Casey was someone who used his entire roster."[1]

One story about Brown from his Yankees days involving Yogi Berra has made the rounds for years, though some doubt its authenticity. Brown says it is true. Berra and Brown spent the evening in their hotel room reading and finished at the same time. Berra was reading comic books. Brown was reading medical books (it may have been *Gray's Anatomy*). Berra turned to Brown and said, "How did yours come out?" Brown said, "Like I was reading a novel or something."[2]

Brown had his medical practice for more than a quarter of a century, was about to turn 60, and was becoming weary of his job when he was offered the American League executive job. "This looks like a very irrational act by a supposedly rational person," Brown said when he was hired. "I've been in practice for 26 years, and it's a tough specialty, cardiology. You deal with the worst types of catastrophic medical emergencies. I reached a point when I thought I could do it for another two-to-five years. When this came along, it offered me an opportunity unusual for most doctors. Few have options of moving in a lateral direction to a different field."[3]

Coleman had longevity with the Yankees, also lost playing time while in military service, but later had a high-profile, off-field baseball career as a broadcaster before passing away at 89. His nine playing seasons were spent with New York, including the part-time ones, but his effectiveness was diminished after returning from his stint as a U.S. Marine captain (and later Lt. Colonel), flying 69 missions in the Korean War. That was after combat flying in World War II. In all, Coleman received 18 medals.

Although Coleman's abbreviated second base career enabled him to play in six World Series with the Yankees, from 1960–2014 (except one season, in 1980), Coleman worked in broadcasting with the Yankees, the California Angels, and from 1972–2014 with the San Diego Padres. His one-year intermission was spent as manager of the Padres. Coleman was ultimately recognized by the Baseball Hall of Fame for his broadcast work. The Padres constructed a statue of Coleman outside their home park to honor his contributions to the team.

Others gained a measure of fame as Stengel's bench players, guys like Bob Cerv, a back-up outfielder who first showed up for the Yankees in 1951 and stayed with the team through 1956 without playing in more than 56 games in a season. Stengel was like a mechanic who had a wealth of spare parts in his garage that he could locate when the need arose. The loss of Coleman and Brown for lengthy stretches would have hampered a lesser team.

Cerv was a relief hitter and fielder, coming to the plate just 96 times in 1952 with a .241 batting average. Cerv didn't get a chance to play regularly in the majors until his early 30s in the late 1950s after being sent to the Kansas City Athletics. He had the season of his career in 1958 with 38 home runs, 104 runs batted in, and a .305 average and made his only All-Star team that year.

Although he derived much pleasure and satisfaction playing for championship teams, Cerv recognized that it was the best thing for his career when he was traded to Kansas for the 1957 season, or else he may never have played in 100 games in a year. But come 1958, Cerv was nearly sidetracked by injury.

Early in that season, Cerv was tagged hard at home plate by Detroit Tigers catcher Red Wilson. He suffered a broken jaw. Yet after three days on the bench (he had had enough of that), Cerv returned to the lineup. It was an ordeal, but he did not wish to forfeit any more playing time.

"I Played Without Eating," was the headline on a magazine story quoting Cerv about how he overcame it. In a first-person, as-told-to-article, Cerv said, "When for a whole month recently I played ball with a broken jaw, I wasn't trying to be a hero. I was only trying to keep from going out of my mind. With my teeth wired together so tightly that I couldn't open my mouth, I had to live on a liquid diet. I couldn't chew, talk clearly, breathe properly, cough, laugh, yawn, or even sneeze like a human being."[4]

A guy with a spirit like that couldn't even break into the Yankees' lineup. For all of the talent the Yankees fielded as they kept winning championships during this era, maybe some of the success was attributable to attitude.

For all of his longevity, stardom, tremendous hitting success, and now a fourth season in pinstripes, Mize was being eased out of the big picture, becoming more of a fill-in like Cerv, someone Stengel still had some faith in, yet was being used less and less. This 1952 season, Mize got into just 78 games and had only 150 plate appearances, or an average of about one per game the team played. Mize hit just four home runs and drove in 29 runs while his average slipped to .263. These were not the kind of statistics that were usually written alongside his name. His career was on a ticking clock.

However, if the Yankees were willing to keep paying him for some of those specialty moments when he was needed to win a game, Mize was game. He knew the end was close, but why not go for a fourth World Series ring? By the end of that season, Mize had clouted 355 career home runs. That left him behind only Babe Ruth, Jimmie Foxx, Mel Ott, Lou Gehrig, and Joe DiMaggio. DiMaggio retired with 361. As befitting a player who was a league-leader in home runs four times, Mize was viewed as a slugger. But when he talked hitting, he very much emphasized the smooth stroke, making good contact, and not necessarily belting the long ball.

Mize differentiated between hitting a home and hitting in the clutch, meaning delivering timely, helpful hits. They could be home runs, but they were not automatically home runs. "Hitting in the clutch is not relegated to alone hitting home runs with the bases loaded," Mize said. "A single, or a bases on balls, is just as important. And I have seen some players who didn't mind purposely getting in the way of a pitch if the situation was crucial enough."[5]

It did not get any easier to repeat. The Yankees were aiming for a fourth straight pennant and World Series in 1952, and they had many enemies along the way to whom the "Anybody but the Yankees" mantra would have appealed. Yankees fans had reached such a point of blind allegiance that they assumed anyone general manager George Weiss and manager Casey Stengel threw on the field for their viewing pleasure at Yankee Stadium was going to win it all.

But that is not at all how the season began. The Yankees posted a losing April, 5–6. They did not catch fire when May arrived either, struggling to an 11–12 mark on May 13 after crossing to the good side of .500 for only one day in April. The next time New York had a winning record was on May 16, when Allie Reynolds beat the Detroit Tigers, 3–2. The Yanks were in fourth place, though just 3½ games out of first.

The Yankees ended May 18–17 but did not seem like a superpower. Then came June, and the warm weather agreed with New York. It was an explosive month for the Yankees. They went 21–9, captured first place for the first time on June 11, fell out on June 13, and then steamrolled the American League over the rest of the season, not for a day falling back out of first. When the gong sounded ending the campaign, the Yankees were 95–59. Only the Cleveland Indians stayed close, finishing 93–61, two games back. Third place went to the Chicago White Sox, 14 games out of first.

If Mize hadn't been slowing down, or the Yankees had gotten off to a hotter start as team, he might have played more. After all, he started at first base on Opening Day and went one-for-three. He added another hit playing full-time in the second game of the year. After two days of pinch-hitting only, Mize had a three-for-five, four-RBI day. Mize was batting .300 at the end of April and .323 in early May. His single at-bat days as a pinch-hitter, though, meant that his average could fluctuate wildly.

As the season wore on, Stengel used Joe Collins more at first base, and he finished with 18 home runs and a .280 average. Sometimes Stengel wrote in Irv Noren, normally an outfielder. Mize would pinch-hit, and if he got a hit, Stengel pinch-ran for him. With his reputation, Mize could still scare pitchers, but he did not do an abundance of damage. It was not always easy to tell if Mize figured into Stengel's plans anymore, and once the Yankees won the pennant, if Mize would even get out of the dugout for the 1952 World Series.

In any case, the Yankees were headed back to the Series, again facing the Brooklyn Dodgers, who felt as if they would never get over Bobby Thomson's "Miracle at Coogan's Bluff" home run in 1951, but somehow managed to pull their act together to win another National League pennant. This time the Dodgers edged the Giants by four games and did not have to face down another playoff series. When the Dodgers wrote out a fresh scouting report on the Yankees of 1952, it is not likely they devoted more than a sentence to Johnny Mize. They probably doubted he would start, doubted he would play much, and were skeptical that he would play any kind of major role in the Yankees' offense.

The Yankees went with Allie Reynolds as their starting pitcher in Game 1. Coming off his finest season, Reynolds went 20–8 with a 2.06 earned run average. The Dodgers countered with Joe Black, a 28-year-old rookie who was phenomenal in the regular season, going 15–4 with 15 (retroactive) saves and a 2.15 ERA. Black won the Rookie of the Year Award for the NL and led the league in games finished with 41.

Black had toiled in the Negro Leagues, served during World War II, and recorded this exceptional season at the right time for the Dodgers, who were the most progressive Major League Baseball franchise on race. On this day, October 1, at Ebbets Field, Black was masterful. He was the winner, 4–2, allowing just two hits, although one was a Gil McDougald homer. Black became the first African American pitcher to win a World Series game. Mickey Mantle had two hits for New York, and Mize did not get into the game.

New York made a turnaround in Game 2, also at Ebbets Field. This was a 7–1 rout, with Vic Raschi pitching a complete game for the Yankees, who scored five runs in the top of the sixth inning. Mantle smacked three hits, and Yogi Berra and Billy Martin had two hits apiece. Martin even hit a homer. This was a tremendous Dodgers team, so hungry for a championship, so hungry to make up for previous losses to the Yankees and the stinging playoff loss to the Giants in 1951. Duke Snider, Pee Wee Reese, Jackie Robinson, Gil Hodges, and Roy Campanella were all future Hall of Famers. They were supplemented by such great players as Billy Cox, Carl Furillo, and Andy Pafko. Yet these were the stocked Yankees.

It was Preacher Roe against Ed Lopat in Game 3. Refusing to be demoralized, Reese, Robinson and Pafko accounted for seven hits, and Brooklyn won, 5–3. Johnny Mize was almost too much for them, however. Mize got into the game late, in the bottom of the ninth, nearly sparking a rally with a solo home run off Roe with one away. But Roe shut down Phil Rizzuto at the plate, followed by Johnny Sain, a pitcher pinch-hitting for first baseman Joe Collins, certainly one of Stengel's most unorthodox calls. The combination of those developments, though, made Stengel's next move, for Game 4, more predictable. Collins was cold at the plate, and Stengel started Mize at first base, that home run shot to right field perhaps giving the manager enough of a glimpse to play a hunch.

So there was Mize, starting for the first time in the Series, presiding over the first-base bag instead of Collins, for Game 4, on a Saturday afternoon at Yankee Stadium before a crowd of 71,787. The Dodgers led the Series, 2–1, so this was a pivotal moment. Brooklyn started Joe Black again. New York started Reynolds. This was the Reynolds of vintage form. He tossed a complete-game, four-hit shutout with 10 strikeouts as the Yankees knotted the Series with a 2–0 win.

It was not as if Black was out of sorts or pitched badly, hurling seven innings, allowing three hits and one run. It was basically that he couldn't solve Mize. Mize led off the bottom of the fourth inning with a home run (his second of the Series), ripping the ball out of the park in deep left field. Mize also collected a ground-rule double leading off the sixth. Both hits came off Black. As a throw-in, Mize walked off reliever Johnny Rutherford. While Mize's home run was the winning run, the Yankees put up an insurance run in the eighth inning when Mantle tripled to center and came home on the poor throw to the plate.

For all of his individual achievements, from winning home-run titles and a batting title, Mize always ranked his performance in the 1952 World Series as a special one that may have excited him more than all of the others. From a guy who wasn't starting and wasn't even pinch-hitting much, Mize became a hurry-up starter and played a huge part in ruining Brooklyn's dreams. "The 1952 World Series against the Dodgers was also a big thrill for me," Mize said in comparing his clutch performance to other highlights. "Casey Stengel sent me up to pinch-hit in the third game and I homered off Preacher Roe. Stengel started me the next day and I homered again [off Black]. We won, 2–0, and then I hit a third Series homer off [Carl] Erskine the following day."[6]

The following day. Of course, the Series continued without interruption, day after day without a break in those days. The following day was October 5, Game 5. The Series was now at 2–2, with an overriding feeling, certainly among the Yankees believers, that Brooklyn had had its fun and now was the time to step on the gas and run the Dodgers off the track. Only these were more seasoned Dodgers, not starry-eyed about merely being part of the big show. The Dodgers scored three runs in the top of the fifth inning off New York's Ewell Blackwell for a 4–0 lead heading into the home half.

The bottom of the fifth was fueled by Mize. New York put together a five-run rally, and Mize smote the big blow. Mize, the scientific hitter, turned Carl Erskine's best pitch into a laboratory study project, sending one toss out of play to deep right field with Gil McDougald and Phil Rizzuto scoring ahead of him. Some Yankees supporters might have suggested that was a message shot, a demoralizing strike at the heart of the Dodgers.

But the Yankees could not hold onto the lead. Brooklyn tied the game, 5–5, in the top of the seventh inning on Duke Snider's RBI single. This was Snider's game to shine, with three hits and four RBI. The game went to extra innings, and Brooklyn scratched out a 6–5 victory in the 11th.

One of the biggest thrills in Mize's long baseball career was homering off Erskine. But Mize actually thought he should have had a second home run that would have rescued the day, at least temporarily, in the bottom of the 11th inning. "I might even say that one of my disappointments came in this same game when Carl Furillo's great catch took a second home run away from me in the ninth inning [Mize misremembered the inning]," Mize said. "This would have tied the score."[7]

After dropping the game in extra innings, suddenly the Yankees were the ones on the brink, trailing 3–2 in games with Game 6 at Ebbets Field. The Yankees had squandered Mize's gift.

It was up to Raschi to straighten out his team. The Dodgers put the weight on young right-hander Billy Loes, who was 13–8 in the regular season after missing the 1951 campaign due to military service. Mize was no factor in this one, although he started. He went 0-for-three. The Dodgers took a 1–0 lead on a solo homer by Snider in the sixth inning. The Yankees retaliated with a solo homer by Yogi Berra in the seventh. Then, after Gene Woodling singled and was balked to second, Raschi, of all batsmen, scored him on a single. That made it 2–1 New York, which became 3–1 in the eighth inning when Mickey Mantle hit a home run. Snider, aka "The Duke of Flatbush," smacked another homer in the eighth to renew the threat. Mulling the situation, Casey Stengel pulled Raschi from the mound and inserted Allie Reynolds. Reynolds struck out Roy Campanella to end the eighth inning and made it through the ninth to send the Series to a seventh game.

October 7, Game 7, an all-hands-on-deck circumstance. If someone showed a sign of weakness, they had their chance and they were out. The pitching matchup was Lopat for New York versus Black for Brooklyn. Stengel would use 15 players, Dodgers manager Charlie Dressen also 15.

The game was scoreless into the fourth inning, when each team scored a run. Again, Mize was at the center of the action. His hard-hit ball deep in the hole at shortstop drove in Rizzuto and was one of his two safeties in the game. Lopat took an early shower in the bottom of the fourth after giving up three straight singles that loaded the bases. Reynolds came on in relief again and, although he got out of the inning without much damage, a line drive to left field scored the one run.

Over four straight innings, the fourth, fifth, sixth, and seventh, the Yankees scored one run each time up. Woodling and Mantle each homered, and Mantle knocked in another run with a single. Reynolds pitched three relief innings for the win, although he was followed to the mound by Raschi (briefly) and Bob Kuzava. Kuzava went 2⅔ innings,

Allie Reynolds was one of the so-called "Big Three" pitchers in the starting rotation who led the Yankees to a record straight five World Series titles with Mize on the club at the end of his career.

got the last out of the Series, and would have been credited with a save if they had existed. Final score, 4–2. Yankees win again. Johnny Mize batted .400 for the World Series and kept showing up with key hits at key times as he became the winner of a fourth championship ring.

This was just the second time in history a team had won four straight World Series, and Stengel joined Joe McCarthy (1936–1939), naturally enough with past Yankees teams, as the only manager to do so. Once again, it would have been an easy choice for Mize to retire, sitting on top of the world, but if the Yankees were willing to have him, he was going to stick around for the 1953 season.

20

Last Call

The 1953 season was Johnny Mize's last in the majors. His role kept diminishing in the New York Yankees' lineup as he aged, following the pattern of even the greatest of baseball stars over time. Manager Casey Stengel, who always showed belief in Mize's hitting ability and pulled him out of his bag of tricks much like a magician at the right time to wow audiences, probably kept Mize on deck longer than another manager would have.

It paid off for both field boss and slugger, as evidenced in the 1952 World Series, when Mize was such a useful component in downing the Brooklyn Dodgers in the seven-game Series, even though he had only been a periodic contributor during the regular season.

The 1953 regular season promised more of the same, Mize sitting more than swinging, but thrown into action at crucial moments to bail out the offense on hurry-up, pinch-hitting short notice. The way Mize was used, mostly sitting around for games at a time, had to send a message that the end was nigh. He turned 40 years old a month or so before the start of spring training, and that was a signal. His body, which expanded in weight and slowed in foot speed, sent another message.

Yet when the season began, Mize was on the roster, ready to go, if not expecting to spend much time full-time at first base. Over the course of a 154-game season, though, the occasions would arise when Stengel needed him to start and hold down the bag, or when the moment was ripe for someone to step into the batter's box cold and lift the offense.

The Yankees, of course, were endowed with riches, a roster bursting with talented players, a roster so deep that key men could depart for the Korean War and the team would only miss them spiritually, not tangibly in the standings. Winners of four straight American League pennants and four straight World Series crowns, the Yankees showed no indications of falling off, of being overtaken by the optimistic teams in the league. So in 1953, New York was chasing history, trying to become the first team ever to win its league's pennant five consecutive seasons and take home five championship trophies in a row. Mize had to know he was only going to be a bit player in the saga, but look what he had done to justify his presence in 1952. He won the plaudits of the multitudes in the Yankee Stadium seats, won the applause of the suits in the Yankees' front office, made Stengel look smart for having him available and for knowing when to use him, and gained a huge measure of self-satisfaction from coming through. Playing all game, every game, might be beyond his ken at 40, but living up to his own beliefs in his clutch ability might not be asking for too much at all.

New York's regular starting lineup was as strong as ever. Yogi Berra was a granite fixture at catcher, in 1953 on his way to capturing his second of three Most Valuable Player Awards as temporary votes of approval on his way to Hall of Fame enshrinement. Joe Collins was never going to be as good as Mize was at his peak, but he was an adequate fill-in who played in 127 games, hit 17 home runs, and batted .269. Jerry Coleman was still away at war, but Billy Martin was in his prime, with his fiery demeanor, powerful emotional ties to the Yankees, and his skills, and could do the job covering second base. Phil Rizzuto was aging at 35, but still hit .271. Gil McDougald, at third base, was in his prime at 25, hit .285, and drove in 83 runs.

The outfield was locked down. Gene Woodling was his usual steady self, still only 30, and batting .306, his line-drive swing still producing 10 homers as a byproduct of his spray hits all over the ballpark. Hank Bauer also was still just 30 and was playing his best ball. He batted .304 with 10 homers, too. Then, of course, there was the Second Coming of Greatness, Mickey Mantle in center field, not making fans forget Joe DiMaggio, but making sure they did not pine for him. Mantle, as injury-prone as he was, did not play every game, but in 127 of them slugged 21 home runs, drove in 92 runs, and batted .295. So it was an across-the-board .300-hitting outfield.

If there was any doubt of Mantle's growing stature and enormous promise at 21, *Time* magazine clued in the non-baseball world with its June 15, 1953, issue that featured the golden boy beaming on the cover. Mantle was the sport's future, the weekly news magazine seemed to be saying. Of course, akin to the supposed *Sports Illustrated* cover jinx, Mantle was hurt often enough to miss 27 games.

Illustrating how rarely Mize was used as a starter, rather than merely as a pinch-hitter, during the season while he appeared in 81 games, he had just 118 plate appearances. Only once before during his career, and that was in 1952 when his responsibilities were similar, did Mize go up to hit less frequently. Mize contributed 26 hits for a

.250 average, clouting just four home runs and driving in 27 runs. Actually, given that was about 25 percent of his usual number of visits to the plate, his RBI total was more than respectable.

Along the way, Mize was tapped for a final All-Star appearance by the American League, the 10th time he was selected. The game was played on July 14 at Crosley Field in Cincinnati and was won, 5–1, by the National League. Casey Stengel managed the AL and Charlie Dressen the NL. At that point in the season, the Yankees were leading the pennant race with a 56–26 record, a superb .683 winning percentage. But it was not a rout. The Chicago White Sox were just five games out, winning at a .619 rate. Stengel had joked that the Yankees did not pay him to win every game, just two-thirds of the time. Sometimes it took that frequency of victory to stay ahead.

Mize was employed as a pinch-hitter on July 12, the day before the break, and made an out. He was batting .275 at the time of the All-Star intermission. Stengel, in charge of choosing non-starters, may have rewarded him with a spot on the squad knowing it was his last chance. This was the 20th All-Star game, and Mize had been chosen for half of them. He made it into the game, naturally enough, as a pinch-hitter in the top of the ninth inning, and stroked a single. The American League scored its only run in that inning.

The Yankees were as good as ever in 1953, finishing with a 99–52 mark, winning the flag by 8½ games. During the course of the regular season, Mize fulfilled a long-held goal of reaching 2,000 career hits. The hit, another pinch-hit, was notched in a loss to the St. Louis Browns, and the ball was donated to the Baseball Hall of Fame.

In October, most of the country was raking leaves or following football. In New York City in October, it seemed, sports fans could attend or watch the regularly scheduled World Series. Not only were the Yankees involved for the fifth straight year, but the National League pennant-winner was also from the neighborhood.

This was the 50th World Series, and baseball not only went all red, white and blue, as usual, it invited living players from the first Series in 1903 to attend as special guests to throw out ceremonial first pitches in each game. Among those, albeit slowed by age, who did some throwing were Fred Clarke, the Pittsburgh Pirates Hall of Famer, and Cy Young, the all-time winner with 511 victories, representing the Boston Red Sox. Young actually took the loss in that inaugural game of October 1, 1903. Clarke played the outfield, hit .351 that year, and managed the Pirates as well.

The Brooklyn Dodgers were becoming autumn regulars. It's just that their road to the ultimate payoff was roadblocked by their snooty

Bronx foes every year. The 1953 season was another Brooklyn year in the National League. The Dodgers won the pennant for the fourth time since 1947. They had no World Series hardware to show for those achievements, but they were tired of being referred to as bums, and they were just as sick of playing second banana to the Yankees. They did not wish to contend for Miss Congeniality. They wanted the big prize.

Essentially, the Dodgers toyed with the NL that year, finishing 105–49, a brilliant record that provided a margin of 13 games over the second-place Milwaukee Braves. Roy Campanella (41 homers, 142 RBI), Duke Snider (42 homers, 126 RBI) and Gil Hodges (31 homers, 122 RBI), knocked the stitches loose on the ball all season. Throw in Jackie Robinson (95 RBI) and Carl Furillo (92 RBI), and the Dodgers were fearsome to face. And that didn't even include Billy Cox, Jim Gilliam, and Pee Wee Reese, who brought their own skills to the offense.

Carl Erskine won 20 games, Russ Meyer won 15, Billy Loes 14, and Preacher Roe and Clem Labine 11 apiece. The pitching was not too shabby. Still, the Yankees seemed stronger than ever on the mound. At 16–4, Ed Lopat had one of his best seasons. Vic Raschi and Allie Reynolds were still holding down spots in the rotation. Johnny Sain, who won 14 games, could go both ways, starting or relieving. But the new staff ace was Whitey Ford, back from his military service. Ford went 18–6, and his 207 innings was a remarkably low total to lead the staff during that era.

In Game 1, Reynolds got the start, but when he appeared fallible, Stengel pulled him and gave the ball to Sain, whose 3 2/3 innings of one-run relief earned him the win in the 9–5 decision. The Yankees jumped on Erskine from the first, sending four runners home in the opening inning and forcing him out of the game in the second. When the Dodgers inched back to within 6–5, the Yankees put up a three-spot in the eighth inning.

The Yankees went up 2–0 in games when Lopat scattered nine hits and limited his runs in a 4–2 victory at the Stadium. Roe went the distance for the loss. Uncharacteristically, Stengel did not mess around with his lineup, leaving it unchanged and deploying no pinch-hitters. Mize sat for both games.

All of the pressure was on Brooklyn for Game 3 at Ebbets Field, and this affair was low-scoring and close. Raschi allowed three runs in a complete game, but Erskine permitted just two to win the 3–2 must-have contest. He also struck out 14 batters.

Mize seemed to groan louder than his teammates on the field as Erskine ran up the Ks. Erskine's curves were breaking so sharply they often bounced in the dirt, and Mize was beside himself, telling his teammates not to swing. Stengel and he were in synch, the manager yelling, "He's killin' worms. He's killin' worms. Lay off the pitch." Mize was an echo, shouting, "Make him get it up."[1]

Second baseman Billy Martin, who hit .500 in the Series but, like just about everyone else in the New York lineup this day, was fooled by Erskine, did not take kindly to Mize's critique. In the ninth inning, Stengel, hopeful that Mize would follow his own eyes and Stengel's advice, pinch-hit him for Raschi, and Mize faced Erskine himself. Erskine threw another of his curves that broke so sharply it dug dirt. Mize swung and missed for strike three, just as the other Yankees had. When Mize returned to the dugout, Martin sarcastically chanted, "Make him get it up. Make him get it up."[2]

So one of the victims was Mize. When he struck out, that made two down. The game ended soon after when Joe Collins grounded out. The Dodgers were not safe, but they could exhale.

Game 4 belonged to Brooklyn. Ford was battered early, lasting just one inning as the Dodgers evened the Series with a 7–3 victory that began with a three-run first inning. Snider drove in four of the runs and Gilliam two. Mize again pinch-hit in the ninth inning and this time flied out to center. Brooklyn had scratched back into contention. Was it possible they could topple the mighty Yankees?

New York had been challenged before, including by the Dodgers, and the Yankees were resolute. Game 5 presented a pitching conundrum for both teams. Since there were no off-days, it was difficult for the regular corps of starters to be adequately rested enough to come back very quickly and start again. The Dodgers went with Johnny Podres, who won nine games during the regular season as a 20-year-old rookie. Stengel's choice might have come to him in a dream.

Although not a well-remembered member of the Yankees Dynasty, right-hander Jim McDonald's 1953 record was 9–7, accompanied by a 3.82 earned run average. McDonald fared better than Podres on a hitter's day that ended up as an 11–7 New York win. He lasted 7 2/3 innings, though he gave up 12 hits and six runs, five earned. However, despite allowing just one hit, Podres gave up five runs in 2 2/3 innings, just one earned. New York made four home runs pay off to boost the Series lead to 3–2. The Dodgers mustered 14 hits, three by Campanella, and they still couldn't get a win.

October 6 brought Game 6 and the end of many things. It was the final game of this year's World Series. It was the final win in the Yankees' streak of five straight titles. It was the final game of Johnny Mize's career. New York won, 4–2, and after a 1–0 start in the first inning, the Yankees didn't retake the lead until the bottom of the eighth inning.

Billy Martin and Mickey Mantle homered, Lopat pitched the distance, and Mize was a spectator for his final time dressing for a game.

Immediately after the triumph, rather than revel in the moment of five World Series titles in a row, Yankees team president Dan Topping gushed that New York would win eight in a row. "This club can go on winning for another three years with a replacement here and there," Topping said. "We will win as long as Casey Stengel's brains hold out."[3]

Mize was still in the locker room post-game when, for the first time, he told the world he was retiring. Depending on which organization was reporting and how it interpreted his words, he either sounded resigned to his time being up or angry because he didn't feel top management of the team would pay him enough money to stick around.

During the 1952 season, Mize made $20,900 in salary, down from his original annual payday of $35,000 when the Yankees first acquired him. In 1953, this current season, Mize was down to $17,000 a year. He was being used about half as often in 1953 as he was when he first came over from the New York Giants. "After the Series I had in 1952, they cut my pay $4,000," Mize said. "So you can imagine what they'd offer me for next year."[4] He made it sound as if he didn't even want to find out for fear of being insulted. At 40, he could see the end, and when asked if he would play for any other team, Mize did not flat-out say that he would not. "It would have to be a hell of an offer," he said.[5]

In announcing Mize's decision, the *New York Post* delivered a strong headline, calling his comments "a blast" at Yankees management. The *Philadelphia Bulletin* used a story written by United Press International containing the same news, adorned with the headline, "Mize Retires: Feels He'd Get Little Pay in '54." The story contained the same quote about having his pay sliced the year before. But also, "Well, I've already made up my mind. I guess I'll talk to someone on the Yankees before I leave for home, but this is definite."[6]

There was also much discussion about the possibility of Allie Reynolds retiring after the fifth straight championship. Reynolds made no declarations when the 1953 Series ended and did end up playing another season.

The *New York Times* took a gentler approach with Mize's pronouncement an extra day later. "Yes, I guess this is the end of the trail for me," he said.

I finally had my mind made up for me at our victory dinner last night when Dan Topping, on meeting my mother for the first time, said, "Why, you look younger than John." That settled it for me.

However, it has been wonderful playing with the Yankees these past five seasons, and in particular I want to thank Casey Stengel for his fine treatment. He gave me every possible chance to keep going, but when you're past 40, the going gets pretty tough. So I guess it's time for me to step out and let the youngsters take over.[7]

Mize said he was going to stay in New York for a few days and then return to his off-season home in Georgia. Mize had some business investments but wished to stay in baseball if the opportunity was there, and this is where he broached the subject of perhaps managing in the minors or coaching hitting, his specialty. His book on hitting hit the bookstores in 1953 and might well serve as an advertisement for his skills in communicating those techniques.

"I guess you can say I'm available," Mize said.[8]

When he retired, Mize had spent 15 seasons in the majors and played in 1,884 games with 2,011 hits, 359 of them home runs, accompanied

Some years after Johnny Mize retired from baseball, he returned to his hometown of Demorest, Georgia, where he maintained a keen interest in the sport through the local youth, helping to raise money for the Boy Scout troop and encouraging the local Little Leaguers.

by 1,337 runs batted in and a .305 average. He led the National League in home runs four times, led the NL in RBI three times, and won one batting crown. He four times led the league in slugging percentage. The numbers led Mize to 10 All-Star game selections. It was probably felt by many that it would not take long for him to be voted into the Baseball Hall of Fame, though that would become a drawn-out issue of some disappointment.

The talk of retirement was in the open and had been reported, but officially Mize did not part with the New York Yankees until November 25, about six weeks after the World Series ended. The team announced that he was being released.

21

Retirement

Johnny Mize, it should be remembered, was nicknamed "the Big Cat" for his grace in the field early in his career, even if at the end of it he was much slower and hardly ever protected first base. If he had come along later, of course, when the designated hitter was in vogue in the American League, Mize would never have ventured near first base except passing by from the batter's box.

After he won some renown with his glove, Mize established his power with the bat and was viewed as one of the top sluggers in the National League. At the end, with the Yankees, as age encroached and he turned 40, Mize was hailed as a pinch-hitter deluxe. On the talent-rich Yankees, that's what kept him going, what kept him employed. Even if his times at bat dwindled, Mize made the most of the ones he was assigned, and people noticed.

In September of 1953, his last active season, Mize's ability to come off the bench without warming up and smack the ball around was highlighted by at least one journalist. This story referred to him as "the New York Yankees' 40-year-old pinch-hitting specialist."[1] Noted was a 10-day block of time in May during which Mize pinch-hit seven times and stunningly produced key results, from a walk with the bases loaded to a timely single to getting hit by a pitched ball. He set a record by reaching base seven straight times as a pinch-hitter, five of them via a hit.

It was as if Mize did not need to bother stretching or taking swings, but as the old adage went, he could fall out of bed and hit safely. It was no wonder manager Casey Stengel put the game on the line with Mize so often. He pondered whether Mize was the greatest pinch-hitter ever. "Maybe there was," Stengel said of any other pinch-hitter being better, "but I can't remember him. He [Mize] has control of that bat and if the ball is this much off, Mize won't go after it. And he hits into very few double plays for a big man."[2]

That seemed to return the issue to Mize's remarkable batting eye

172

and his sharp judgment of what to bother swinging at. Even after so many years in the bigs, Mize fooled people. They saw his body, listened to his reputation, and read his record, and all they could think was that he must be this big galoot who would unleash a mighty swing on a big risk rather than comprehending what a cautious hitter he was.

"What gets me about him," said Cleveland Indians manager Al Lopez,

> is that he can beat you so many ways in the clutch. He is an ideal pinch-hitter because he doesn't run to type. If you want to start a rally and you have a big guy like [Yogi] Berra, say, coming up behind him, he can work the pitcher for a walk. If you have the winning run on third, he can get the long ball to the outfield. If the winning run is on second, he can dump the ball into left field and get it across that way. If the bases are loaded, with the winning run on third, you have to pitch so carefully to him that you stand the danger of hitting him or walking him. And if the score is tied, and if he's up there with nobody on and two out, he can still ruin you by hitting one into the seats.[3]

Indeed, Mize had done all of that. And Lopez was no idle observer. Once a widely respected catcher, in 1954 he would manage the Indians to the American League pennant, breaking the Yankees' streak.

As his major league career was approaching its end in this off-the-bench role, Mize reminisced, recalling how in his youth, as an over-sized teenager, he gained attention because he could knock the ball around as a pinch-hitter. That ability gave him his start. "I had pretty good luck as a pinch-hitter then," Mize said of those years in Georgia before turning pro. "So they stuck me in the regular lineup."[4]

Even though he had made a study of hitting and had the knack for sharing his wisdom with other players, Mize did not discount the challenge of coming into a game after sitting around in the dugout for several innings and being expected to come through under pressure.

> The big difference between pinch-hitting and playing regularly is that you only get one look at a pitcher as a pinch-hitter, while you get three or four shots at him as a regular. You can't tell how fast he is that day, or whether his curve is good. You can't read a pitcher from the bench, though of course you try to all day long.
>
> If you know your pitcher, you know what pitches are his strong ones. You can bet that he's going to go to "his pitch" in the clutch. Of course, what you try to remember is that the pitcher is in a pretty tough spot himself. If he gets behind you, he's going to have to come in with one and it's your advantage.[5]

Given that more than 60 years have passed since Mize retired from playing, and a couple of home-run eras have come and gone, it doesn't seem to count for much that in 1953, when he exited the game, he was the leading active home run hitter. His total of 359 seems somewhat pedestrian now, especially since even the 500-home-run club, once so exalted, has become crowded.

Only some of those stalwarts, so many of them great players for years, who waltzed into the Hall of Fame, including Stan Musial, Ted Williams, Mickey Mantle, Willie Mays, Hank Aaron, and more, scared the soapsuds out of pitchers when they settled into the batter's box and casually wiggled their bats. They all collected compliments, but few gained accolades in the manner Stengel described Mize. "Mize is a cleanup hitter who hits like a leadoff man."[6] He could be characterized as discerning in his pitch selection.

Musial, Mize's early teammate with the St. Louis Cardinals, opined in similar fashion about the impression Mize made on him with his stroke. "I was impressed mostly with that sweet swing and the fact that he was a power hitter who rarely struck out," said Stan "the Man." "He had the greatest eyes I've ever seen."[7]

In those early days of his big-league career, Mize was partnered in the Cardinals lineup with Joe Medwick, and the two ultimately became partners in the Baseball Hall of Fame. However, in the 1930s, when they were slugging the ball around the lot, broadcaster Bob Elson, basically affiliated with Chicago, would steel his listeners with the comment, "Ah, here they come—the mighty Medwick and the mighty Mize."[8]

Mize's career played out in a peculiar shape. He was one of the finest hitters in the National League when he was young, but when middle-aged athleticism approached, it seemed he was not worthy of a nod until the well-stocked Yankees picked him up. He played well for New York for a few years, but his body felt the creaks. It was of great moment, serendipity and of life coming full circle that Mize became a 39-year-old World Series hero.

It was not spoken of much until later, but Mize had decided over the early winter of 1952 that it was time to retire. Stengel lobbied him out of the notion of eschewing a visit to St. Petersburg, Florida, altogether. Still, he was reluctant. "I had my things loaded in the car," Mize said of preparing for his drive from Georgia to Florida.

I said goodbye to Mrs. Mize and walked out of the house to be on my way. I got into the car, took the wheel, and then asked myself, "What am I doing? Why should I punish myself all over again?" I am going to take all this stuff back to the house and call Casey and tell him it's all off.

Then I reminded myself of my January promise to Casey, and I felt in all fairness, the least I could do was to report to St. Pete and see how things went.[9]

Months later, he was the toast of Broadway after hitting three home runs in the World Series and batting .400 against the Dodgers, Mize's greatest performance on the Series stage. "So I reported, and look at me now," Mize said. "Not bad for a kid."[10]

A humorous quasi-review of Mize's decision to write his book on hitting offered a delicious observation on the timing of the effort immediately following his attention-getting World Series explosion of 1952. "The man certainly qualifies as an authority on the subject," one writer's comment went. "By way of insuring a brisk sale for his volume, he engaged in a most clever promotional campaign during the first week in October. When the World Series was over, there hardly was a person in the country who wasn't aware of the existence of Big Jawn Mize and his booming bat."[11]

That World Series showing stuck to Mize like fly paper, though there were worse things that were impossible to shake. One tidbit rarely discussed was that Mize was the recipient of the New York chapter of the Baseball Writers Association of America award as the outstanding player for the Series. It happened to be named after Mize's distant relative, Babe Ruth.

Between the heroics in the Series, his return to the Yankees for spring training the next year, and the publication of his hitting book, Mize, who had sometimes had irascible relations with sportswriters and was known for spitting tobacco juice on their shoes, became a sought-after conversationalist and seemed to be getting along better than ever with the scribes. Months after the Series, sports guys would sidle up next to him, wishing to discuss that performance.

He switched back and forth in each setting about a desire to stay in the game or to try something fresh. "I might go into something far removed from baseball," Mize said. "What I will do after I retire depends on what's offered. If my work is to continue in the game, I want to work with kids, to teach them to hit [the target audience of his book]. If you see a youngster pick up in the averages as a result of your coaching, you get a tremendous thrill."[12]

As seemed logical and appropriate, Mize did remain connected to Major League Baseball after retiring from playing. Between 1955–1960, he was associated with the New York Giants, acting as a scout, broadcaster, and hitting coach. He spent 1961 as a coach with the Kansas City Athletics. He hooked up with Kansas City when his old Yankees teammate, Hank Bauer, was managing the team, but spent just one year with that club.

During this time period, Mize split up with his wife, Jene, and she perished tragically in July of 1957 in DeLand, Florida. She was 39 at the time. She fell asleep in a chair while smoking and died at a hospital from burns. By then, Mize was a Florida resident involved in various business ventures. Mize later married for a second time, in DeLand, to Marjorie Pope, who had been working for a radio station.

As a hitting instructor, Mize made news by helping a Giants minor leaguer of promise named Bob Lennon adjust his batting stance during spring training of 1956. "I'll listen to Mize," said Lennon, who was viewed as a difficult subject by his team. "He's a great hitter. I wish he was here last year and I'd have listened to him then." Mize's advice to Lennon was to shorten his wide stance. "Bob cannot handle the low, outside corner pitch the way he was hitting. That needn't have bothered him in the minors because he would see only one pitcher a week who could hit that spot constantly. Up here, he may see six in a row."[13]

The coaching was there, but the results were not. Lennon had a long minor-league career, bashing as many as 31 home runs for Minneapolis in AAA in 1955, but he never quite cut it in the majors, playing small portions of three seasons and finishing with a .165 lifetime average.

When Mize showed up for work on his first day at the Polo Grounds to work with the varsity, he was in street clothes because he hadn't yet been fitted for a uniform. There he was, in short sleeves, providing a tutorial to Giants. He never said he was going to radically change any stances, but he was going to offer tips, much as he did in an unofficial fashion with Phil Rizzuto back in his playing days. Saying he learned from experience, in a way this was a private Mize clinic straight from the pages of his hitting book. He could have passed out copies like a college professor on the first day of class.

Hitting coaches do not make the same type of salary as star hitters, however, and eventually Mize left his clinical instruction behind. Although he still made public appearances, Mize eventually left the baseball world as a profession for business, operating Augustine Shores Country Club on the outskirts of St. Augustine, Florida. He presided over bingo games, a swimming pool, and a card and pool room, plus cookouts. It was far from the limelight.

On one occasion, Mize and Stengel were together again in a baseball confab, and Stengel told stories, as only he could, about what a terrific hitter Mize was for him during his five seasons with the Yankees. "Now, take this big fella," Stengel said. "He was a slugger who had the eagle eye of a leadoff man. He and [Ted] Williams could umpire as well as any man behind the plate. If you pitched Mize inside, my, how he could hit home runs. He hit more [51] in one season [1947] than any left-handed hitter in National League history, and if you don't believe me, you could look it up."[14]

Stengel stuck with Mize as a topic, but he veered off the highway to Boston and what it was like to manage the Braves when Mize came to the plate in old Braves Field, adjacent to the Charles River. "We'd built the fence higher in left field," Stengel said, "the wind was blowing in a gale, and we pitched this fella away and he hit two darn near into the river."[15]

Mize interrupted, taking a turn.

"Yeah, Case," Mize said, "and the next time I came up, you yelled out to your pitcher, 'Pitch to him,' but when I glanced to your bench, you were holding up four fingers." Stengel laughed. "I have to say that I was hoping my young man would understand that the four stood for four balls, not four bases."[16]

Mize retired from the Yankees after the 1953 season, and many, including Mize himself, expected he would soon receive a phone call from the Baseball Hall of Fame informing him that he had been voted in and enshrined. Except as the years passed, the call never came.

For a time, Mize was satisfied with his memories of great baseball accomplishments and the value of his name in the game. Once, he ruminated over the emotions, sounds, and sights of what it was like in a packed Yankee Stadium when he went up to pinch-hit, knowing his team was counting on him.

"Sure, I hear the crowd," he said, "and feel the tension. But somehow I am able to keep pretty cool when I'm hitting. After I get back to the bench, then I have a reaction." When he smashed the big homer off Carl Erskine in the World Series, he said, "I got around the bases and as the guys on the bench got up to greet me, I felt goose pimples. I guess anyone would."[17]

For a time, Mize felt he might have been the only one who recalled his exploits. He felt he belonged in the Hall of Fame, and many sportswriters took up his cause, stumping for him. Yet another period would pass with no election. When he was out at a baseball event, he would be asked why it could be that he was excluded, and he would end up in discussions about the Hall.

"When I got out of baseball, they put in a five-year waiting rule," Mize said in 1976. "Then, when I became ineligible for the regular vote by the writers, they put in another five-year wait. Half of the time when I was eligible, the vote was only every other year. I guess they've forgotten who I was. I can show you hundreds of letters people write to me all the time. Four out of five say they can't understand why I'm not in."[18] The others? They asked for autographs to be sent back on a card.

It continued that way for some time. One writer who was a Mize believer, Hal Bock, wrote about him being overlooked a year later, in

1977, when that year's class was inducted. "Johnny Mize missed the ceremonies," the piece read. "He was at home in Demorest, Georgia, and there are some people who'll tell you that Mize was not in the right small town yesterday. His absence from the Hall of Fame remains one of the larger injustices perpetrated by the shrine's electors."[19]

Those electors were members of the Baseball Writers' Association of America, and although cordial with many, he did not pal around with any. Some deemed him cranky and were resentful of any practical jokes, such as spitting tobacco juice on their shoes.

Mize was candid, and if asked how he felt when his ballot tally fell short, he was truthful. He didn't think it was justice. He felt he belonged in the Hall of Fame. And he told you so.

Epilogue: The Hall at Last

Some bitterness built up in Johnny Mize over his lack of support for induction into the Baseball Hall of Fame. He was reminded of the hole on his resume every time a vote was taken and he came up short of the 75 percent required of votes cast. He was reminded when he appeared at baseball functions and sportswriters interviewed him. It was obvious to those he spoke with, as well, that he was reminded in his own head of this slight.

"It's nothing but a popularity poll," Mize said in an interview in 1972.

> If I got in tomorrow I wouldn't change my mind. [Lou] Boudreau finished behind me in some ballots in recent years and now he's in. How does a player suddenly jump over another when both are retired? [Enos] Slaughter was ahead of me, now he's behind me. I've been in the top ten the last 10 years or so in the voting. ... But how does it figure that some writers didn't even have Ted Williams in their top ten? Now, even if you couldn't stand the guy, you'd have to have him at least 10th, wouldn't you?[1]

The procedures changed over time and have even changed some more in recent years since that era, but there always seem to be questions about the how and why in the manner some players are considered. "It seems strange to me that some fellows have passed me on the ballot without any of us getting any more hits," Mize said in another interview in 1973.[2] Convinced he belonged, bewildered as to why he was overlooked, his dismay bubbled to the surface when asked to chat about the elephant in the room.

Until everything finally changed, and his perceived slight was remedied. Mize was voted into the Hall of Fame 28 years after he played his last big-league game and was inducted in the annual ceremony conducted on August 2, 1981. He was chosen by the Veterans Committee, which convened periodically to weigh possible oversights by the baseball writers. He still needed 75 percent of those voting to back him, but it was a much smaller electorate, a group of a dozen, if often enough just as hard to sway.

179

One sports columnist of note who chimed in about Mize's ascension was the closest big-city guy to his roots, Furman Bisher of Atlanta. It was a subject of some sensitivity in Georgia, Bisher commented, that Mize was on the outside for so long. In Mize's hometown of Demorest, Bisher said, "they still talk of his long and mighty drives. One day, it's said, a blast by Big Jawn struck a hickory tree with such force that it created a rain of hickory nuts on the ground that sounded like a hail storm."[3]

Could have happened. Or it could have been apocryphal. It was the type of tale that tagged along behind power hitters, where witnesses spoke of what they saw with their own eyes rather than what was recorded by technology and spread by video.

Mize was at home when he learned by telephone call that he had become a member of the Hall of Fame. His second wife, Marjorie, was right there, and his first comment was a simple one, just saying that he had made it. Others were left to say more at first, probe for more. When a baseball writer reached him, Mize was not shy about expressing his true thoughts. "It's about time," he said.[4] No one blamed him for making the statement. The comment was not second-guessed.

Joe Reichler, the longtime baseball reporter for the Associated Press, had taken up Mize's cause and lobbied for him, saying, "This man Mize would hit more home runs in a season than he would strike out."[5] That resonated with some people.

On the day Mize was inducted and fans gathered on a wide lawn in Cooperstown, New York, to welcome the newcomers to the exclusive Hall of Fame club, the crowd was somewhat surly. That was because it was a summer of discontent all around. Baseball was on strike, bogged down by a labor relations war between owners and employees, and it would not end soon. It was hoped that the feel-good nature of this occasion would temper some of the feeling of being deprived of the sport for the time being. Some booed when faces of authority like Commissioner Bowie Kuhn were visible, but the fans were receptive to the honorees.

Mize took his place in the Hall as part of the class of 1981, with stalwart St. Louis Cardinals pitcher Bob Gibson and Rube Foster, one of the legends of the Negro Leagues. Foster had passed away long before, in 1930, some 17 years before Major League Baseball integrated in the 20th century. Talk about a long wait for such recognition.

Mize, whose name was back in the public eye because of the Hall of Fame attention, and also because he was a regular participant in baseball card shows and mailed autographs back to those who wrote him at home (as long as they enclosed return postage) was the center of much attention in the upstate New York village that is never more alive than during induction week festivities.

The player was asked if he had saved much memorabilia from his days in the majors, and he had, including autographed World Series caps from each of his championship years with the Yankees. He also revealed that he had in his possession a watch worn by Babe Ruth, a gift from Ruth's wife to Mize, passed down from that side of the family. The way the memorabilia market was taking off, Mize seemed to lament the distribution of some other items from his career that were once mere pieces of personal nostalgia but had become valuable nostalgia.

"But the bat I got my 2,000th hit with, I gave away to the Hall of Fame like a damned fool," Mize said. It was not clear if he was making fun of himself or deadly serious when he added, "I could have given them another one, like so many other guys have done."[6]

Some sportswriters said there was testiness in the air at Cooperstown because of the labor dispute, but it was noted that Mize struck a strong conciliatory note with fans who came out to the Hall, and they responded with gusto.

> Without you baseball fans, none of us would be here today. So I made a prepared speech, but somewhere along the way, it got lost. I've been asked if being elected by the Veterans Committee means going in the back door. To them I say, "Look who's on it—ex-players, managers and executives, most of whom are in the Hall of Fame. Who else would you want to pick you? They were my peers."[7]

Mize did joke about his own background, taking his fans back to his early days playing ball in Georgia when he was first noticed in the most unusual of manners. Mize explained his Piedmont College connection and how Harry Forrester helped him as his first coach. "I guess that's one record that will never be broken," Mize said, "playing three years of college ball while still in high school."[8]

When Mize was inducted, he was able to bring a sizeable crowd of relatives to the festivities, including wife Marjorie, her daughter (whom Mize had adopted, along with her son from her previous marriage) and her husband, a grandson, and Zell Miller, who was lieutenant governor of Georgia. When Mize told fans he would like them to meet his wife, he added, "I think she had a little more faith than I did [that he would get into the Hall]."[9]

Mize also acknowledged the fans specifically from his playing days and those who stayed in his corner for years as he fell short on the vote to obtain Hall status.

I take this opportunity to thank all the people who have been sending me letters, calls from all over the country and they were stickin' with me even when I failed. They kept on writing. So this will be an opportunity to thank all of those people who worked so hard trying to get me into the Hall of Fame. And I just want to thank everybody. I can't do it personally, but this may be—this will get to a few of them—and I want to thank all of the ones who have come here from different places.

I want to thank 'em again for inviting me to Cooperstown. It's a little better invitation when you're goin' into the Hall of Fame and it is a lot better when you are able to smell the roses.[10]

Mize was a bigger star with the St. Louis Cardinals and New York Giants, though still a major contributor with the New York Yankees. But when asked which was his favorite team allegiance, Mize gave the nod to the big winners over the personal achievements. His biggest individual thrills, though, were hitting three home runs in a game a record six times, hitting a home run in every ballpark in use during his career, and his outstanding showing in the 1952 World Series. Yet Mize was not above being humble enough to relay other memories that didn't portray him in a glorious light. It was just part of his forthright nature when asked a question. "In my first pro game," Mize recalled about his 1930 minor-league stint, "I was used as a pinch hitter. So I started out as a pinch hitter and ended up as a pinch hitter. I remember my first game very well. I fell over the first-base bag after my first hit. I wanted to watch that ball every minute and that probably made me a better hitter."[11]

After years spent in the business world in Florida, Mize moved back to Demorest, Georgia, his birthplace, in 1974, where old-timers remembered his career with enthusiasm and where he made new friends among younger generations, supporting local kids in their baseball endeavors. Mize played golf frequently, and when he signed autographs for pay, he gave the money to the local Boy Scout troop in Demorest.

A little more than a year after his induction into the Hall of Fame, in December of 1982, Mize, then 69, underwent heart bypass surgery. In Demorest, Mize moved into the home of his late grandmother, the house where he spent much of his youth. Demorest, in Habersham County, in the northeast section of Georgia, never grew very much. Even two decades into the 21st century, its estimated population was 2,125 people. A quiet location with little to lure the tourist, Demorest eventually opened "The Johnny Mize Athletic Center and Museum," operated by Piedmont College, the school he represented on the baseball diamond. The museum honoring "the Big Cat" is situated on the school's campus.

Fan mail received by Mize was collected there, and some was shared with the Hall of Fame in Cooperstown. Many of the handwritten notes were from youngsters, thanking Mize for his autograph and for sending advice about baseball. One was signed, "Your best fran and pal."[12]

Mize not only gave proceeds from his autograph sales at shows around the country to the Boy Scouts, he also helped the group raise money by selling Mize authenticated and autographed memorabilia. The money Mize helped raise and donated helped fund the Boy Scouts' educational trips. "Oh, Johnny is such a good guy," said Patsy Allen, manager of a local bank selling autographed balls and photographs. "We get along just great. He sure does help the community. We couldn't do it without Johnny Mize."[13]

At age 80, Mize entertained a visit from Greg Graber, then the sports information director at Piedmont, for a brief interview. The piece appeared in the college's newspaper, "The Lion's Roar." At the close of the interview, Mize was asked what advice he had for young players. "Just the regular stuff," Mize said. "Listen to your coaches. And you can't ever practice too much. I don't know if I could coach today because kids think the know everything."[14]

That was Mize's last interview. On June 2, 1993, Mize suffered a heart attack and died in his sleep at home. Officially, the coroner said the cause of death was cardiac arrest.

Mize, who was buried at Yonah Memorial Gardens Cemetery in Demorest, was first honored with a funeral service conducted at the Demorest Baptist Church with about 250 people in attendance. One of those in the church was Gov. Zell Miller, who when lieutenant governor had attended Mize's Hall of Fame induction. "He was my hero, he was my friend," Miller said. "He brought a great deal of credit to baseball and to our Georgia mountains area. He was a man of few words. He let his actions speak for him."[15]

Others spoke for Mize after he passed away. At the funeral, one Demorest Boy Scout, Jason Stribling, addressed the full-house crowd in the church. "When you hear the name, most people think of baseball," Stribling said. "For the kids in Demorest, it goes much deeper. It is through Johnny Mize that we come together as Scouts. Whenever you see the smile of accomplishment, see a Scout advance, or hear a Scout sharing his experience, think of Johnny Mize. It is through him that we have built on dreams and helped carve out tomorrow."[16]

Also, writing in *The Sporting News*, Stan Musial, Mize's old friend and teammate, referred to him as "really one of the greatest hitters ever."[17]

In 2014, long after he represented the team on a baseball field, Mize was selected as one of the original 22 members of the St. Louis Cardinals Hall of Fame. That same year, the Demorest City Council named a street after the former ball player, calling it "Johnny Mize Drive."

"This is a fitting tribute to a baseball legend," said the town's mayor, Rick Austin, when the action was voted. "We are proud to call him one of our hometown heroes."[18]

Demorest, Georgia, was truly Johnny Mize's hometown. But for those who watched the gifted hitter in his prime of his youth swinging a baseball bat, they too claimed him in St. Louis and New York (twice over). The Hall of Famer belonged to them, too.

Chapter Notes

Preface

1. BrainyQuote/Johnny Mize. https://brainyquote.com/authors/johnny-mize-quotes
2. Johnny Mize website. www.johnnymize.com.
3. National Baseball Hall of Fame, Johnny Mize, https://baseballhall.org/hall-of-famers/mizejohnny.

Introduction

1. Jeffrey Sisk, "Mize Legend Continues On," *The Northeast Georgian* (Cornelia, GA), June 8, 1993.
2. Baseball in Wartime, https://actofvalorward.org/johnny-mize-n-y-giants/
3. *Ibid.*

Chapter 1

1. Johnny Mize and Maury Kaufman, *How to Hit* (New York: Henry Holt, 1953), 3.
2. *Ibid.*
3. *Ibid.*, 4.
4. *Ibid.*, 6.
5. *Ibid.*
6. *Ibid.*, 7.
7. Jerry Grillo, "Johnny Mize," Society for American Baseball Research, https://sabr.org/bioproj/person/johnny-mize.
8. *Ibid.*
9. Cort Vitty, "Ripper Collins," Society for American Baseball Research, sabr.org/bioproj/person/ripper-collins/.

Chapter 2

1. Mike Eisenbath, "Doctor Saved Mize's Career Before It Started," *St. Louis Post-Dispatch*, May 22, 1992.
2. David Craft, "Known As 'Big Cat,' Mize Hit, Fielded His Way Into the Baseball Hall of Fame," *Sports Collectors Digest*, September 25, 1987.

Chapter 3

1. *Ibid.*
2. Mike Eisenbath, "Doctor Saved Mize's Career Before It Started," *St. Louis Post-Dispatch*, May 22, 1992.
3. Donald Honig, *Baseball: When the Grass Was Green* (New York: Berkley Medallion Books, 1975), 90.
4. Jerry Grillo, "Johnny Mize," Society for American Baseball Research, https://sabr.org/bioproj/person/johnny-mize.
5. Robert L. Burnes, "'Me and Paul' The Best of the Gas-House Gang," *St. Louis Globe-Democrat*, March 18, 1981.
6. *Ibid.*
7. Craft, "Known as Big Cat."
8. Johnny Mize and Maury Kaufman, *How to Hit* (New York: Henry Holt, 1953), 7.

Chapter 4

1. Jerry Grillo, "Johnny Mize," Society for American Baseball Research, https://sabr.org/bioproj/person/johnny-mize.

2. Donald Honig, *Baseball: When the Grass Was Green* (New York: Berkley Medallion Books, 1975), p. 90.

3. *Ibid.*, 90–91.

4. "Dizzy Gives In for Half His Original Demand," United Press International, March 19, 1937.

5. "Fifty Grand Or 'We Don't Pitch,' Mrs. Dizzy Dean Warns Cards," *United Press International*, January 26, 1937.

6. *Ibid.*

7. "Dizzy Gives In for Half His Original Demand."

8. Mat Kovach, "The Dizzy Dean Injury Cascade," *The Hardball Times*, March 3, 2011. https://tht.fangraphs.com/tht-live/the-dizzy-dean-injury-cascade/

9. Honig, 91.

10. Bob Broeg, "King Carl: Superb Mound Craftsman," *The Sporting News*, May 2, 1970.

11. Thomas Barthel, *Pepper Martin: A Baseball Biography* (Jefferson, NC: McFarland, 2003), 122.

Chapter 5

1. Robert Gregory, *Diz: Dizzy Dean and Baseball During the Great Depression* (New York: Viking, 1992), 327.

2. Roscoe McGowen, "Dizzy Denies Slur, But Not in Writing," *New York Times*, June 4, 1937.

3. *Ibid.*

4. David Craft, "Known As 'Big Cat,' Mize Hit, Fielded His Way Into the Baseball Hall of Fame," *Sports Collectors Digest*, September 25, 1987.

5. John Kieran, "Sports of the Times: The Mad Musicians," *New York Times*, May 13, 1937.

6. "Gutteridge Finds Batting Eye After Frisch Issues Ultimatum," Don Gutteridge vertical file, Baseball Hall of Fame Research Library (newspaper name missing), May 14, 1937.

7. Leonard Cohen, "The Sports Parade," *New York Post*, August 29, 1944.

8. *Ibid.*

9. Johnny Mize and Maury Kaufman, *How to Hit* (New York: Henry Holt, 1953), 12.

10. *Ibid.*

11. Mize and Kaufman, *How to Hit*, 15.

Chapter 6

1. J. Roy Stockton, "Lord Medwick, Of Carteret," *Saturday Evening Post*, March 5, 1938.

2. Leonard Koppett, "Medwick Recalls Vegetable Shower," *The Sporting News*, December 26, 1970.

3. Bob Broeg, "Fiery Medwick Took No Gaff from Friend or Foe," *St. Louis Post-Dispatch*, March 23, 1975.

4. *Ibid.*

5. *Ibid.*

6. *Ibid.*

7. Daniel, "Home Life Did It—Medwick," *New York Daily Mirror*, November 10, 1937.

8. J. Roy Stockton, "Lord Medwick, of Carteret," *Saturday Evening Post*, March 5, 1938.

9. Johnny Mize, "My Greatest Day in Baseball," Baseball Hall of Fame Newsletter, January, 1981.

Chapter 7

1. *Ibid.*

2. *Ibid.*

3. Joseph Gerard, "Mike Gonzalez," Society for American Baseball Research. https://sabr.org/bioproj/person/mike-gonzalez-2/

4. *Ibid.*

5. Rick Hummel, "Schoendienst on Moore: 'He Knew How to Win,'" *St. Louis Post-Dispatch*, March 31, 1995.

6. Rich Westcott, "A Defensive Wizard in Center Field," *Baseball Card Monthly*, May 1990.

7. *Ibid.*

8. *Ibid.*

9. Dick Farrington, "North Carolina Lad, With Arm Again in Shape, Regarded as Strongest Candidate for Shortstop, Vulnerable Spot on Club; Improved as Hitter After Learning to Swing Left-Handed," *The Sporting News*, March 9, 1939.

10. Bill Ballew, "Enos 'Country' Slaughter: HOFer Was the Original 'Charlie Hustle,'" *Sports Collectors Digest*, May 31, 1991.

11. Joseph Wancho, "Enos Slaughter," Society for American Baseball Research. https://sabr.org/bioproj/person/enos-slaughter/

12. *Ibid.*
13. "Derringer Puts Mize on Most Feared List," National Baseball Hall of Fame Research Library, Paul Derringer vertical file, newspaper name missing, July 20, 1939.

Chapter 8

1. *Ibid.*
2. Mize and Kaufman, *How to Hit*, 44.
3. Dave Condon, "In the Wake of the News," *Chicago Tribune*, September 14, 1959.
4. *Ibid.*
5. "Last of the Gas House Gang," *Baltimore Sun*, September 8, 2008.
6. Warren Corbett, "Curt Davis," Society for American Baseball Research. https://sabr.org/bioproj/person/curt-davis/
7. *Ibid.*
8. John J. Ward, "Baseball's Second Best Rookie Pitcher," *Folio Magazine*, February 1935.
9. David Condon, "In the Wake of the News," *Chicago Tribune*, November 19, 1958.
10. "Breakfast Dizzy Dean Style," *Collier's Magazine*, September 17, 1938.
11. Mize and Kaufman, 46.
12. Mize and Kaufman, 90.
13. Johnny Mize, "My Greatest Day in Baseball," Baseball Hall of Fame Newsletter, January 1981.
14. Donald Honig, *Baseball: When the Grass Was Green* (New York: Berkley Medallion Books, 1975), 91.
15. Arthur Daley, "Sports of the Times: A Man Who Collects Hairpins," *New York Times*, September 3, 1944.

Chapter 9

1. *Ibid.*
2. John C. Skipper, *Billy Southworth: A Biography of the Hall of Fame Manager and Ballplayer* (Jefferson, NC: McFarland, 2013), 97.
3. Johnny Mize, "My Greatest Day in Baseball," Baseball Hall of Fame Newsletter, January, 1981.
4. *Ibid.*
5. Richard Goldstein, "Marty Marion,

93, Cardinals Shortstop," *New York Times*, March 17, 2011.
6. Rick Hines, "Marty Marion: 'Mr. Shortstop' Tells It Like Is," *Sports Collectors Digest*, April 26, 1991.
7. *Ibid.*
8. Bob Broeg and Stan Musial, *Stan Musial: The Man's Own Story* (Garden City, NY: Doubleday, 1964), 38.
9. *Ibid.*
10. *Ibid.*, 50.
11. *Ibid.*, 251.
12. *Ibid.*, 282–283.
13. Donald Honig, *Baseball: When the Grass Was Green* (New York: Berkley Medallion Books, 1975), 92.

Chapter 10

1. *Ibid.*, 92.
2. *Ibid.*, 94.
3. *Ibid.*
4. *Ibid.*
5. *Ibid.*
6. *Ibid.*
7. *Ibid.*
8. Harry T. Brundidge, "Ott Wore His First Pair of Long Pants When He Broke into Professional Ball," *The Sporting News*, December 19, 1929.
9. Lee Greene, "The Little Giant," *Sport Magazine*, May 1961.
10. Roscoe McGowen, "Giants Interest in Dahlgren Grows," *New York Times*, March 3, 1943.
11. John Drebinger, "Induction of Star Blow to Ott Team," *New York Times*, March 20, 1943.
12. David Craft, "Known As 'Big Cat,' Mize Hit, Fielded His Way Into the Baseball Hall of Fame," *Sports Collectors Digest*, September 25, 1987.
13. *Ibid.*
14. Ken Smith, "Sailor Mize Is Back, Returns to Giant Deck," *New York Mirror*, October 12, 1945.

Chapter 11

1. *Ibid.*
2. *Ibid.*
3. *Ibid.*
4. *Ibid.*
5. Mize and Kaufman, *How to Hit*, 80.

6. *Ibid.*
7. *Ibid.,* 81.
8. Leonard Koppett, "Hal Schumacher, Ex-Hurler, Turns Traitor, Now Sells Bats," *New York Herald-Tribune* (National Baseball Hall of Fame Library Archives, Hal Schumacher vertical file, date missing).
9. *Ibid.*
10. Mize and Kaufman, 13.

Chapter 12

1. Frank Graham, "Graham's Corner: The Way to Hit," *New York Journal-American,* June 1947.
2. *Ibid.*
3. *Ibid.*
4. Rich Marazzi, "Willard Marshall Was Part of Record-Setting Giants Homer Brigade in 1947," *Sports Collectors Digest,* January 12, 1996.
5. Lew Freedman, *The 50 Greatest Pirates Every Fan Should Know* (Indianapolis: Blue River Press, 2014), 31.
6. George Vecsey, *Stan Musial: An American Life* (New York: Ballantine Books, 2011), 201.
7. John A. Ross, "Big Jawn Mize," *Sportfolio,* September 1947.
8. *Ibid.*

Chapter 13

1. Fred Stein, *Mel Ott: The Little Giant of Baseball* (Jefferson, NC: McFarland, 1999), 172.
2. *Ibid.,* 175.
3. *Ibid.,* 178.
4. Paul Dickson, *Leo Durocher: Baseball's Prodigal Son* (New York: Bloomsbury, 2017), 190.
5. Roger Kahn, *The Era: 1947–1957, When the Yankees, the Giants and the Dodgers Ruled the World* (New York: Ticknor and Fields, 1993), 154.
6. *Ibid.*
7. *Ibid.,* 156.
8. "Cooper Happier Away from Lippy," *New York Sun,* June 29, 1949.
9. Rich Marazzi, "Willard Marshall Was Part of Record-Setting Giants Homer Brigade In 1947," *Sports Collectors Digest,* January 12, 1996.

10. Donald Honig, *Baseball: When the Grass Was Green* (New York: Berkley Medallion Books, 1975), 94.
11. *Ibid.*
12. *Ibid.,* 95.

Chapter 14

1. William J. Briordry, "Giants Sell Veteran First Sacker to Bombers for Undisclosed Sum," *New York Times,* August 23, 1949.
2. *Ibid.*
3. *Ibid.*
4. Dan Daniel, "DiMag Resting, Casey Ponders Mize at First, Heinrich Back in Right," *New York World-Telegram,* August 24, 1949.
5. Dan Daniel, "Daniel's Dope: Sick Yanks Travel with Own Hospital," *New York World-Telegram,* August 31, 1949.
6. *Ibid.*
7. Maury Allen, *You Could Look It Up: The Life of Casey Stengel* (New York: Times Books, 1979), 13.
8. Joe DiMaggio, "Read Joe DiMaggio ... On the Pennant Race," *New York World-Telegram,* September 10, 1949.
9. *Ibid.*
10. *Ibid.*

Chapter 15

1. Gene Schoor, *The History of the World Series* (New York: William Morrow, 1990), 220.
2. Roger Kahn, *The Era: 1947–1957, When the Yankees, the Giants and the Dodgers Ruled the World* (New York: Ticknor and Fields, 1993), 220.
3. "Yanks, Bums (Cross Out 1) a Cinch!" *Newsday,* October 4, 1949.
4. Ed Comerford, "Calmest W-S Fans Those at Park," *Newsday,* October 5, 1949.
5. Jene (Mrs. Johnny) Mize, "From the Feminine Viewpoint: Yell of 'Hit Him in the Head,' Worst Worry of Player's Wife," *The Sporting News,* November 19, 1942.
6. Bob Broeg, "Big John: As a Hitter, Mize Had Size for Power, Eyes for Contact," *St. Louis Post-Dispatch,* June 4, 1953.
7. *Ibid.*

8. Marty Appel, *Casey Stengel: Baseball's Greatest Character* (New York: Doubleday, 2017), 166.

Chapter 16

1. Joe Durso, *DiMaggio: The Last American Knight* (New York: Little, Brown, 1995), 176.
2. *Ibid.*
3. Richard Ben Cramer, *Joe DiMaggio: The Hero's Life* (New York: Simon & Shuster, 2000), 274.
4. Roger Kahn, *The Era*, 234.
5. Rick Van Blair, "Tommy Byrne: Yankee Southpaw Flirted with Greatness," *Sports Collectors Digest*, February 11, 1994.
6. *Ibid.*
7. Van Blair, *ibid.*
8. Ed Comerford, "Yanks Spell Mize-ry for Flock, 4–3," *Newsday*, October 8, 1949.
9. Joe DiMaggio, "Mize Knows 'Em, Too, Joe Reminds," *New York World-Telegram*, October 4, 1949.
10. James P. Dawson, "Mize, World Series Hero at Long Last, Likes Those Fences at Ebbets Field," *New York Times*, October 8, 1949.
11. *Ibid.*
12. *Ibid.*
13. *Ibid.*
14. *Ibid.*
15. Don Harrison, "Rex Barney," Society for American Baseball Research. https://sabr.org/bioproj/person/rex-barney/
16. Donald Honig, *Baseball: When the Grass Was Green* (New York: Berkley Medallion Books, 1975), 95.

Chapter 17

1. Roger Kahn, *The Era*, 236.
2. Carlo DeVito, *Scooter: The Biography of Phil Rizzuto* (Chicago: Triumph Books, 2010), 110.
3. *Ibid.*, 155.
4. *Ibid.*
5. *Ibid.*
6. Kahn, 176.
7. Sol Gittleman, *Reynolds, Raschi and Lopat: New York's Big Three and the Great Yankee Dynasty of 1949–1953* (Jefferson, NC: McFarland, 2007), 65.
8. *Ibid.*, 86.
9. *Ibid.*, 159.
10. C. Paul Rogers and Bill Nowlin, editors, *The Whiz Kids Take the Pennant: The 1950 Phillies* (Phoenix: Society for American Baseball Research, 2008), 1.
11. Josh Leventhal, "Take Me Out to the Ballpark" (New York: Black Dog and Leventhal, 2006), 48.
12. Mize and Kaufman, *How to Hit*, 13–14.

Chapter 18

1. Marty Appel, *Casey Stengel: Baseball's Greatest Character* (New York: Doubleday, 2017), 169.
2. *Ibid.*
3. Carlo DeVito, *Yogi Berra: The Life of an American Original* (Chicago: Triumph Books, 2008), 199.
4. *Ibid.*, 285.
5. Bob Broeg, "Only One Yogi...Pitchers Glad of That," *The Sporting News*, August 7, 1971.
6. Harold Rosenthal, "St. Louis Clubs Refused $500 Bonus to Berra," *New York Post*, July 31, 1957.
7. Rich Marazzi, "Hank Bauer Was the Classic, Hard-Nosed Ballplayer," *Sports Collectors Digest*, February 7, 1997.
8. "Hank Bauer, 84, World Series Star, Dies," *New York Times*, February 10, 2007.
9. Ed McAuley, "'It Was Nothing Really,' and Allie Isn't Kidding," *Cleveland News*, July 12, 1951.
10. *Ibid.*
11. Dan Daniel, "Reynolds Steps Over Feller into Record Book," *The Sporting News*, July 25, 191.
12. Lou Miller, "Ancient Mize Just Won't Shed That Old Home Run Wallop," *New York World-Telegram*, July 25, 1951.
13. *Ibid.*
14. Dan Daniel, "Allie Blazed Double No-Hit Trail in A.L.," *The Sporting News*, October 10, 1951.
15. Jimmy Cannon, "Jimmy Cannon Says" (syndicated column), October 5, 1951.
16. Roger Kahn, *The Era*, 289.
17. James P. Dawson, "McDougald's

Grand Slam Matches Smith's Wallop of 1920, Lazzeri's of 1936," *New York Times*, October 10, 1951.
    18. *Ibid.*

Chapter 19

    1. Rich Marazzi, "A.L. President Bobby Brown Profiled," *Sports Collectors Digest*, December 17, 1993.
    2. *Ibid.*
    3. Hal Bodley, "Brown Put His Heart in AL Presidency," *USA Today*, December 13, 1983.
    4. Bob Cerv and Al Hirshberg, "I Played Without Eating," *Saturday Evening Post*, July 10, 1953.
    5. Mize and Kaufman, *How to Hit*, 76.
    6. Johnny Mize, "My Greatest Day in Baseball," Baseball Hall of Fame Newsletter, January, 1981.
    7. Mize and Kaufman, 98.

Chapter 20

    1. Maury Allen, *You Could Look It Up: The Life of Casey Stengel* (New York: Times Books, 1979), 165.
    2. *Ibid.*
    3. Al Buck, "And Who Says Yankees Won't Win 8 in Row?," *New York Post*, October 6, 1953.
    4. "Mize Quits in Blast at Yankee Brass," *New York Post*, October 6, 1953.
    5. *Ibid.*
    6. "Mize Retires: Feels He'd Get Little Pay in '54," *Philadelphia Bulletin*, October 6, 1953.
    7. John Drebinger, "Mize Retires: 'End of the Trail,' Says Yankee At 40," *New York Times*, October 7, 1953.
    8. *Ibid.*

Chapter 21

    1. Bruce Connors, "Big Man in a Pinch," *Sport Magazine*, September, 1953.
    2. *Ibid.*
    3. *Ibid.*
    4. *Ibid.*
    5. *Ibid.*
    6. Bob Broeg, "M&M's Bats Didn't

Melt in Their Hands," *St. Louis Post-Dispatch*, March 1981.
    7. *Ibid.*
    8. *Ibid.*
    9. Dan Daniel, "'Not Bad for a Kid,' Says Amazing Mize," *The Sporting News*, October 15, 1952.
    10. *Ibid.*
    11. Arthur Daley, "Sports of the Times: Among the Literary Set," *New York Times*, October 28, 1952.
    12. Dan Daniel, "Mize Says He Got Lucky Swinging in Big Series," *New York World-Telegram*, March 16, 1953.
    13. Joe King, "Mize Alters Stance of Slugger Lennon," *New York World-Telegram*, March 1, 1956.
    14. "Stengel Has High Praise for Mize" (National Baseball Hall of Fame Library Archives, Casey Stengel vertical file, newspaper name missing), August 12, 1972.
    15. *Ibid.*
    16. *Ibid.*
    17. Connors, "Big Man in a Pinch."
    18. "'Big Cat' Still Waiting for Cooperstown Call," *Associated Press*, August 22, 1976.
    19. Hal Bock, "Mize Among the Uninvited," *Associated Press*, August 9, 1971.

Epilogue

    1. Craig Stolze, "Hall of Fame Skips Great Slugger Mize," *Rochester Democrat*, September 29, 1972.
    2. "Insiders Say," *The Sporting News*, March 10, 1973.
    3. Furman Bisher, "A Belated Honor for Mize—Other Greats Still Shunned," *Atlanta Constitution*, May 2, 1980.
    4. Dick Young, "Elect Mize to Hall of Fame," *New York Daily News*, March 13, 1981.
    5. *Ibid.*
    6. Bill Madden, "Yankee-Dodger Oldtimers Hear the Cheers, But Wonder Where Their Mementoes Rest," *New York Daily News*, August 23, 1981.
    7. Bill Madden, "Hall of Famers Win the Cheers of Bitter Crowd," *New York Daily News*, August 23, 1981.
    8. *Ibid.*
    9. Johnny Mize Baseball Hall of Fame Acceptance Speech, August 2, 1981.

https://www.mlb.com/video/mizes-hall-of-fame-speech
10. *Ibid.*
11. Jim Hone, "Mize Ends Long Waiting Game," *Oneonta (NY) Star,* August 3, 1981.
12. Child's letter sent to Johnny Mize, curated by Piedmont College, Demorest, Georgia.
13. "Mize a Role Model for Children in Small Town," *New York Daily News,* July 15, 1991.
14. Greg Garber, "The Big Cat's Final Interview" (reprinted from Piedmont College, "The Lion's Roar"), *The North-east Georgian* (Cornelia, GA), June 8, 1993.
15. Jeffrey Sisk, "Mize Legend Continues On," *The Northeast Georgian* (Cornelia, GA), June 8, 1993.
16. Demorest Scout Troop 660, *The Northeast Georgian* (Cornelia, GA), June 8, 1993.
17. Stan Musial, "The Man's Memories of Mize and a Bad Move," *The Sporting News,* June 14, 1993.
18. Staff Report, "Demorest Council Designates 'Johnny Mize Drive,'" *The Northeast Georgian* (Cornelia, GA), July 2, 2014.

Bibliography

Books

Allen, Maury. *You Could Look It Up: The Life of Casey Stengel.* New York: Times Books, 1979.

Appel, Marty. *Casey Stengel: Baseball's Greatest Character.* New York: Doubleday, 2017.

Barthel, Thomas. *Pepper Martin: A Baseball Biography.* Jefferson, NC: McFarland, 2003.

Broeg, Bob, and Stan Musial. *Stan Musial: The Man's Own Story.* Garden City, NY: Doubleday, 1964.

Cramer, Richard Ben. *Joe DiMaggio: The Hero's Life.* New York: Simon & Shuster, 2000.

DeVito, Carlo. *Scooter: The Biography of Phil Rizzuto.* Chicago: Triumph Books, 2010.

_____. *Yogi Berra: The Life of an American Original.* Chicago: Triumph Books, 2008.

Dickson, Paul. *Leo Durocher: Baseball's Prodigal Son.* New York: Bloomsbury, 2017.

Durso, Joe. *DiMaggio: The Last American Knight.* New York: Little, Brown, 1995.

Freedman, Lew. *The 50 Greatest Pirates Every Fan Should Know.* Indianapolis: Blue River Press, 2014.

Gittleman, Sol. *Reynolds, Raschi and Lopat: New York's Big Three and the Great Yankee Dynasty of 1949–1953.* Jefferson, NC: McFarland, 2007.

Gregory, Robert. *Diz: Dizzy Dean and Baseball During the Great Depression.* New York: Viking, 1992.

Honig, Donald. *Baseball: When the Grass Was Green.* New York: Berkley Medallion Books, 1975.

Kahn, Roger. *The Era: 1947–1957, When the Yankees, the Giants and the Dodgers Ruled the World.* New York: Ticknor and Fields, 1993.

Leventhal, Josh. *Take Me Out to the Ballpark.* New York: Black Dog and Leventhal, 2006.

Mize, Johnny, and Maury Kaufman. *How to Hit.* New York: Henry Holt, 1953.

Rogers, C. Paul III, and Bill Nowlin, eds. *The Whiz Kids Take the Pennant: The 1950 Phillies.* Phoenix: Society for American Baseball Research, 2008.

Schoor, Gene. *The History of the World Series.* New York: William Morrow, 1990.

Skipper, John C. *Billy Southworth: A Biography of the Hall of Fame Manager and Ballplayer.* Jefferson, NC: McFarland, 2013.

Stein, Fred. *Mel Ott: The Little Giant of Baseball.* Jefferson, NC: McFarland, 1999.

Vecsey, George. *Stan Musial: An American Life.* New York: Ballantine Books, 2011.

Newspapers

Atlanta Constitution
Baltimore Sun
Chicago Tribune
Cleveland News
New York Daily News
New York Herald-Tribune
New York Journal-American
New York Mirror
New York Post
New York Sun
New York Times

New York World-Telegram.
Newsday
The Northeast Georgian (Cornelia, GA)
Oneonta (NY) Star
Rochester (NY) Democrat.
St. Louis Globe-Democrat
St. Louis Post-Dispatch
USA Today

Magazines

Baseball Card Monthly
Baseball Hall of Fame Newsletter
Collier's
Folio
The Saturday Evening Post
Sport
Sportfolio
The Sporting News
Sports Collectors Digest

Wire Services

Associated Press
United Press International

Internet

Baseball in Wartime: https://www.base
ballinwartime.com/
The Hardball Times: https://tht.fangra
phs.com/
Johnny Mize website: http://johnnymize.
com/
National Baseball Hall of Fame: https://
baseballhall.org/
Society for American Baseball Research:
https://sabr.org/

Index